# Book 2 | Starting off systemically in environmental decision making

*by Ray Ison, Chris Blackmore and Dick Morris
with the course team*

**T863 Environmental decision making: a systems approach**

This publication forms part of an Open University course T863 *Environmental decision making: a systems approach*. Details of this and other Open University courses can be obtained from the Student Registration and Enquiry Service, The Open University, PO Box 197, Milton Keynes, MK7 6BJ, United Kingdom: tel. +44 (0)870 333 4340, email general-enquiries@open.ac.uk

Alternatively, you may visit the Open University website at http://www.open.ac.uk where you can learn more about the wide range of courses and packs offered at all levels by The Open University.

To purchase a selection of Open University course materials visit http://www.ouw.co.uk, or contact Open University Worldwide, Michael Young Building, Walton Hall, Milton Keynes MK7 6AA, United Kingdom for a brochure. tel. +44 (0)1908 858785; fax +44 (0)1908 858787; email ouwenq@open.ac.uk

This course is printed on New Revive Matt Paper and Board. At least 75% of the furnish is made from 100% de-inked consumer waste. The remainder is made from mill broke to improve the whiteness and print characteristics of this grade.

The Open University
Walton Hall, Milton Keynes
MK7 6AA

First published 2006.

Copyright © 2006 The Open University

All rights reserved. No part of this publication may be reproduced, stored in a retrieval system, transmitted or utilised in any form or by any means, electronic, mechanical, photocopying, recording or otherwise, without written permission from the publisher or a licence from the Copyright Licensing Agency Ltd. Details of such licences (for reprographic reproduction) may be obtained from the Copyright Licensing Agency Ltd of 90 Tottenham Court Road, London W1T 4LP.

Open University course materials may also be made available in electronic formats for use by students of the University. All rights, including copyright and related rights and database rights, in electronic course materials and their contents are owned by or licensed to The Open University, or otherwise used by The Open University as permitted by applicable law.

In using electronic course materials and their contents you agree that your use will be solely for the purposes of following an Open University course of study or otherwise as licensed by The Open University or its assigns.

Except as permitted above you undertake not to copy, store in any medium (including electronic storage or use in a website), distribute, transmit or retransmit, broadcast, modify or show in public such electronic materials in whole or in part without the prior written consent of The Open University or in accordance with the Copyright, Designs and Patents Act 1988.

Edited and designed by The Open University.

Typeset by The Open University.

Printed and bound in the United Kingdom by Halstan Printing Group, Amersham.

ISBN N978 07492 02651

1.1

# Contents

Course Team — 5
Aims — 6
Overview of this book — 7

Part One  Developing your systemic awareness — 9

1 Introduction — 9

2 Being equipped to explore and re-explore — 14
  2.1 Creating a 'rich picture' of a situation — 14
  2.2 Climate change and the carbon cycle — 19
  2.3 The carbon cycle: ecosystems, oceans and geology — 20

3 Exploring and re-exploring through modelling — 24
  3.1 An introduction to modelling — 24
  3.2 A general typology of models — 27
  3.3 Systems maps — 29
  3.4 Influence diagrams — 29
  3.5 Multiple cause diagrams — 30
  3.6 Sign graphs — 32
  3.7 System dynamics diagramming — 33
  3.8 A review of modelling — 36

4 Systems thinking for exploring and re-exploring — 39
  4.1 Systems thinking and environmental thinking — 42
  4.2 Understanding environmental decision making as a systemic practice — 44
  4.3 The relationship between understanding and practice — 57
  4.4 Stakeholders and stakeholding — 71

5 Perspectives on a situation — 74
  5.1 Valuing multiple perspectives — 74
  5.2 Knowing what the problem or opportunity is — 82
  5.3 Knowing how we know — 85
  5.4 Relating the social and the biophysical — 89
  5.5 Initial starting conditions — 90

6 Formulating problems, opportunities and systems of interest in environmental decision-making situations — 93
  6.1 From exploring to formulating — 93
  6.2 Consultation or participation? — 94
  6.3 Generating systems of interest for environmental decision making — 104
  6.4 Review – moving on — 116

| | Part Two Exploring and formulating through environmental legislation and schemes | 118 |
|---|---|---|
| 7 | Exploring and formulating what? The scope of Part Two | 118 |
| 7.1 | The overall trajectory of environmental legislation and schemes – past, present and future | 118 |
| 7.2 | Auditing experiences of environmental legislation and schemes | 126 |
| 7.3 | Some questions of purpose of environmental legislation and schemes | 129 |
| 8 | How specific environmental legislation and schemes frame a situation and our practices | 132 |
| 8.1 | The Aarhus Convention – more information, participation and justice? | 132 |
| 8.2 | Environmental impact assessment and its broader evolution | 134 |
| 8.3 | Strategic environmental assessment | 158 |
| 8.4 | Regulatory impact assessment | 160 |
| 8.5 | Environmental management systems standards: ISO 14001 and EMAS | 163 |
| 8.6 | Corporate social (and environmental) responsibility | 174 |
| 8.7 | The future for environmental legislation and schemes and systemic decision making | 180 |
| | Part Three Monitoring and evaluating your own learning | 183 |
| 9 | Managing a learning system | 183 |
| 9.1 | Evaluation | 184 |
| 9.2 | Monitoring | 186 |
| 9.3 | Evaluation of a system of interest | 189 |
| 9.4 | Evaluating the course framework and your use of it so far | 196 |
| 9.5 | Monitoring and evaluating your systemic awareness | 198 |
| 9.6 | Taking control action with respect to your own learning | 202 |
| Learning outcomes | | 203 |
| References | | 205 |
| Responses to Activities | | 215 |
| Answers to Self-Assessment Questions | | 248 |
| Acknowledgements | | 266 |

Ray Ison was largely responsible for Parts 1 and 3, Chris Blackmore wrote Part 2, and Dick Morris contributed the material on the carbon cycle and modelling in Sections 2 and 3.

# Course Team

## Academic staff

| | |
|---|---|
| Andrea Berardi | *Author* |
| Chris Blackmore | *Author* |
| Kevin Collins | *Author* |
| Ray Corrigan | *Critical Reader* |
| Pam Furniss | *Course Chair/Author* |
| Ray Ison | *Author* |
| Dick Morris | *Author/Consultant* |
| Paul Murphy | *Critical Reader* |
| Martin Reynolds | *Author* |
| Sandrine Simon | *Author* |
| Carolyn Baxter | *Course Manager (to February 2005)* |
| Suzanne Brown | *Course Manager (from February 2005)* |
| Mark Yoxon | *Critical Reader for Book 2* |

## External Assessor

Professor Barry Dent, FRSE, OBE

## Production Team

| | |
|---|---|
| Tammy Alexander | *Graphic Designer* |
| Annette Booz | *Compositor* |
| Philippa Broadbent | *Buyer, Materials Procurement* |
| Sarah Crompton | *Graphic Designer* |
| Andrew Cupples | *Editor* |
| Henry Dougherty | *Editor* |
| Vicky Eves | *Graphic Artist* |
| Zoe Gipson | *Editor* |
| Carol Houghton | *Media Assistant* |
| Simon Lawson | *Producer, Sound and Vision* |
| Jonathan Martyn | *Media Assistant* |
| Carol Morgan | *Course Secretary* |
| Stewart Nixon | *Project Manager* |
| Lynn Short | *Software Designer* |

## Aims

In Book 2 we aim to:

- engage you in a case study and other examples of complex environmental decision-making situations
- introduce a range of systems concepts and techniques
- raise your awareness of some aspects of biophysical environments that are a cause of concern
- raise your systemic awareness for understanding complex situations
- demonstrate what is involved in starting off systemically in environmental decision making
- build on your understanding of models and how they can be used to describe situations concerned with environmental decision making
- enable you to recognise how a range of modelling types can aid your exploration of situations and systemic awareness
- develop your practice in formulating problems, opportunities and systems of interest in complex situations
- raise your awareness and understanding of a range of environmental legislation and schemes
- examine how more formalised approaches to environmental decision making can enhance or constrain systemic action
- develop your capacity to act (be response-able) in environmental decision-making situations (including monitoring and evaluating your own learning).

# Overview of this book

The title of this course, *Environmental decision making: a systems approach*, includes several concepts. Book 1 introduced environmental decision making and detailed the aviation expansion case study. This book will introduce and develop what we mean by taking 'a systems approach' to environmental decision making. The focus of Book 2 is the first two stages of the T863 environmental decision-making framework (Figure 1). These stages are not sequential but iterative, and the boundaries between the two are not as clear-cut as our model might convey. (Note: the iterative process between these two stages is depicted by the arrows going through the 'techniques and skills' rectangle in the centre.) I recognise that the descriptions of these two stages, 'explore (or re-explore) the situation' and 'formulate problems, opportunities and systems of interest', may not be familiar to you. The language, and associated understanding and skills, are concerned with starting off the process of environmental decision making in a particular way, i.e. starting off systemically. The case for taking a systems approach will be developed by considering the complexity of most environmental issues.

Book 2 will draw heavily on the 'Freedom to fly?' case study presented in Book 1, using new material as well as a range of activities to capture and build on some of your main insights and questions from Book 1. In Part 1 of this book, the case study is used to introduce and explore:

1 what it means to start off systemically; this includes being aware of the biophysical dynamics in, and modelling of, the situation. You are introduced to different types of models and modelling; modelling is usually integral to taking a systems approach;

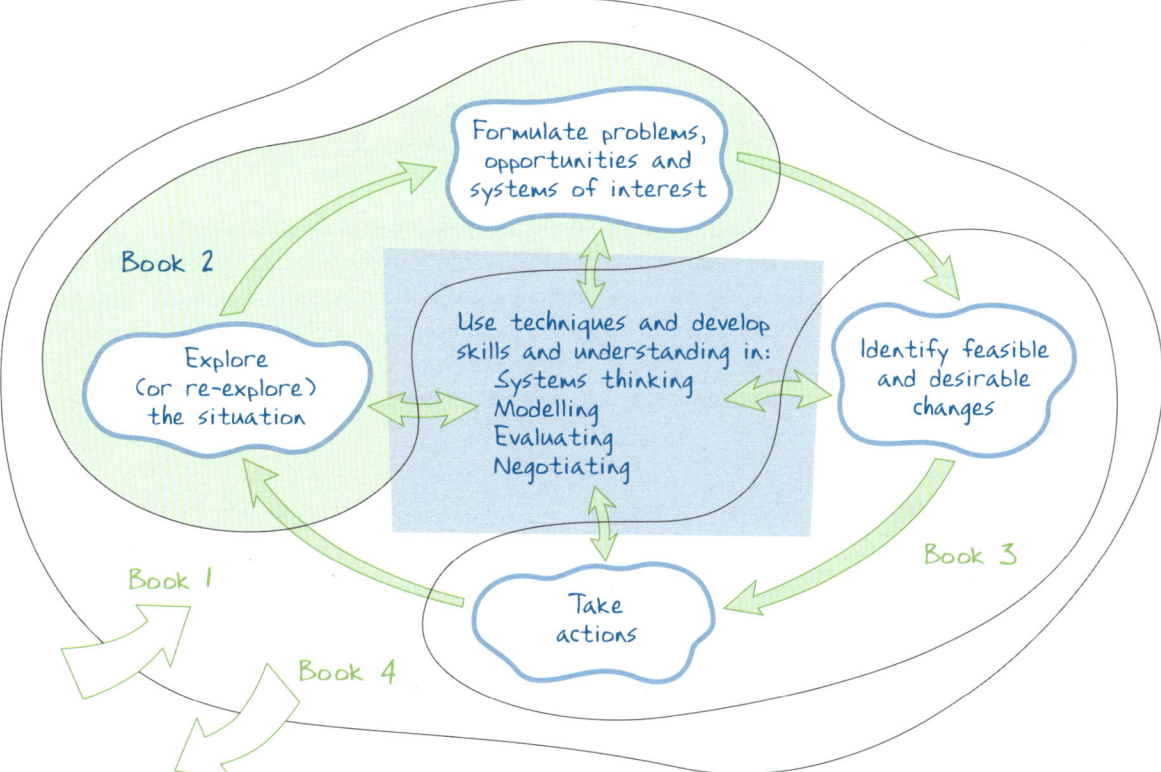

Figure 1    The T863 framework with the contents of this book highlighted

2   whether different environmental decisions are likely to be reached if more attention is paid to how the process is started and who participates; and

3   what creative tools for thinking and action can be used to start and sustain processes of environmental decision making. The DVD and *Techniques* book will be major resources for your study.

The skills needed in taking a systems approach in these first two stages include:

1   using systems concepts as tools for thought, creativity, communication, representation and process design

2   appreciating the significance of modelling

3   conducting stakeholder analyses

4   recognising and accommodating multiple perspectives

5   starting off the decision-making process in a participatory manner

6   becoming aware that evaluation of any planned action starts at the beginning, not the end, and that to evaluate some form of monitoring is required throughout to check how you are going.

You may have started this course with some awareness of, or desire to learn about, more formalised decision-making approaches such as Environmental Impact Assessment or the international standard for environmental management systems, ISO 14001. There is now a wide range of legislation and schemes which are important for environmental decision making. In Part 2, we want you to critically engage with some examples of current environmental legislation and schemes. You are asked to consider and judge how they might be used in relation to the first two stages of the T863 framework. Part of your critical engagement will concern the question of whether or not these current initiatives can be used as part of systemic environmental decision making, and if so, how.

By the end of the book you will have had a chance to further develop understanding and skills in systems thinking, modelling and evaluating (Figure 1). In Part 3 you are asked to monitor and evaluate your own learning to date.

Twelve readings are included with this book. They explore contemporary environmental decision-making situations, and introduce and develop systems ideas. Throughout the book, tools and techniques which can be used to start off systemically will be introduced; you will be guided to appropriate sections of the *Techniques* book and DVD when needed. Whilst the focus of Book 2 is the first two stages of the framework, you are invited to keep the whole framework in mind at all times.

## Study note

The book is designed so that Part 1 takes three weeks of study, Part 2 takes two weeks of study and Part 3 (including time for the TMA) takes one week.

# Part One  Developing your systemic awareness

# Introduction

Starting off systemically means being both systemic and systematic – these are the two adjectives that arise from the word 'system'. The word system comes from the Greek verb *synhistanai*, meaning 'to place together'. A system is a perceived whole whose elements are 'interconnected'. Someone who pays particular attention to the interconnections is said to be systemic (a systemic family therapist is someone who considers the interconnections amongst the whole family; the emerging discipline of Earth Systems Science is concerned with the interconnections between the geological and biological features of the earth).

On the other hand, if I follow a recipe in a step-by-step manner then I am being systematic. Medical students in traditional courses on anatomy often take a systematic approach to their study of the human body – the hand, leg, internal organs, etc. – but at the end of their study they may have very little understanding of the human body as a whole because the whole is different from the sum of the parts.

Systemic awareness comes from understanding:

1. 'Cycles', such as the cycle between life and death, various nutrient cycles and the water cycle – the connections between rainfall, plant growth, evaporation, flooding, run-off, percolation, etc. (Figure 2). Through this sort of systemic logic, water availability for plant growth can ultimately be linked to the milk production of grazing animals and such things as profit and other human motivations. Sometimes an awareness of connectivity is described in the language of chains, as in 'the food chain' and sometimes as networks, as in the 'web of life'. Other phrases include 'joined up', 'linked', 'holistic', 'whole systems', 'complex adaptive systems', etc.

2. Counterintuitive effects, such as realising that floods can represent times when you need to be even more careful about conserving water, for example the shortages of drinking water in the New Orleans floods that followed Hurricane Katrina in 2005.

3. Unintended consequences. Thinking about things systemically can often minimise these. For example the designers of England's motorways did not plan for what is now experienced on a daily basis – congestion, traffic jams, emissions, etc. These unintended consequences are a result of the gaps in thinking that went into designing and building new motorways as part of a broader 'transport system'.

Peter Senge (1999) captures the idea of systemic complexity in the following terms:

> Businesses and other human endeavours [can also be viewed as] systems. They, too, are bound by invisible fabrics of interrelated actions, which often take years to play out their full effects on each other. Since we are part of that lacework ourselves, it's doubly hard to see the whole pattern of change. Instead, we tend to focus on

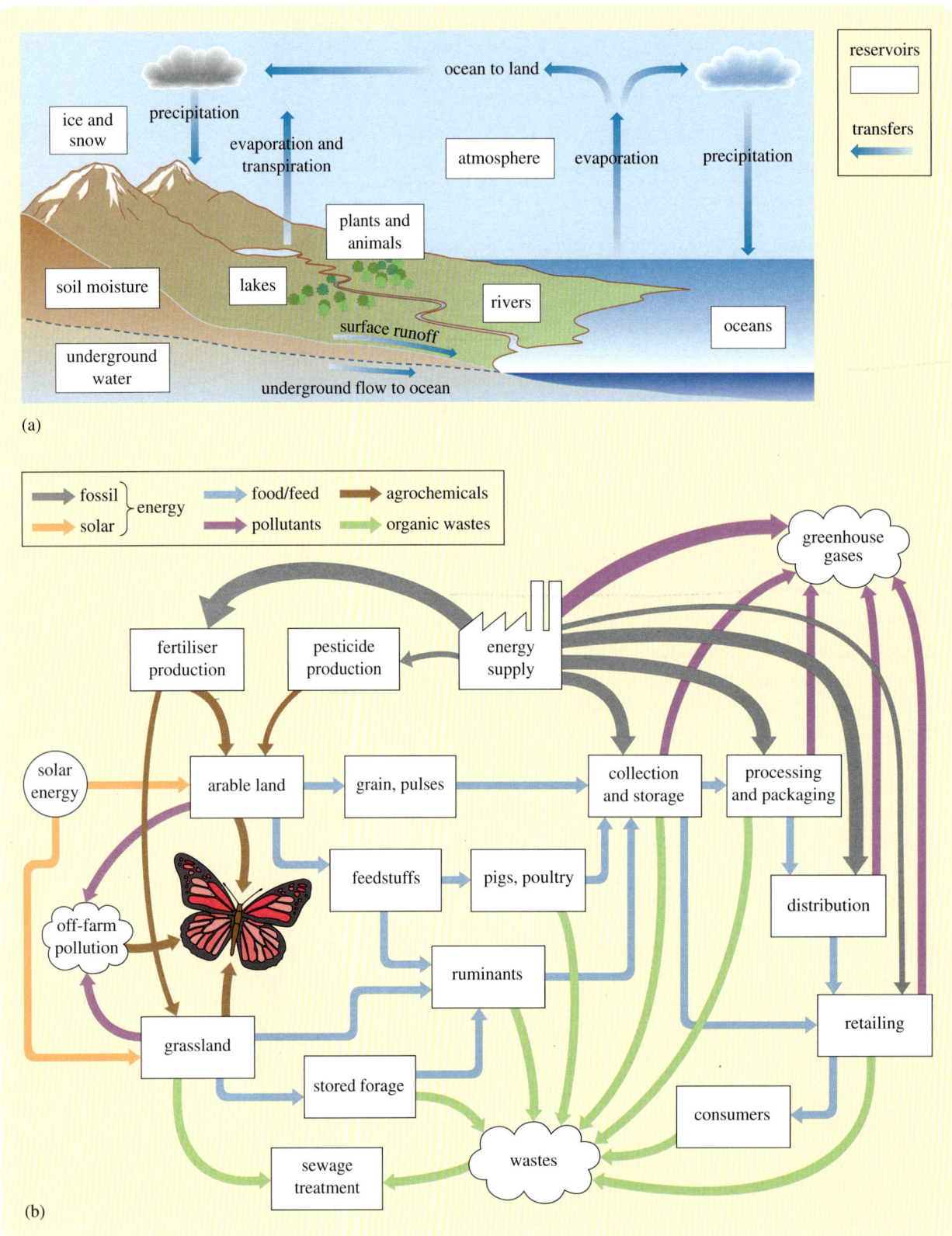

Figure 2 (a) A model of the water cycle depicting the connections between the different elements and (b) a model of a food chain (Sources: a: The Open University, 2003; b: Morris, 2005)

snapshots of isolated parts ... and wonder why our deepest problems never seem to get solved. Systems thinking is a conceptual framework, a body of knowledge and tools that has been developed over the past fifty years, to make the full patterns clearer and help us see how to change them effectively.

(Senge, 1999)

A primary aim I have for Part 1 is to help you to develop your systemic awareness for analysing and understanding complex environmental decision-making issues. To test out your own systemic awareness of an everyday activity, try Activity 1; it is not essential that you complete this activity before moving on but it is worth trying it at some time. I will return to the notion of 'systemic awareness' in Part 3, after you have had an opportunity to develop your own understanding and skills based on the 'Freedom to fly?' case study, material on climate change and the carbon cycle and other examples.

### Activity 1   The food on your table – an environmental web

Following a meal, take time, with your fellow diners, to explore the material and money flows and connections that brought two or three specific food items to your plate. Discuss the systemic connections and possible unintended consequences. As you do so, note some potential or actual environmental issues that you or others around the table are aware of. To highlight systemic connections you might care to think about various elements (things, products, people) and connections (links between elements, e.g. transporting).

This activity is best done with friends or family, i.e. in a group.

Make some notes in your learning journal about what you learned from doing this activity. You may also like to post to the T863 computer conference about how you found this activity.

### Study note

If you haven't yet made use of the T863 computer conferencing facility, now would be a good time to start. Instructions and software are provided. Look in the Course Guide for further details.

The stage of the T863 framework called 'exploring and re-exploring a situation' is a particular approach to engaging with a situation that is experienced as complex. It involves stepping back from the hasty naming of a problem or opportunity within that situation, particularly if the naming is done by those with a narrow perspective or vested interests. An example might be the naming of the problem which led to the flooding of New Orleans following Hurricane Katrina in 2005 as 'the failure of levees' and thus purely a question of engineering. Most would agree that the situation was more complex than this as the following quote exemplifies:

> Katrina was a man-made disaster even more than a natural one. It was not the hurricane alone that caused the devastation in New Orleans. It was the hurricane plus the absence of the wetlands that should have buffered the city from the storm.

Every 2.7 miles of wetlands reduces a storm surge by about one foot. Louisiana has been losing wetlands equal to the size of Manhattan every year. You don't need a slide rule to see where that calculus leads.

It's not malls and vacation homes that are destroying these wetlands, as in other parts of the country. In Louisiana it's largely oil. Offshore drilling has required the dredging of large canals, which enable salt water to flow into the marshes and cause land to sink. The other culprit is the extensive system of levees built to protect New Orleans from the Mississippi floods. These floods used to carry sediment into the marshlands which nourished and replenished them.

No floods means no replenishment. What used to be a buffer zone is now just open water, and a clear shot for the hurricane that experts have been warning of for years.

(Rowe, 2005)

Consider Figure 3. What I particularly like about this cartoon is that it conveys a number of systemic insights which can be connected to the first stages of the T863 framework. A simple systematic reading of the cartoon could be that tourism causes development which in turn causes pollution. Such a reading would be simplistic, though. The cartoon reveals the following insights for me:

1   The interconnectedness of human action with environmental change.
2   The image of the sun reminds me that life on earth is driven by photosynthesis and is carbon-based; each scene depicts different aspects of human modification of the carbon cycle.

Figure 3   The consequences of not engaging in environmental decision making using a systemic approach? (Source: O'Brien, 1990)

3   The notion that human behaviours co-evolve with their environment, i.e. the final scene depicts the use of technology (gas masks) to maintain adaptation to the situation (I take the perspective that evolution unfolds every day, even though it can only be seen in hindsight over long periods).

4   The operation of what is known as feedback processes – an ideal setting becomes popular (possibly by the use of cheap air travel), is increasingly spoiled by the influx and impact of tourists on infrastructure, natural environment, costs, congestion, pollution, etc., and ultimately destroys itself as a desirable destination (you will be asked to look at feedback processes in more detail in Section 3).

5   The cartoon also implicitly invites the reader to reflect on what we humans do to our surroundings when we act in particular ways and resort to technology to maintain behaviour which degrades our environment.

6   A simple systematic or deterministic reading of the cartoon would also conceal the idea that we humans are capable of learning and thus changing behaviour in purposeful ways. Examples might include taxing aviation, the design of an ecotourism resort or putting quotas on visitors to a particular location.

The material in Book 2 will equip you not only to understand situations such as that depicted by Figure 3, but also to begin to move beyond understanding to action. However, before asking you once again to engage with the case study, I want to raise your awareness of the systemic nature of climate change and the underpinning carbon cycle.

# 2 Being equipped to explore and re-explore

To fully come to grips with the systemic dimensions of the 'Freedom to fly?' case study, you will need to understand some of the main processes associated with the enhanced greenhouse effect and climate change. These are covered in this section. I will also begin to introduce or re-introduce some modelling techniques, to enable you to re-explore the case study (modelling will be covered in more detail in Section 3 and Book 3). In Book 1 you did a series of spray diagrams. Book 1 also included a systems map and a multiple cause diagram, and suggested that Klein's diagram could be thought of as a rich picture. In this section you will begin to do these diagrams for yourself.

One of my main points in this introductory part of Book 2 is that the way in which we read a situation, such as that depicted in Figure 3, determines how we understand it and thus how we name particular problems or opportunities. Depending on your particular background and interest, you may well have begun to form the conclusion that airport expansion is largely an 'economic problem' or a 'climate change problem'. To an economist or scientist either of these might seem sensible, but each is only part of the situation. My claim is that 'reading' a situation has as much to do with the reader as with what is read. Later, I will consider the social processes by which issues arise and problems and opportunities become named. Resisting pressures to rush towards a preconceived 'solution' involves standing back from the situation and exploring or re-exploring the wider context, and formulating and re-formulating systems of interest. Formulating systems of interest is a particular way of doing this when starting off systemically, for which modelling is a key practice. Only after this stage is it sensible to stabilise particular formulations of problems or opportunities. I shall explain more about what I mean by 'standing back', 'formulating' and 're-formulating' and 'system of interest' throughout Part 1.

## 2.1 Creating a 'rich picture' of a situation

To begin this process of standing back, I would like you to do Activity 2 which concerns the case study from Book 1. I suggest you have ready access to the case study (Book 1 and DVD) and your learning journal or blog before attempting this activity. It is designed to capture some of your main insights and questions about the case study, using a rich picture and spray diagram.

The techniques of 'rich picturing' and 'spray diagramming' are described in the *Techniques* book (see Diagramming) and in the Techniques section of the DVD. You will need to familiarise yourself with the guidelines for developing these diagrams before completing the activity. An advantage I find with both spray diagramming and rich picturing is that you can develop or add to them while watching a DVD or video.

## Activity 2  Spray diagramming and rich picturing

Depict in a spray diagram and a rich picture the main insights and questions that you had after engaging with the case study in Book 1.

You will need to be familiar with (i) the case study material in Book 1, (ii) the *Reach for the Sky* video and (iii) the *Heathrow Terminal 5* video. Preparing a rich picture might be helped by having another look at the cartoon images that have been used in Book 1, but wherever possible try to use your own images rather than those belonging to someone else.

---

To produce my own answer to this activity, firstly, I jotted down questions and insights that occurred to me as I read the case study and watched the videos. A list of these, in no particular order, is shown below, and from these I constructed a spray diagram and rich picture of the situation. My rich picture and spray diagram are depicted in Figure 4, and some of my reflections on what insights I gained from doing the rich picture follow. Some of what I have learnt has also found its way into the remaining teaching text in Part 1 of Book 2.

### The case study: some questions and insights

Why in the UK is so much investment going into air travel compared to what is happening with rail, especially high-speed rail as in France?

What did the designers of the consultation process want to gain from it, if anything? (i.e. what was its purpose?)

Were the design of the consultation process and the subsequent analysis and interpretation of the results adequate for the circumstances?

Health and safety was seen not just as a technical problem. Why? Was the environment seen as just a technical problem?

Usage of the terminal is expected to be 30 million passengers each year – that is half the population of the UK! What 'externalities' or unintended consequences will this produce?

'Nature' in the UK has been designed by humans for hundreds if not thousands of years, e.g. the rivers designed by Henry VIII and Charles I.

Attention has been paid to the habitat of a range of wildlife – but what about the habitat of people? Are we not part of nature?

The Terminal 5 project was ambitious in engineering and logistical terms and is being managed successfully, it would seem, using sophisticated software (and modelling tools) and a reductionist project management approach (16 separate projects further divided into 170 sub-projects).

Despite its planned focus as an integrated public transport hub, it plans for an extra 4000 car parking spaces with only one exit/entrance from the M25 motorway. What are the implications for me travelling to Terminal 5 from Milton Keynes (an hour north of London)? It is already very difficult to go by public transport (because of the need to change trains several times in London), and if I go by road, I can miss my flights because it can take anywhere between 50 minutes and three hours depending on whether the motorway system becomes jammed or not – and this is unpredictable!

What would an input/output or an ecological footprint analysis of the Terminal 5 development reveal about the situation?

*Reach for the Sky* starts and finishes by mentioning 'commons' issues, e.g. loss of access to common land in Wales and Sussex and then concern that carbon trading will transfer ownership of the atmosphere (a common) to multinationals. What do I need to know about current thinking on commons issues?

History shapes what we do now and it is sometimes difficult to break out of the determinism of history, e.g. an airport near Swansea developed in a time of war, a national emergency, but the airport continues to be a focus for development because it exists.

There is an important distinction between landscape designations and conservation designations (in terms of planning/development).

There are a wide range of stakeholders with varying perspectives concerned with airport expansion and they seem to draw the boundary around their concerns in different ways.

Planning Inspectors seem to have a critical role in UK decisions which affect planning and the environment – who are these people and what are the 'rules of the game' that they have to follow or choose to follow?

Who receives the benefits from the environmental levy on passengers, and how does this benefit those most affected?

Global warming seems much more accepted as 'scientific fact' compared to when I wrote a similar course 10 years ago. Is this really the case and how did this happen?

What is the right place to draw the boundary around an assessment of economic impact, e.g. level of project, tax paid to the Treasury, national economy, balance of payments of a country, whole earth system, etc?

What questionable assumptions have been built into the decision-making process? (An obvious answer is the assumed price of oil stabilised at $25 per barrel.)

If the assumptions subsequently prove unfounded, will the decisions be altered?

Why is it so difficult to get concerted action by different stakeholders when there appears to be scientific consensus that climate change is a significant issue?

---

Please remember that these are my themes/questions; some, but not all, of these themes will be addressed as the course unfolds. My answer to this activity is based on my experience; I would expect it to differ in many ways from your own because we each have a different history which conditions how we think and act – I call these different traditions of understanding. An environmental scientist will see things differently from a politician! The differences in our traditions of understanding explain why people doing the same thing, e.g. listening to the same speaker, can lead to many different outcomes – different interpretations of what is happening, what is,

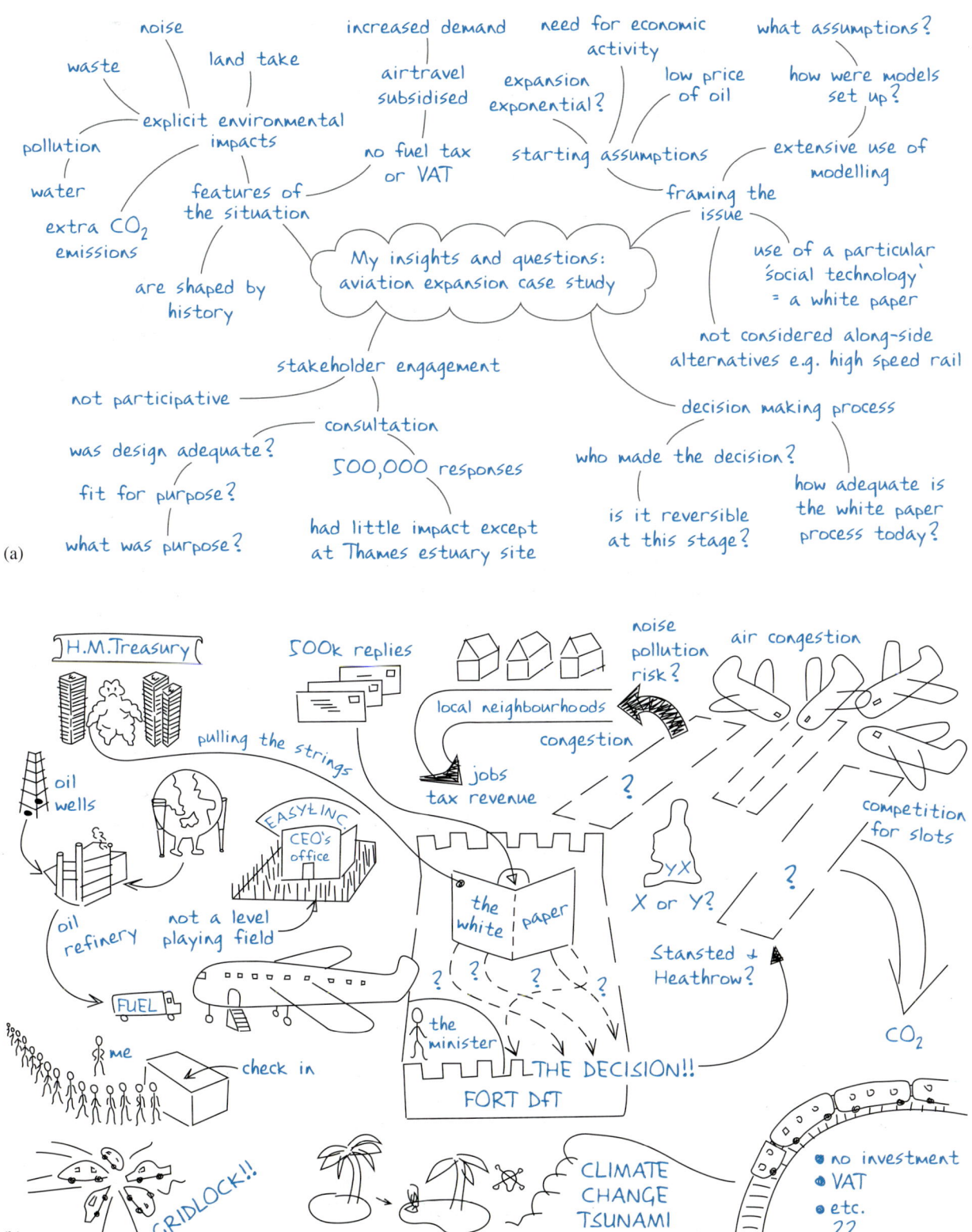

Figure 4  (a) A spray diagram and (b) rich picture of the situation as I experienced it from my engagement with the aviation expansion case study

or is not, important, etc. For this reason it is important to explore, and re-explore, a situation from a number of different perspectives as you engage in and monitor and evaluate environmental decision making.

When I constructed my spray diagram, I found that my main concerns could be captured in four higher-level headings: 1, features of the situation; 2, framing the issue; 3, decision-making process; and 4, stakeholder engagement. As shown in Figure 4a, I then recognised a set of other sub-headings within each of these higher-level headings. As I developed the diagram, I began to realise that stakeholder engagement could have been included as a branch in 'framing the issue'. My rich picture is shown in Figure 4b. As the protocol for rich pictures requires, I have included myself in the picture – as someone who also queues for cheap flights but perhaps slightly outside the mainstream! What did I learn from doing my rich picture? I became concerned that perhaps I was not representing the dominant view as fairly as I might.

This then led me to think about other forms of economic activity that may be less problematic than airport expansion, and made me feel more confident that my rich picture captured the idea that there is too much siege-mentality thinking. I have depicted cars in one corner, rail in another corner and air in another and this caused me to wonder further why governments have found it so hard to develop an integrated transport strategy (both nationally, Europe-wide and internationally). This led me to hypothesise that the White Paper process is not conducive to delivering systemic outcomes. I became conscious of some of the metaphors in my picture, e.g. airline companies not on a level playing field; climate change as a tsunami; the Treasury pulling the decision-making strings, etc. Most importantly my rich picture has illuminated a number of themes that I could pick up on if I wanted to do more about the situation through further inquiry. These themes concern content and process issues as well as political and emotionally charged personal aspects.

You may have noticed that in my list of questions and my two diagrams, I have not dwelt on the detail of the environmental decision making. I did this because I wanted to stand back from some of the detail of the case study and to explore/re-explore the case study situation. However, to begin systemically, we also need to have some means of exploring the effects of some of these details, and the connections between them. In particular, we need to consider some specific aspects of the wider biophysical environment, and its relation to the decision-making process.

### SAQ 1  Biophysical environments

What examples of taking the biophysical environment into account are presented in the *Heathrow Terminal 5* video?

### SAQ 2  Environmental impacts

In the *Reach for the Sky* video what existing, or potential, environmental impacts as a result of aviation expansion are mentioned that were not mentioned in the BAA production?

To begin exploring aspects of the biophysical environment, I am going to look in more detail at some of the issues surrounding climate change and in particular the systemic processes that affect the amount of carbon dioxide (the major 'greenhouse gas') in the atmosphere. Working with this material, and with other aspects of the case study, requires further ideas about modelling and some concepts associated with the way that systems can change, that is, their dynamics.

## 2.2   Climate change and the carbon cycle

In this section I aim to (i) introduce some of the key processes that affect the movement of carbon around the earth system and (ii) explain why it may be difficult to make predictions about future events associated with atmospheric carbon dioxide levels.

Some of the predictions of the possible hazards associated with climate change, and suggestions about the cause of climate change, are given in the video *Reach for the Sky* and the topic is further examined in Reading 1.

### Reading 1a and 1b

Read 'Climate change: scientific certainties and uncertainties' by the Natural Environment Research Council and 'Condemned to death by degrees' by Robin McKie. These readings set out some of the important aspects of climate change – a major environmental issue. You should read them now, and make notes in your learning journal. You should then be able to answer the following SAQs.

---

**SAQ 3   Earth and the greenhouse effect**

What determines the temperature of the earth, and how is this related to the 'greenhouse effect'?

---

**SAQ 4   Evidence for climate change**

List some of the factors that suggest that climate change is occurring.

---

**SAQ 5   Key uncertainties about climate**

Describe in your own words some of the key uncertainties about climate change.

---

One of the few studies that gives data on the changes in carbon dioxide in the atmosphere over a relatively long period comes from the Mauna Loa observatory in Hawaii (Figure 5). This clearly shows the increase since 1958. Ironically, given the stance of the US regime in 2005 to climate change science, the Mauna Loa observatory is operated by the USA.

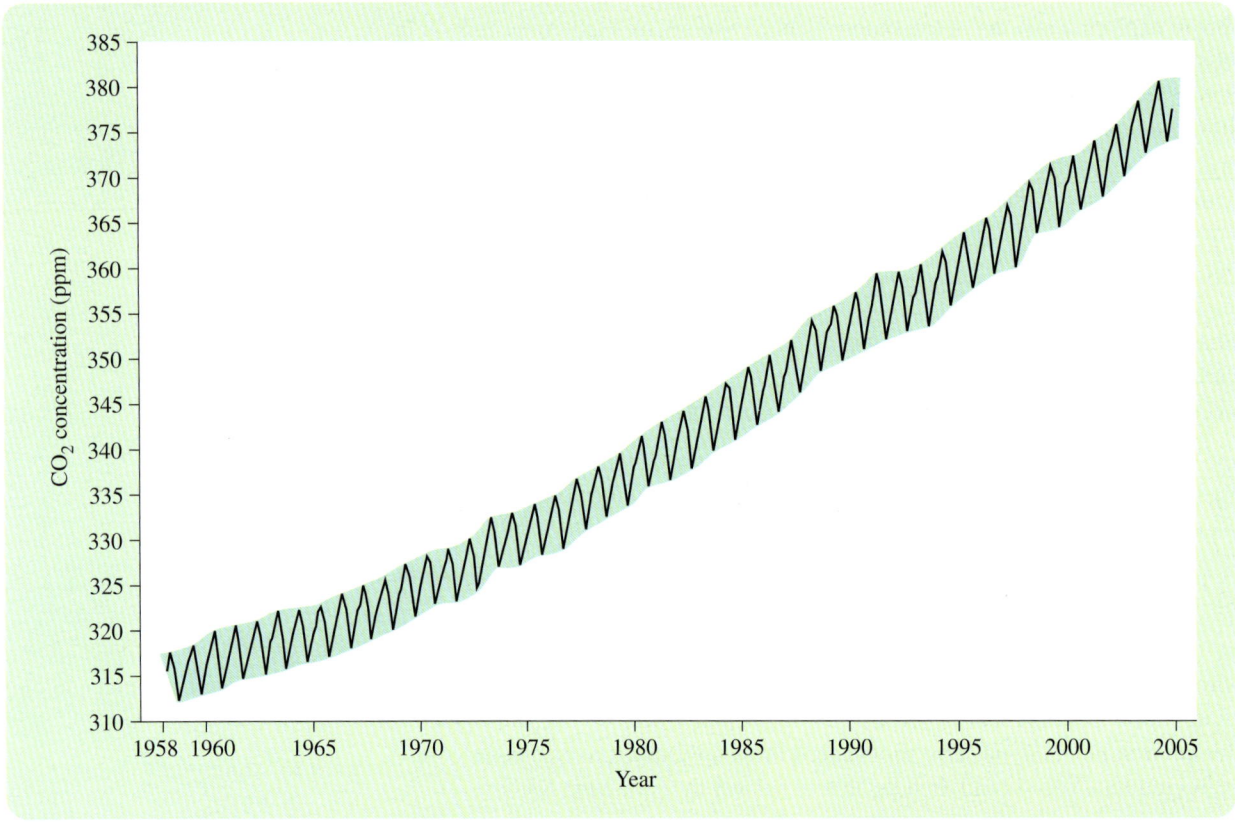

Figure 5   The historic series of carbon dioxide measurements from Mauna Loa, Hawaii (Source: http://cdiac.esd.ornl.gov/trends/co2/sio-mlo.htm)

From Reading 1, it appears that the cycling of carbon around the globe is a vital but complex environmental process, and an understanding of the basics of this will help to illuminate a major aspect of the airport expansion study. It also provides concrete examples of some further concepts associated with systems that will be useful later in the course.

### Study note

At this point, if you have studied environmental science, you may want to skip directly to SAQ 6.

## 2.3   The carbon cycle: ecosystems, oceans and geology

To read some coverage of the issue, it might appear that the changes in atmospheric carbon dioxide are simply the result of the burning of fossil fuels (which all contain carbon) in engines, releasing carbon dioxide into the atmosphere. However, that is only one of a number of other processes involved, and to examine the implications of ever increasing use of aircraft, we need to have a general understanding of these processes. Many of them depend on the presence of living organisms (including ourselves), and they also underlie many other aspects of our environment, such as biodiversity. One way of understanding these processes systemically is in terms of **ecosystems**, defined as the interdependent groupings of plants, animals and other living organisms with non-living components such as water, soil minerals, etc. that use energy and process materials (Tansley, 1935). Nearly all ecosystems share a common structure and set of processes involving carbon. These are represented schematically in Figure 6 and we can trace the movements of carbon around this generalised ecosystem. Plants absorb light and grow in size as they absorb simple raw materials, including carbon dioxide from the air and water from the soil, to produce new leaves and other tissues. Growth of living organisms generally involves increasing the amount of carbon stored in them, but when they die, the carbon is mostly released through decomposition.

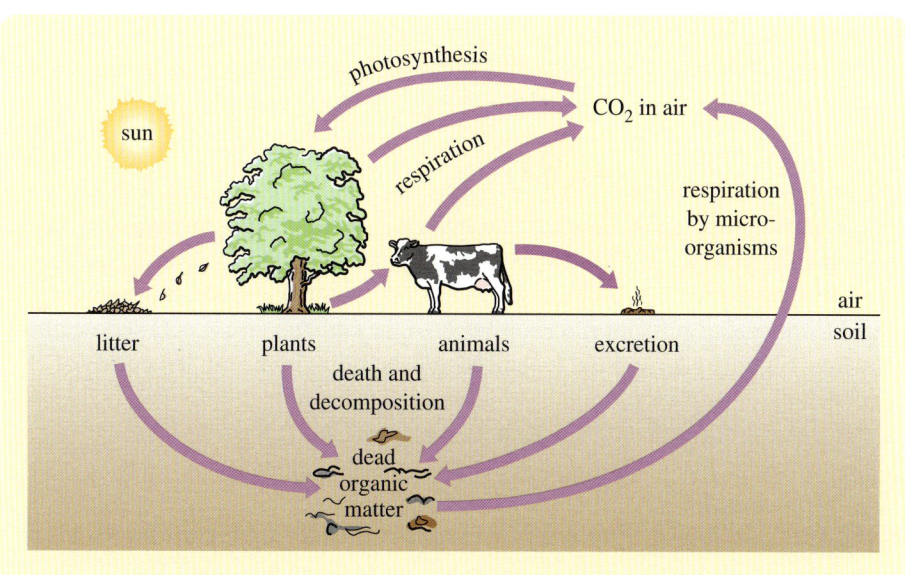

Figure 6  Some basic components and interlinkages in a stylised terrestrial ecosystem

Some plant material is consumed by herbivores, but some of it passes to less familiar compartments. Dead organic matter represents the remains of living organisms which have died but have not (yet) been consumed by detrivores (animals that feed on dead material) or the microbial decomposers that break down dead material outside their cells. Dead organic matter includes, for example, the dead heartwood standing in the trunks of living trees, the peat which accumulates in bogs and the 'humus' and other dead organic matter in soil.

### Box 1  Photosynthesis and respiration

These two fundamental life processes are, in effect, mirror images. In photosynthesis, carbon dioxide is combined with water to produce a complex carbon-containing compound (carbohydrate) plus oxygen; and in respiration, the complex compound breaks down, with oxygen being taken in and carbon dioxide and water released. The processes are essentially:

carbon dioxide + water ↔ complex carbon compounds + oxygen.

In photosynthesis, light energy absorbed by plants drives the process from left to right; in respiration, the process goes from right to left releasing water, carbon dioxide gas and energy in different forms.

Building up new living materials requires energy, breaking them down releases it.

Animals such as ourselves and most micro-organisms cannot photosynthesise, but rely on consuming material from other organisms for both carbon and energy. Animal movement requires energy, and energy is continually lost from organisms as heat and dissipated into the surroundings and out into space. Solar energy trapped through photosynthesis replaces energy lost to the ecosystem, so there is a continual flow of energy through any functioning ecosystem. In contrast, much of the carbon involved is cycled around the compartments, as one organism feeds on another. In our urbanised world, the importance of these two sets of processes is sometimes obscure, but they are critical to the existence of all life. Without the building-up of ordered structures that results from the trapping of solar energy by plants, the basic laws of thermodynamics dictate that the prevailing state of matter on earth would be complete disorder.

The ecosystem processes in Figure 6 are only part of the story of carbon. Carbon dioxide in the atmosphere is absorbed into the water in the oceans, but is also released from the oceans as water is moved around as a result of differences in temperature, wind effects and the rotation of the earth. Figure 7 shows the range of processes involved in the global and longer term version of the carbon cycle. Local scale carbon movements (Figure 6) correspond to the generalised flows in the top left corner of Figure 7.

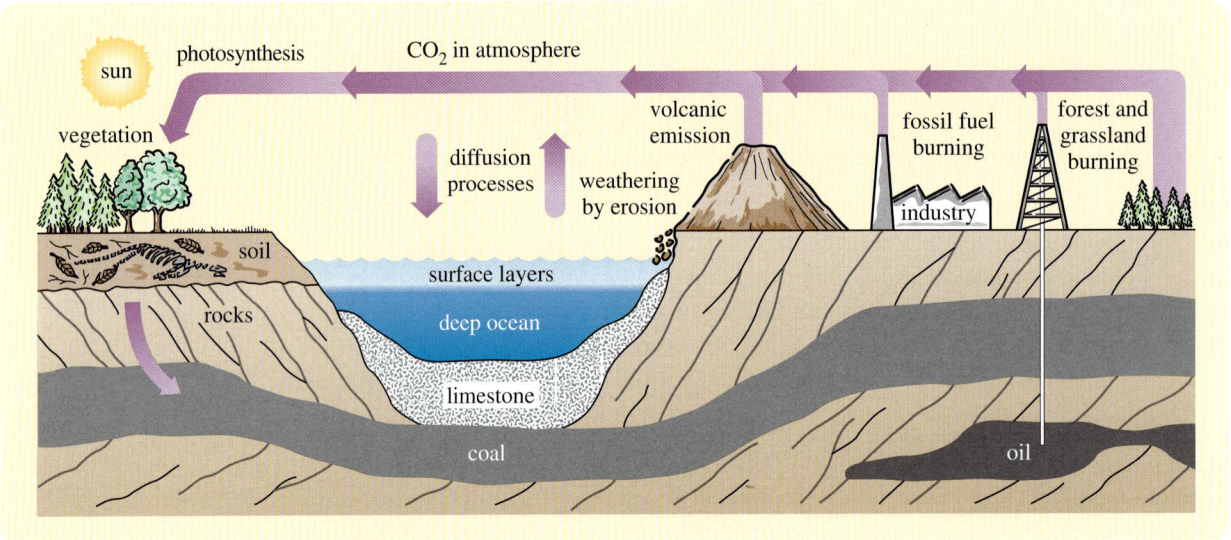

Figure 7    The global, long term carbon cycle

Human activities add carbon dioxide to the atmosphere mainly by burning carbon-containing materials, either recently produced (<200 years) biomass such as wood or straw, or items like oil and coal that are extracted from the ground. Oil and coal are generally accepted as being the remains of biomass from millions of years ago that have been transformed into their present form by the effects of pressure and temperature as overlying layers of rock built up over them and were moved around by geological processes. (There is a school of thought that claims that oil and coal are continually being formed by totally different processes deep within the earth. The evidence for this is generally believed to be spurious, but its attractiveness to some sections of society are obvious!)

For all practical purposes, carbon cannot be created or destroyed within the earth system boundary, so it should not be impossible to measure and/or calculate the flows of carbon between, and amounts present in, the items in Figure 7. However, there are some major difficulties in doing this. The first is the spatial scale of observation required to document the stocks and flows of carbon across the whole globe. Secondly, there is the problem of distinguishing short term fluctuations from longer term trends.

It is theoretically possible to measure the rates of flow of carbon between the different compartments in Figures 6 and 7, and to use these values as if it were a simple cash flow analysis. Unfortunately, this would be of little help in looking at longer term changes because the rates of flow are not constant over time, but depend on the amounts present in the different compartments. The rate of global photosynthesis and of solution into the oceans depends on the amount of carbon dioxide present in the atmosphere (as well as on temperature). For example, within limits, the maximum rate of photosynthesis, and hence the average rate across the world, increases as the amount of $CO_2$ in the atmosphere increases, provided there is sufficient light, water and soil-derived nutrients available. In formal terms, there is feedback within the system, and we will examine this concept further in Section 3.5.

To estimate future values of the carbon storage in different compartments including the atmosphere, and hence to make estimates of the likely magnitude of climate change, it's necessary to create a quantitative, mathematical model of the chosen system. Mathematical models are an important class of models for exploring systems of interest (see below), but they are just one of a range of possibilities. In the following section, we will look in more general terms at the use of models as a part of starting out systemically. Modelling takes many forms and is an important skill in environmental decision making – but not all modelling is necessarily systemic!

### SAQ 6 Key processes affecting $CO_2$

Summarise the key processes that affect the amount of carbon dioxide in the earth's atmosphere, and relate these to some of the 'uncertainties' that were mentioned in Reading 1.

# 3 Exploring and re-exploring through modelling

In this section you will be introduced to various ways of using models to explore aspects of situations where environmental decision making occurs. Book 3 will then consider some of the ways in which models can be used to represent and analyse criteria for making environmental decisions before taking action. Remember that modelling is a central activity in the overall framework (Figure 1) that relates closely to all of the stages.

### Study note

As you work through this section, you will be asked to look again at some sections of the course DVD to examine the way that models have been used to present possible configurations of the expansion of aviation in the UK.

## 3.1 An introduction to modelling

Although you may not immediately have recognised them as such, you will certainly have already encountered many examples of models in everyday life. You have also been doing modelling in some of your activity answers, such as the spray diagrams and rich picture in Activity 2. Maps and plans are models of the layout of roads or buildings, and photographs are models of the scene that the camera user saw when the button was pressed. The word modelling itself has a range of colloquial and technical interpretations, so we need first to establish the way in which the course team is using the term. As a start, consider Figure 8, part of an Ordnance Survey map of the UK. This shows selected features of an area of land, and provides a simplified and stylised representation of the real roads, buildings and landforms that we would encounter if we went to explore that area (though, of course, we would not expect to find the actual letters 'London Stansted Airport' in the position shown!).

One definition of a model might therefore be 'a simplified representation of reality', but that actually raises some quite significant philosophical questions, relating to the distinction between a positivist and constructivist epistemology. Put simply, the positivist view is that there exists an objective 'reality' that we can explore in more or less detail, and that with sufficient time, we would all reach a description (model) of that reality that would be the same. The contrasting, constructivist position concentrates much more on the way in which each individual experiences and perceives events. Without necessarily denying the existence of concrete objects in our surroundings, this view would suggest that each of us has only a particular, internal conception of objects, events and the links between them.

Put another way, we each have internal mental models of situations, and it is these rather than the situation itself (which in its entirety is almost certainly unknowable) that affect, and are determined by, the outcomes of our actions. It may therefore be better to define a model as a simplified representation of a person's/group's view of a situation. We also need to expand the simple definition further, to stress that the sorts

Figure 8   A section of the 1:50,000 OS map of the area around Stansted Airport

of models we are dealing with in this course are intended for a specific purpose. That could be as limited as 'to summarise my understanding of a situation' but, in the present context, we are concerned with decision making. For this course, a fuller definition of a model, and the one on which this section is based, is:

**A simplified representation of a person's/group's view of a situation, constructed to assist in making environmental decisions.**

In the airport expansion case study, several types of models were mentioned. Many runway configuration studies carried out within the Aviation White Paper used maps of the possible noise contours around an airport. A similar map is reproduced as Figure 9. These were models, representing the different noise levels as contours, but the maps themselves were derived from mathematical models of the relationships between frequency of flight movements, types of aircraft, their flight paths, etc. and the level of noise that would be perceived by someone standing on the ground at a given point. The units used in Figure 9 are in dBA (decibels A-scale) which is a frequency-weighted noise unit used for traffic, industrial noise measurement, etc. Leq is a measure of the equivalent continuous noise level over a specific period; thus it is an averaging technique in which the noise levels are averaged through, for example, an operating day. This means that quiet periods can hide extreme events of noise nuisance during peak operation (usually in the morning and early evening), which could give a misleading impression.

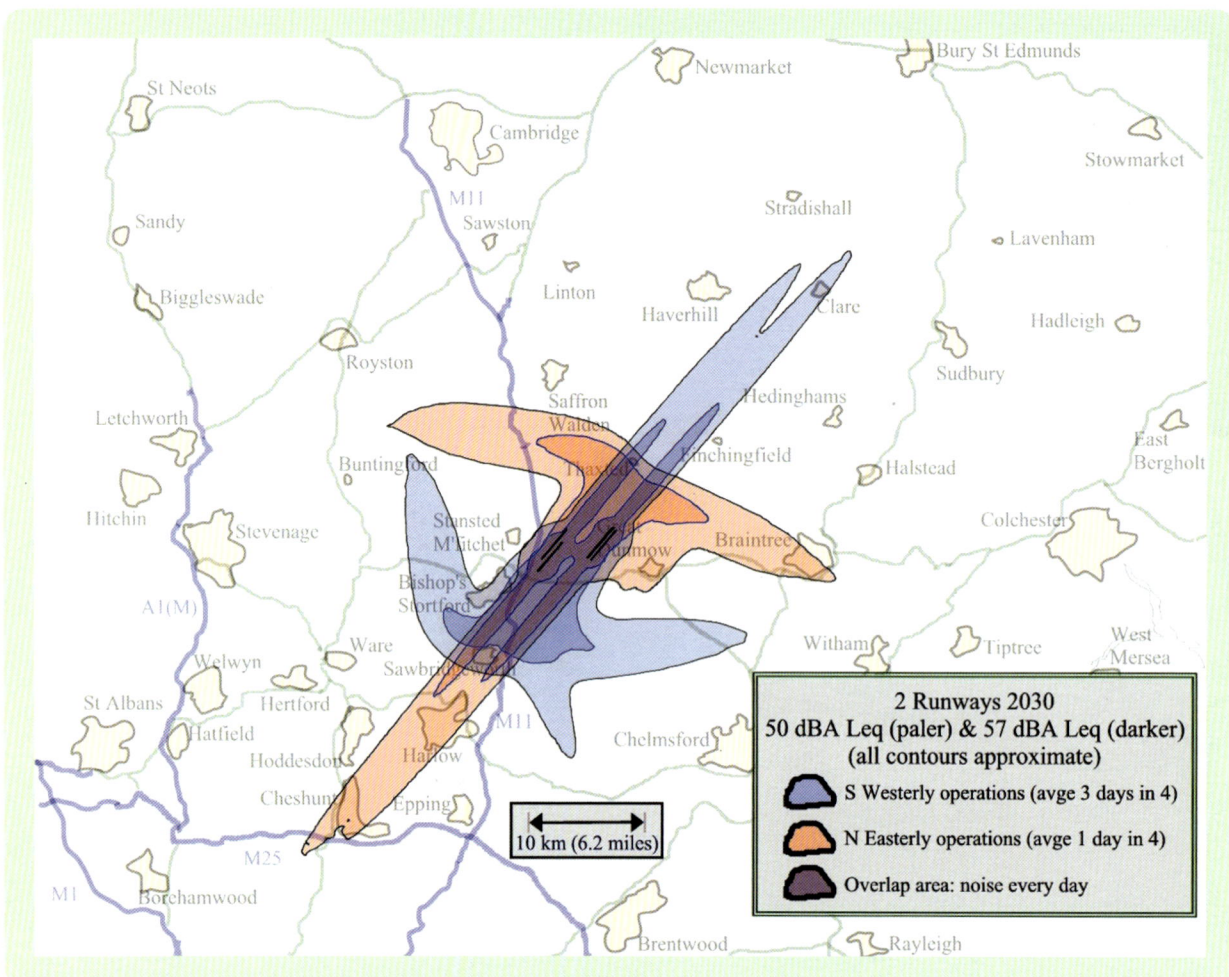

Figure 9  A representation of the predicted noise levels around the expanded Stansted Airport with the two-runway option. 50 dBA Leq is the level that the World Health Organization states should not be exceeded in order to 'protect the majority of people from being moderately annoyed in the daytime', while 57 dBA Leq is the level that the UK Government states 'marks the approximate onset of significant community annoyance' (WHO, 1999; DfT, 2003). (Source: Stop Stansted Expansion, 2005).

One of the important factors in the decisions about siting the expansion was the use of cost–benefit analysis, which is another specific form of mathematical model, described in the *Techniques* book and examined in more detail in Book 3.

Each of the examples provided a simplified representation of different aspects of the situation that existed, or might exist, as a result of the airport expansion. They have been used to explore possible future configurations of quite complex situations. Without some of these modelling techniques, it would be difficult – if not impossible – to visualise the outcomes of decisions. Humans have a limit to their information-processing capacity, and so we have to simplify situations in order to make decisions. This gives modelling a vital role in framing possible decisions, since each model will vary in the extent of the simplification involved, and in the different aspects of the situation that it represents. It also means that the perspectives of the persons doing the modelling (or paying for it to be done) can have a major effect on what emerges. Therefore it is essential that we understand how models are constructed, how they can be used and for what purposes and, in particular, what their limitations are.

> ### Activity 3  Use of models in the *Terminal 5* example
>
> View the sequence on the *Heathrow Terminal 5* video entitled 'Passenger experience'. See if you can identify at least two different models that have been used in the first few minutes of this track.

In addition to the models listed in the response to this activity, I would also suggest that the commentary on that track illustrated another aspect of modelling. The terminal was described as a 'public transport interchange'. To me, this was an example of using words to imply a particular conceptual model of the terminal. It is an accurate, but partial, metaphor for the way the terminal system is intended to operate, one which might be expected to appeal to (or appease?) any viewers who had doubts about the increase in private car use that the terminal might generate.

## 3.2  A general typology of models

In order to consider different modelling activities, it is helpful to try to categorise the types of models that we are likely to encounter in dealing with environmental issues and the uses that are made of them in this context. Two important uses are for prediction and for communication. The virtual-reality models of the new Terminal 5 in the case study showed predictions of the appearances of as-yet-unconstructed facilities, based on the designers' assumptions (in themselves, models) about the terminal. The models were being used as a tool for communication, in the sense of informing the public and official decision makers about the benefits that the terminal would provide for its users. Prediction and communication of possible configurations of a situation or system of interest are an essential part of the framing and exploring in environmental decision making.

Behind the virtual-reality model of the terminal, there is another way in which models are extensively used – for optimisation. The architects and engineers involved in designing the new terminal could not do this work entirely by trial and error, although trial assembly of parts of the terminal off-site was actually used in the process. Nor could they work on the basis of the sort of craft knowledge used by the medieval masons who constructed the great churches, which in themselves were probably just as much symbols and drivers of economic success in their period as are airports today! Modern design makes use of mathematical models of the relationships between materials, their form, their strength and other properties, to choose realisations that have what is considered to be the best combination of cost, convenience for users, safety, etc. We will look in some more detail at this general use of models for choosing desirable alternatives in Book 3.

Different models may be more, or less, useful for the different purposes identified above. Table 1 represents a general indication of the likely usefulness of the four basic model types for communication, prediction and optimisation.

Table 1  The four general types of model and their suitability for different uses

| Use | Type of model | | | |
|---|---|---|---|---|
| | Iconic | Conceptual | Graphical | Mathematical |
| Communication | ✓ | ✓ | ✓ | ?/✓ |
| Prediction | ✓ | x | ? | ✓ |
| Optimisation | ? | x | ? | ✓ |

Key: x = cannot be used; ? = may be usable; ✓ = can be readily used for this purpose

You have already encountered a number of conceptual models, which mainly use words and pictures or images to express internal mental processes. Metaphors are a particularly important example within this general area. Conceptual modelling and metaphors are dealt with later in this book. Graphical models include maps and plans, but also more abstract forms such as systems maps, multiple cause diagrams and sign graphs. Mathematical models, such as those used in the design of Terminal 5 and in the aviation cost–benefit study, are usually now computer-based and much of the professional literature concerned with modelling seems to regard the term 'model' as synonymous with this aspect. In practice the use of computers has begun to blur the distinction between graphical and mathematical models, with the computer providing the means both to undertake the calculations and present the graphical images. Colloquially, the word 'model' also applies to the scaled-down models of aircraft shown at the beginning of *Reach for the Sky*, or to an architect's model of a new development. These, the province of the model engineer, are termed iconic models and are the most direct representation of part of the world, changed mainly in terms of scale or material from the physical object.

In the following sections, we are going to concentrate on graphical models and their use for communication and, to a limited extent, for prediction.

### SAQ 7  Models used in the case study

Recall your study of the whole case study and list some further examples of models that were used either explicitly or implicitly and for what purpose.

I would recommend that before undertaking this SAQ, you read briefly through all the various modelling techniques, both qualitative and quantitative, within the *Techniques* book (see Diagramming and Modelling), so that you can recognise examples of these.

You have already worked with three sorts of graphical model – maps, spray diagrams and rich pictures. In the following section, you will be asked to do some more modelling, linked to the case study. For obvious reasons, you won't be making any physical, iconic models, but will use some further graphical models and the early stages of one type of mathematical model. The first graphical model technique I want to explore further here is that of systems maps.

## 3.3 Systems maps

Systems maps are an important technique for capturing a snapshot of a complex situation at a particular moment in time. They also force you into some rigorous thinking about a situation by making you combine similar elements together in sub-systems and making boundary judgements (i.e. what is in or out of a sub-system or what is in your system of interest and what is outside, in the environment of the system). Try this for yourself by attempting Activity 4.

### Activity 4  Developing a systems map

Develop a systems map of the airport expansion environmental decision-making situation. Before you start, you should become familiar with the protocols for developing systems maps in the *Techniques* book (see Diagramming: systems maps) and on the DVD. It is important to follow 'the rules' as they make your thinking more rigorous.

You might like to compare your systems map with mine, which is at the back of the book. I do not expect them to be the same because (i) you have a different perspective from me and thus you are likely to see different things and group them differently and (ii) you will make different boundary judgements, i.e. put your boundary in a different place, which will result in different things being inside and outside of your system of interest. I use the term 'interest' to make the point that there is no right or wrong 'system' but that a range of different ones are possible based on your perspective and interests. The process of formulating (or constructing) a system of interest is one which aims to help you learn about a complex situation. I would hope that at the end of this activity you will have learnt something more about the case study and have a better understanding of the important systems concepts of boundary, boundary judgements, and levels, or hierarchy (i.e. system, sub-system, element).

## 3.4 Influence diagrams

A systems map derived from a situation identifies the major items that comprise the perceived system, but does not say much about the influences that are at work within that situation. An influence diagram is one way of representing this, and a second is a multiple cause diagram. Let's start with an influence diagram (see Diagramming: influence diagrams in the *Techniques* book).

### Activity 5  Patterns of influence – influence diagramming

From your perspective what are the main set of influences that have led to the decision to expand airports in the south east of England?

Make some notes on what you learnt about the situation by developing an influence diagram.

#### Study note

I recommend you work your way through several iterations of your diagram. You may like to share ideas about the set of influences on the course conference, because it is inevitable that others will have different perspectives on the situation.

My response to this activity is at the back of the book, and also features in a DVD activity that you will work through in Section 3.8.

## 3.5  Multiple cause diagrams

A multiple cause diagram (MCD) was used in Book 1 to provide a model of the factors influencing road traffic growth (Figure 9 in Book 1). I now want you to develop a multiple cause diagram for yourself. For the diagram, I want you to consider as the central topic the volume of air traffic using Swansea Airport described in the video *Reach for the Sky*. The range of factors affecting this is enormous, and could even be taken to include the decisions of the UK Air Ministry in the 1950s to retain the airport land, rather than handing it back to local farmers as proposed in the original agreement. But the most immediate factors are the demand for flights and the cost of flights. (If you need to remind yourself of the content of this sequence, take time now to review it, and to read the material on multiple cause diagrams in the *Techniques* book (see Diagramming) and on the DVD.)

### Activity 6  A simple multiple cause diagram

Draw a part of a multiple cause diagram that shows plausible relationships between the three factors identified above (volume of air traffic, demand for flights and cost of flights).

This diagram really adds very little to a verbal description and the diagramming technique only becomes useful when extended to include more factors. Demand itself is affected by several factors beside cost. These might include the attractiveness/ availability of alternative modes of travel, attitudes to air travel and local/regional/ national prosperity. Cost will depend on fuel price, and to some extent on demand. Because many of the costs of an aircraft journey are fixed, and do not vary with number of passengers, the higher the load factor (that is, the average proportion of seats occupied), the lower the airline can make prices per seat to the passengers.

One important aspect of multiple cause diagrams is that they can help to identify feedback loops, where cause and effect are linked both ways, so that A affects B and B can also affect A. The idea of feedback is a very important one in looking at systems; feedback effects are often responsible for the unexpected behaviour that occurs.

### Activity 7  Multiple cause diagrams and feedback loops

Identify at least two feedback loops implicit in the text above and in Government beliefs that have been expressed in the Aviation White Paper. Extend your earlier multiple cause diagram to show the feedback loops you have identified.

Feedback loops of the sort shown in my response to Activity 7 (see Figure 55 at the back) have an important bearing on the way that the situation modelled will change over time. If you think logically around the second loop, an increase in air traffic causes an increase in prosperity and that causes an increase in air traffic. To show this formally, we would need to convert the multiple cause diagram into a sign graph, but it represents a classic example of *positive feedback*, which implies that the two items concerned would just go on growing for ever and ever. This is the phenomenon of *exponential growth*, and the Aviation White Paper is based on the assumption that this will occur over the foreseeable future. Of course, in reality, there are limits to any real example such as the growth of air traffic, even if it is the situation where everyone in the world is flying around all the time! We can probably assume that is unlikely to occur, and other factors will intervene to prevent this. To fully understand the mathematics of feedback is beyond the scope of this course, but before moving on to the material on system dynamics diagramming in Section 3.7, I recommend that you work through Activity 8 using the DVD, to make sure you have a good grasp of the implications of feedback loops.

### Activity 8  Investigating feedback

Using the Feedback model provided on the DVD, view the graphs of the change in the item called 'amount' that show the differences between:

- high and low strength of positive feedback
- positive and negative feedback.

One of the factors that will probably limit the growth of air traffic is the cost of fuel. In the period between the publication of the White Paper and the time of writing in 2005, fuel costs have almost trebled, and it is at least plausible that prices will remain at such a level or even increase further. This may occur because of physical shortages of the fossil fuels on which aviation currently depends. It is perhaps more plausible that fears over climate change will at some point force governments to introduce policies that are designed to limit fossil fuel burning. These might include imposing taxes that will increase fuel cost.

Other factors that look to be important in restraining the growth of aviation include public attitudes to flying. Terrorist attacks, changes in the value attributed to the disbenefits of noise, pollution and some of the cultural effects of mass aviation and the occurrence of air accidents are just some of the possible factors. What we cannot know is the balance between these restraining factors and the general positive feedback relationship that appears to hold at the moment – that the more people who have flown, the more seem to want to fly.

> ### SAQ 8  Factors affecting air traffic in south east England
>
>
>
> From the preceding text, from your work with the case study and from general knowledge, draw up a more extensive multiple cause diagram of the factors you regard as important in affecting air traffic in the south east of England.

If you look at my answer to this SAQ, and compare it with your own, you will almost certainly notice differences. Although I do fly several times a year, including journeys where the train would almost certainly be a less environmentally damaging alternative, you may notice that my multiple cause diagram includes some items concerned with damage to the local and global biophysical environment. This is a reflection of my particular perspective, and a desire to draw attention to these effects. This emphasises the point that no model is an objective representation but each one is representative of the values, knowledge and skills of the person(s) producing the model.

Remember that an MCD does not tell us anything more than that there is a relationship between the factors in the diagram. It does not directly tell us anything about the nature of this relationship. To make this more explicit, and to begin to investigate the possible implications of a multiple cause diagram, we need to redraw it as a sign graph. This will also enable us to identify more clearly where feedback loops, with their potential for unchecked growth, may occur.

## 3.6  Sign graphs

### Study note

Before reading the next section, check that you understand the conventions of a sign graph by reading the *Techniques* book (see Diagramming: sign graphs) and watching the relevant sequence in the Techniques section of the DVD.

In a sign graph, the arrow linking any two factors has a plus sign if a change in the factor at the tail of the arrow results in a change, in the same direction, in the factor at the head of the arrow. That is, an increase in one causes an increase in the other and a decrease causes a decrease. So, in the example above, an increase in prosperity causes an increase in air traffic (+). The converse, negative effect is exemplified by costs, where an increase in costs causes a decrease in traffic (–).

Use of this convention enables us to explore in a systematic and systemic manner how a situation may change over time.

## Activity 9  Sign graphs

Work through your multiple cause diagram in answer to Activity 7, and convert it into a sign graph by adding + or − signs to the links where you feel it is appropriate. Where you are uncertain, use ? to show this.

You may well have had difficulty in adding the signs on several of the relationships. This may be because the relationship is inherently unclear, in which case it may indicate that further investigation of the situation is warranted to clarify the point. However, a common problem occurs where factors themselves are given an explicit direction of change. A common error is to give factors names like 'increase in cost' or 'increase in global temperature'. It is then potentially confusing to decide whether something like 'availability of fuel' has a positive or negative relationship with 'increase in cost'. While this can be accommodated in a sign graph, it is much clearer to state each item neutrally, as 'availability of fuel', 'cost', etc. Based on this advice, you might like to modify some of the terms in your MCD.

In all the graphical models so far considered, the main purpose is communication. Such graphical models can be used to a limited extent to give qualitative indications of what may happen in the future (prediction), but their most important role is as a focus for exploring a situation, both in your own mind and in debate with others. Their value lies in making explicit each set of perspectives and beliefs about what is occurring or possibly what should occur. My MCD showed my understanding and interpretation of the case study situation, in a way that I hope you found clear and easy to question. This exploration and questioning is an essential part of 'starting off systemically', getting away from over-concentration on single causal sequences. (I would rate the UK Government's focus on economic growth in the context of aviation expansion as a classic example of single cause thinking. However, your perspective may be different.)

## 3.7  System dynamics diagramming

System dynamics diagrams are a development from sign graphs, allowing for some additional detail in relationships, and form the basis of some more formal mathematical models. They were originally associated with chemical engineering, where there were often 'flows' of some physical substance between different 'compartments', and as such, offer a relatively obvious way to model the carbon cycle introduced earlier. Plants, animals, the soil, the atmosphere, etc. can all be conceptualised as compartments in our generalised picture of an ecosystem in Figure 6.

## Activity 10  Drawing a system dynamics diagram

By to Figure 6 and to the *Techniques* book (Diagramming: system dynamics diagrams), draw a section of a system dynamics diagram of the relationships between carbon in the atmosphere, in the terrestrial biosphere and in the soil.

One version of such a model is given in Figure 10.

Note that this version regards carbon in the soil as being separate from carbon in the 'terrestrial biosphere'. This is somewhat arbitrary (many would argue that the soil is an essential component of the biosphere) but has the merit of distinguishing between carbon in living organisms (the biosphere component) and that sitting in dead material in the soil.

Figure 10 includes four feedback loops. The rate of incorporation of carbon into plants by photosynthesis depends on the amount of photosynthetic tissue available in the biosphere, which in itself depends on the rate of photosynthesis. The rate of photosynthesis also depends on the amount of carbon (as carbon dioxide) in the atmosphere, forming the second feedback loop.

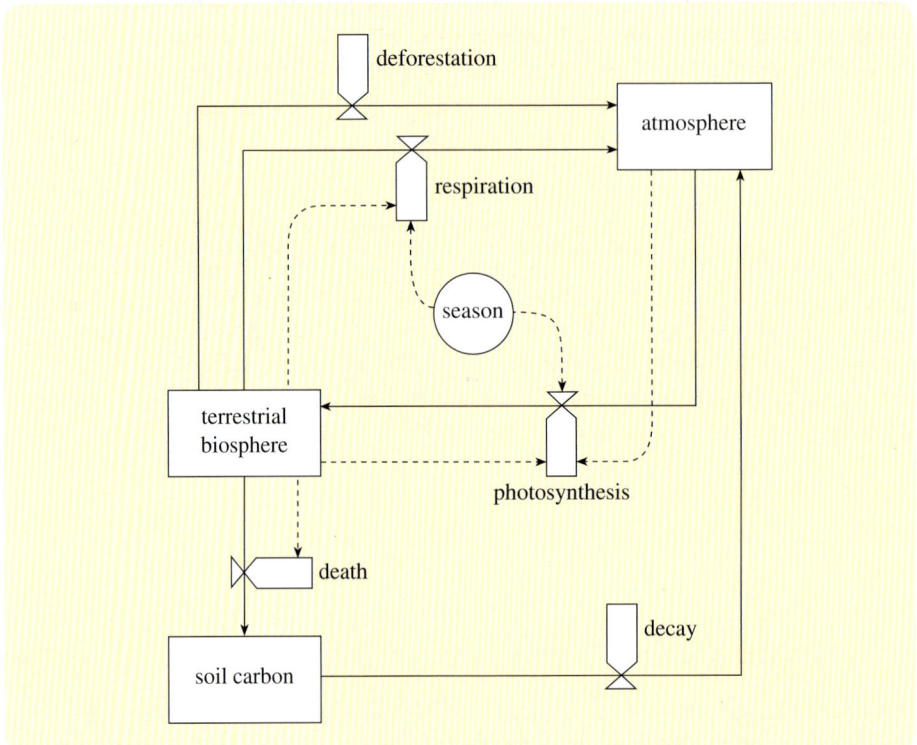

Figure 10   System dynamics diagram of the parts of the global carbon cycle involving the terrestrial biosphere, soil and the atmosphere (Source: adapted from http://www.shodor.org/mvhs/carbon.sif)

## SAQ 9   Feedback loops

Identify, and explain in words, one other feedback loop shown in Figure 10.

Using the system dynamics diagramming convention, a very simplified model of the processes in the carbon cycle is shown in Figure 11. This model has also been provided as a program on the course DVD, and in Book 3 you will have the opportunity to work with this model to examine its behaviour.

> ### SAQ 10  More feedback loops
>
> Identify at least two other feedback processes in Figure 11 whereby the rate of movement of carbon between compartments depends on the quantity present in one or other compartment.

Using a much more complex version of this model, it is possible to estimate the amounts of carbon dioxide likely to be present in the atmosphere in the future as a result of different policies for controlling human induced emissions. Of course, this is only a part of the story, because there are further complications in predicting the likely effects of increases in atmospheric $CO_2$ on the global mean temperature, on local variations of temperature and on other aspects of climate and weather. Much of the uncertainty outlined in the NERC reading (Reading 1a) concerns both the structure of the models available (are enough of the causal factors included, are the relationships between them understood, are there connections that have been omitted?) and the precise numerical values that are used when these models are expressed mathematically in order to make predictions. Some of these major modelling issues will be addressed further in Book 3.

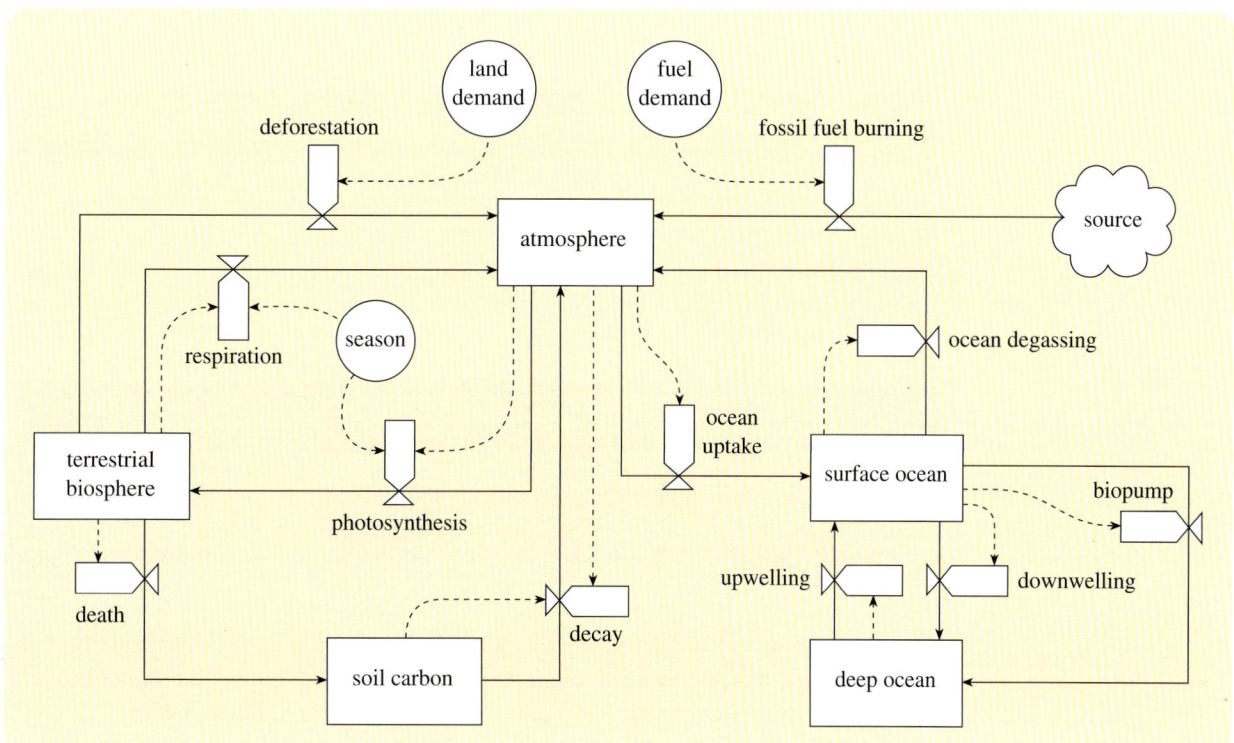

Figure 11  A highly simplified system dynamics diagram of the major processes in the carbon cycle (Source: adapted from http://www.shodor.org/mvhs/carbon.gif)

## 3.8 A review of modelling

You have now seen examples of several types of models that we suggested were useful for descriptive analysis of situations and for communication as part of the process of framing issues for consideration. Even as descriptions, there are some important general questions which you ought to ask on the basis of your study of the various examples. To help you do this, there is an activity on the DVD that compares the different models that have been used so far in the context of the 'Freedom to fly?' case study. You should now work through this activity, and then answer the following SAQs.

### Activity 11 Developing diagrams

View the Developing diagrams animation on the DVD. Make notes on how you saw the diagramming techniques complementing and feeding into each other. Also note down the various restrictions and constraints that each diagramming technique imposed.

### SAQ 11 Diagram differences

Explain in your own words the main distinctions between an influence diagram and a multiple cause diagram.

### SAQ 12 Diagrams – compare and contrast

Using systems maps and multiple cause diagrams as an example, compare and contrast the effect that using only one of these in a situation may have on the process of exploring and re-exploring an issue.

### SAQ 13 Boundaries in a system dynamics diagram

What are the implicit boundaries evident in the system dynamics diagram of the carbon cycle?

Activity 11 should have alerted you to the way that choosing to use a particular model can affect what is 'seen' in a particular situation. One further issue with modelling concerns the treatment of space and time. Nearly all models associated with environmental decision making have temporal and spatial components, yet these are not always made explicit by the modellers and can have major implications for the interpretation of the models. For example, the cost–benefit models used in the case study use discounting (see Economic evaluation: net present value and discounting in the *Techniques* book) to bring costs and revenues occurring at different times on to a common baseline of their net present value. The implication of this is that events occurring in the more distant future are less important than those in the near future. The models thus make an implicit boundary judgement about when, in time, events become unimportant. While this may be familiar to experts in the field, this is often not pointed out when presenting the results of cost–benefit studies.

Spatial issues also involve boundary judgements. Where a geographic area is being modelled, depending on the way results are presented, spatial averages can conceal local differences that may be important to particular stakeholders. For example, the predicted concentration of oxides of nitrogen resulting from increased traffic could be presented as an average over a whole town, and the values fall within agreed guidelines. However, local concentrations on particular streets may be much higher than the overall average and so the model could conceal a major health hazard to some groups.

Spatial and temporal issues also relate to the classification of levels of decision making mentioned in Book 1. Tables 2 and 3 give another suggested classification of scales of space and time relevant to models of biophysical systems.

Table 2   Spatial scale classification proposed for use in describing natural system models

| Nomenclature | Spatial scale |
|---|---|
| Ecozone | > 6,250,000 ha |
| Ecoprovince | 250,000–6,250,000 ha |
| Ecoregion | 10,000–250,000 ha |
| Ecodistrict | 625–10,000 ha |
| Ecosection | 25–625 ha |
| Ecoseries | 1.5–25 ha |
| Ecotope | 0.25–1.5 ha |
| Ecoelement | < 0.25 ha |

(after Klijn and De Haes, 1994)

Table 3   Timescale classification proposed for use in describing natural system models

| Nomenclature | Timescale |
|---|---|
| Mega | > $10^6$ years |
| Macro | > $10^4$ to < $10^6$ years |
| Micro | < $10^4$ years |

Micro subunits:

| | |
|---|---|
| Kiloyears | 1000 years |
| Centiyears | 100 years |
| Decayears | 10 years |
| Years | 1 year |
| Months | 1 month |
| Days | 1 day |
| Minutes | 1 minute |
| Seconds | 1 second |

(after Delcourt et al., 1983; Woodward, 1987; Dickinson, 1988)

A perhaps more familiar classification of timescales relates to human activities, lifespans, the evolution of the human race and longer periods. Many of our everyday concerns involve short term timescales of at most a few days (the weather, leisure/work activities), but if we have families, we may also have concerns about periods of many years, related to the lifespans of parents and the development of children. In a political system where elections occur at four or five year intervals, politicians often seem to regard consequences beyond this sort of period as being unimportant. Taking a longer view, we may look at changes over historical time (for written history, say 1000–2000 years). Change relative to prehistory is probably of interest only to a few specialists, even more so when talking of geological timescales of millions of years. Different individuals ascribe different importance to different timescales, and this can greatly influence views of the importance of predicted changes. This is another element of the anthropocentric/ecocentric division of human attitudes.

### SAQ 14 Time and space in aviation expansion

Select one of the models used in the aviation expansion case study and try and identify the timescale involved and the spatial area affected.

Given the importance of models in framing issues in environmental decision making, I suggest that when faced with any model as part of a decision-making process, you spend some time studying it, to make sure that you understand what aspects of the situation it represents and, equally importantly, what aspects it conceals. Even without specialist knowledge, you should be able to form some judgement as to how plausibly the model represents the situation of interest and whose perspective it favours. You should be particularly careful when confronted with mathematical models, which are usually developed by 'experts'. While these experts are most probably honest, they have their particular biases and specialisations, which may have limited or coloured their construction of any model. So, even as a layperson, you should try to tease out the simplifications and limitations inherent in the modelling activity, to be sure that it does not invalidate the use to which the model is being put.

# 4 Systems thinking for exploring and re-exploring

You have now experienced a range of systems methods and concepts, in Sections 2 and 3, that are relevant to exploring the issue of airport expansion, so I hope you will have begun to get a feel for what taking a systems approach might be like. I will explain in more detail what I mean by 'systems' and starting off systemically in this section. For the moment, consider the following quote from Lester Brown, Director of the Earth Policy Institute, which is a comment on an updated version of a very famous (perhaps infamous) book called *The Limits to Growth*, by Meadows et al., first published in 1972:

> Reading the 30th-year update reminds me of why the systems approach to thinking about our future is not only valuable, but indispensable. Thirty years ago, it was easy for the critics to dismiss the limits to growth. But in today's world, with its collapsing fisheries, shrinking forests, falling water tables, dying coral reefs, expanding deserts, eroding soils, rising temperatures, and disappearing species, it is not so easy to do so. We are all indebted to the 'Limits' team for reminding us again that time is running out.
>
> (Lester Brown, 2004)

I will say more about the concept 'limits to growth' below; at this stage I am not asking you to agree that starting off systemically is the 'only way' to start environmental decision making, but to acknowledge that there may be something here to take seriously!

I now want to invite you to consolidate what you think you know about the term 'system' by completing Activity 12.

## Activity 12  Your experience of the term 'system'

Jot down some notes in your learning journal on how you have used the word 'system' in your recent work. Make notes on what the word means to you. Questions may have arisen when the topic was briefly introduced in Book 1, or in the introduction to Part 1 of this book. You may wish to comment on how you now understand the adjectives 'systemic' and 'systematic' and also to jot down some ideas about how systems thinking might differ from systems practice. (My own perspective is introduced below.)

As I intimated earlier, many people either implicitly or explicitly refer to things that are interconnected (exhibit connectivity) when they use the word 'system'. A common example is the use of 'transport system' or 'computer system' in everyday speech. At this stage note whether your use of the word 'system' in your answer to Activity 12 implies that you see a 'system' as a set of interconnected 'things'

(elements). Or perhaps your use of the term suggests a way of thinking about the connections between things – hence a process?

My own experience is that it is often difficult to explain to someone else what is entailed in taking a systems approach. In Box 2, I outline how I understand the concept of 'system' for systems thinking and practice. Read through this and underline any points that do not make much sense to you at this stage. Then move on to Activity 13. My aim is to enable you to make better sense of the material in this box by the time you finish Book 2.

### Box 2 Explaining 'systems'

The place to start is with a situation of complexity and uncertainty, where the problem is to know what the problem is. Russell Ackoff, a widely known systems thinker, called such situations 'messes' and argued that they are not amenable to improvement through thinking which is linear, deterministic or reductionist. There is also rarely a single 'right' solution to a mess!

- Reductionism, a common scientific practice, has limitations because it assumes the whole can be understood from knowledge of the component parts. Reductionism is thus unable to deal with complexity and emergence.

- Within complex situations, progress can be made by formulating relevant wholes (systems of interest) as part of a process of systemic inquiry.

- Wholes do not pre-exist. They are selected by someone for a purpose – generally to learn about the complex situation and do something about it (change it, improve it, decide about it). All parts of the whole – and their relationships to one another – evolve from the practice of 'selecting' relevant wholes as an aid to learning.

- The parts, or elements, of a system play their role in light of the purpose for which the whole is seen to exist. The parts are connected.

- Deciding what the 'whole' is in a given context involves making boundary judgements. The outcome of this judgement is a 'system of interest'.

- All judgements must be made by someone.

- Judgements can be made without awareness. This happens all of the time when we use the word system in everyday speech, e.g. to describe the 'education system' or the 'transport system'. This everyday usage can lead to misunderstanding and conflict because different stakeholders will make different boundary judgements based on their different experiences. This is the same as saying that one person's 'education system' will be different to someone else's! Conflict and confusion can also arise because of lack of clarity about the purpose and boundary of a system of interest.

- Someone who is aware of 'systems thinking' recognises the significance of making boundary judgements and exploring purpose as part of their systems practice.

- Systems practitioners are thus well equipped to manage in situations where there is complexity, confusion or conflict particularly around issues of purpose, function, organisation, structures and measures of performance of a system of interest.
- Part of the skill of an aware systems practitioner is their ability to use systems thinking as part of a process of learning (by them or with others), in which the outcome is some improvement to a situation of concern. Modelling, including diagramming, is important in this process.
- The particular form of learning at the core of systems practice is concerned with effective action among stakeholders in complex situations. This involves concerted action or 'social learning'.
- Systems practice can be applied in any domain where complexity is experienced. In addition to environmental decision making, systems practitioners can be found in fields ranging from family therapy to engineering.
- At the OU, our teaching and research is primarily focused on systems practice in relation to 'environmental decision making for sustainable development', 'information systems' and 'critically reflective systems practice'.

Figure 12 depicts some of the key aspects of what I have described in Box 2. It depicts someone who has formulated or distinguished a system of interest in a situation – the situations we are interested in are environmental decision-making situations.

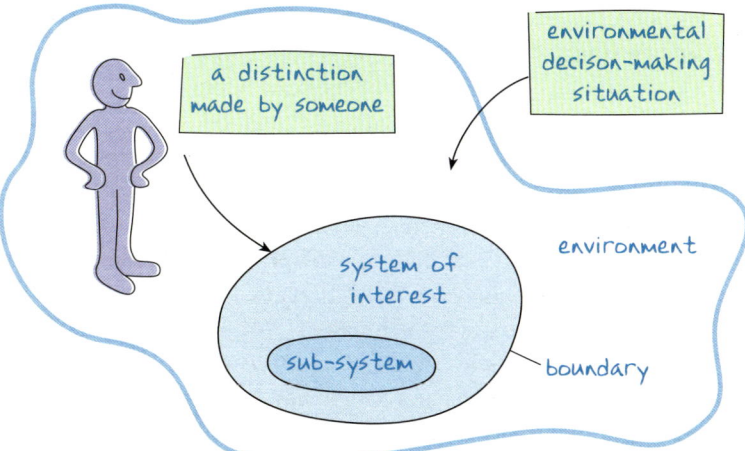

Figure 12  Key elements of systems practice which result from systems thinking within an environmental decision-making situation

> ### Activity 13  Explaining systems
>
>
>
> Look again at the material in Box 2 and what you have underlined whilst reading it. Imagine you were in conversation – how would you respond to the points made? Perhaps you would listen to several points before responding or perhaps you would respond to each point. At times you may have become angry or intrigued? Make notes in your learning journal and if you have questions or comments that you would like to pose to your fellow students, post them to the T863 computer conference.

By now I hope you have some appreciation of 'connectivity', some inkling about feedback processes and that a system is not just a thing but something that someone 'constructs' as part of a process in a situation (e.g. Figure 12). You should be aware, however, that 'systems' is a rich and diverse field of academic and practical activity and, as in many situations, there are a range of perspectives and practices as to how to approach systems. It is generally recognised that systems thinking in the twentieth century was pioneered by biologists who emphasised the view of living organisms as integrated wholes. It was further developed through gestalt psychology, ecology, quantum physics and more recently by the sciences of complexity (Capra, 1996).

I now want to explain a bit more about the relationship between systems thinking and environmental thinking, as well as clarifying the term 'environment' from a systems perspective.

## 4.1  Systems thinking and environmental thinking

The systems use of the term 'environment' was introduced in Book 1. The logic of Figure 12 implies that the word 'system' is always a shorthand description for a system–environment and system–sub-system relationship, that is, a set of nested relationships as depicted in a systems map (Activity 4). Another way of saying this is that a system is always coupled to its environment. In speaking about it in this way, I am trying to point out that I am not referring to an either/or situation – the system and/or the environment (sometimes called a dualism) – but to a situation where the system and its environment together comprise a unity (i.e. one cannot exist without the other, sometimes called a duality). The Chinese yin–yang symbol is often used to depict this unity/duality (Figure 13). Some common examples of a duality include the concepts predator and prey (from ecology), and in physics wave–particle duality is a central concept of quantum mechanics. Wave–particle duality holds that light and matter can exhibit properties of both waves and particles (whereas in the usual formulations of classical mechanics a given object is either a particle or a wave). If you want to understand more about the distinctions between a dualism and a duality, see Box 3.

Figure 13  The Chinese yin–yang symbol depicting a duality – a unity

Taking this systems view of the environment is consistent with the origins of the word 'environment'. It is derived from the Old French word *environer*, a verb meaning to envelop, surround, enclose, wrap, conceal or encircle. As a noun, environment thus means the state of being environed or the action of being environed. Following the logic of a duality (and not a dualism), it is not really appropriate to speak of 'inside' and 'outside' the system because this conveys the notion of a dualism and loses the sense of a related unity – system and environment. The understanding of a phenomenon within the context of a larger whole, or to understand things systemically, literally means to put them into a context, to establish the nature of their relationships (Capra, 1996). Systems thinking is 'contextual' thinking; and since explaining things in terms of their context means explaining them in terms of their environment, we can also say that all systems thinking is environmental thinking.

### Box 3  Duality and dualism

It is now widely known that light can be treated as both a wave and a particle depending on the experiment we, as observers (or experimenters), have decided to use to observe its behaviour. This apparent paradox, i.e. wave-like behaviour and particle-like behaviour, was described for many years as the 'wave–particle dualism' which implied they were separate or opposite phenomena. The term used to describe antagonistic or negating opposites is a *dualism*, e.g. mind/matter, objective/subjective. Two concepts form a dualism when they belong to the same logical level and are viewed as opposites. The logic behind this dialectic is negation. Alfonso Reyes (1995) suggests that dualistic thinking is a product of the prevailing objectivist Cartesian worldview with its orthodox logic under which we are still brought up. He also suggests that dualisms are responsible for ephemeral and endless debates, e.g. centralisation versus decentralisation. Dualistic or either/or thinking can often represent a trap.

It was not until it was recognised that phenomena we observe in 'nature' are not independent of our observing that this paradox was resolved by appreciating that wave-like and particle-like behaviour were complementary behaviours that constitute a *duality*. Taken as a whole they do not negate each other but constitute a unity or whole. A commonly used example of a duality taken from ecology is the predator–prey relationship. Two concepts form a duality when they belong to two different logical levels and one emerges from the other. The logic behind this dialectic is self-reference. The following pairs are examples that can be considered as dualities: environment–system; control–autonomy; constraint–freedom; what–how.

When complementary pairs (a duality) are recognised, rather than self-negating pairs (a dualism), a discussion is potentially more rewarding and creative as it encompasses a higher level of complexity. An implication is that in environmental decision making, some awareness of the difference between a dualism and duality by those responsible for decisions might enable more of the complexity to be addressed.

(Source: adapted from Reyes, 1995)

> ### SAQ 15 Differences between a dualism and a duality
>
>
>
> Summarise in your own words the main differences between a duality and dualism. Suggest why some awareness of the difference might be significant to environmental decision making.

Having briefly reviewed your understanding of the concept of system, and thus systems thinking, I now want to enable you to begin to deepen your appreciation about environmental decision making as a form of systems practice. I will ask you to do this by engaging in more systems practice in relation to the 'Freedom to fly?' case study.

## 4.2 Understanding environmental decision making as a systemic practice

Recognising pattern, connectivity and feedback processes is an important stage in thinking systemically and starting off an environmental decision-making process. What insights did you gain when you identified feedback loops in your multiple cause diagram (Activity 7)? If you are still unclear about the differences then use the *Techniques* book to read up about positive and negative feedback (see Diagramming: sign graphs). The essential things to remember about these two concepts are: (i) they have nothing to do with good and bad; and (ii) positive feedback has opposing effects on two factors whereas negative feedback is associated with balancing effects. Understanding feedback loops is one way of breaking out of the common trap in our society of understanding things in simple, linear cause and effect ways. Feedback processes exemplify a circular, or recursive, pattern of causality in contrast to the more common linear deterministic one. An appreciation of feedback processes has been incorporated into a series of 'systems archetypes' by a sub-field of system practitioners concerned with system dynamics.

### 4.2.1 Systems archetypes

Systems archetypes were developed by a group of systems practitioners in the 1980s and made popular in a book by Peter Senge (Senge, 1990, 1999). Initially eight diagrams were developed that practitioners felt would catalogue 'the most commonly seen behaviours' in situations they had experienced (Senge et al., 1994). It is claimed that 'archetypes are accessible tools with which managers can quickly construct credible and consistent hypotheses about the governing forces' of their situations. 'Archetypes are also a natural vehicle for clarifying and testing mental models' about situations (p. 121).

Here I will deal with the systems archetype called 'limits to growth' which you have already encountered in the quote from Lester Brown at the beginning of Section 4. If you have not encountered the historical context of 'limits to growth' before then read the short overview in Box 4.

### Box 4 'Limits to growth' – a short history

One of the landmark studies that initiated much of the debate that led to the development of the sustainable development concept was that reported in the book referred to earlier, *The Limits to Growth*, by Meadows et al. published in 1972. The authors were all systems practitioners in the sub-field of system dynamics. The book described a model which showed, amongst other things, that:

- economic growth peaks shortly after the year 2000;
- the world population peaks around 2050, falling rapidly as food production declines.

The authors explored the behaviour of the model under a range of assumptions. For example, they found that the collapse in economic growth could be delayed by about 10 years if they presumed that the stock of natural resources was twice as large. The model still showed a cessation of growth and a sharp decline in population by 2050, but this time because pollution absorbed a growing proportion of economic output and also reduced life expectancy. The authors introduced technical 'solutions' including pollution control, birth control and unlimited natural resources. In all cases, the model predicted a cessation of economic growth and dramatic population reductions within the 21st century. In short the authors claimed that their model convincingly demonstrated that there were substantial limits to the growth of human populations and the global economy. Such views had been expressed before, but with considerably less conviction and with less supporting evidence. For example, this was the first time that attention was drawn to the increasing carbon dioxide in the atmosphere and how this could affect global climate.

As may be expected, the book gave rise to a great deal of interest and controversy. Specialists in specific areas such as natural resources or food production raised detailed issues on which they disagreed. Economists questioned the whole basis of the model and asserted that it had underestimated the role of technical progress in avoiding the types of catastrophes predicted by the model. They pointed to the similarly dire predictions of Malthus nearly 200 years earlier that had not been realised. Despite all these objections, the idea that human development would be constrained took root. Ultimately there would be constraints imposed on the growth of human population and industrial development because these were taking place on a finite planet. Exactly where and when these constraints would first 'bite' was not predictable with any certainty, but that did not mean that the limits did not exist.

One reason why this book created such a fuss was that it challenged economic growth, the main vehicle advocated by western governments for solving many problems, including those of poverty and inequality. In a later book the authors stated:

> The predominance of growth in human activity comes as no surprise. In fact most people see it as something to celebrate. Most societies, rich or poor, seek some kind of expansion as a remedy for their most immediate and important problems. In the rich world economic growth is believed to be necessary for employment, social mobility, and technical advance. In the poor world economic growth seems the only way out of poverty. Until other solutions are found for the legitimate problems of the world, people will cling to the idea that growth is the key to a better future, and they would do all they can to produce more growth.
>
> (Source: Meadows et al., 1992, p. 5)

The 'limits to growth' archetype refers to situations in which a reinforcing (amplifying) process is set in motion to produce a desired outcome. The archetype could be used to interpret the cartoon depicted in Figure 3. The amplifying process creates success (more tourists) but also has inadvertent secondary effects (shown as the balancing process), which eventually slow the success (congestion, pollution if left unmanaged or an ecotax). In Figure 14 the growth process is shown as a virtuous reinforcing loop on the left. The limiting process is shown as a balancing process on the right, which reacts to imbalances imposed on it by the growth loop. Note that there is often a time lag (delay) in this balancing loop as it is driven to move towards its target – a limit or constraint on the whole system and often difficult to see as it is so far removed (cognitively, spatially and time-wise) from its founding growth process.

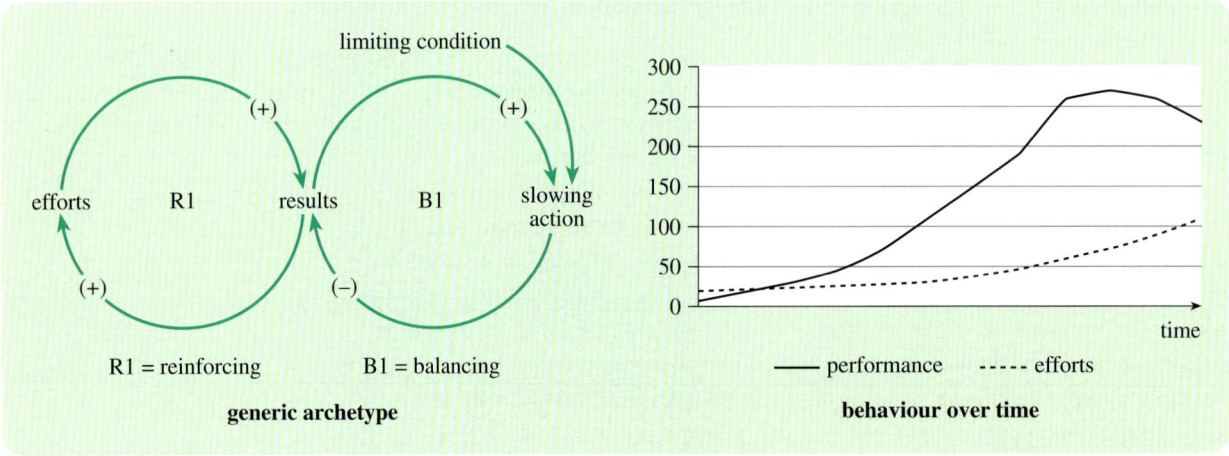

Figure 14   A model depicting the systems archetype called 'limits to growth (Source: Svensson, 2005)

### 4.2.2 Exploring 'mental models' – the role of metaphor

Another concept in systems thinking that Peter Senge did much to popularise is that of 'mental models' – our internal pictures of the world. It is argued that only by reflecting upon, continually clarifying and improving our mental models and seeing how they shape our actions and decisions can systemic improvements be made. With this in mind, I now want to introduce two images to explore the case study situation; these are shown in Figures 15a and b. I would also like you to 'take a step back' and use these images to explore your own practices in exploring the case study. (You might like to read that last sentence again as what I have asked you to do is to operate at two levels at the same time – i.e. at the level of the case study (the situation) as well as at the level of your own thinking/practices in relation to the case study!)

I am proposing the two images in Figure 15 as metaphors for environmental decision making. Metaphors are pervasive in all languages; they are characterised by referring to one thing in terms of another. Whenever the words 'as' and 'is' appear then it is likely that a metaphor is being used – they take the form 'X as Y' or 'X is Y' (Box 5). I am introducing material here on metaphors to (i) provide you with some insights into the power of metaphor in shaping our mental models, or as I prefer to say, our understandings and (ii) to show how an understanding of metaphor can be used to explore and re-explore a situation (see the example described by Schön in Box 5).

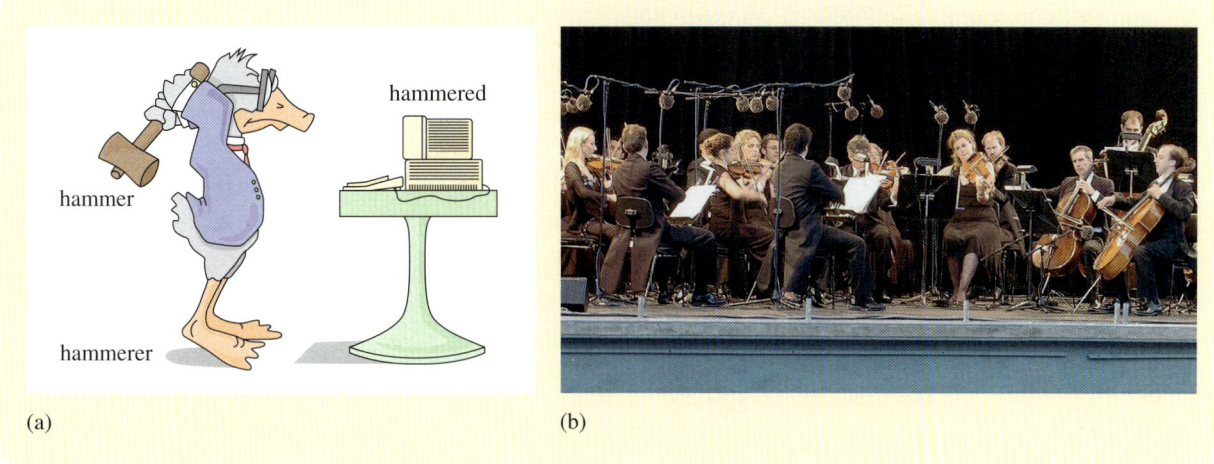

Figure 15   Two images of environmental decision making: (a) as hammering and (b) as a concert performance. Both images act as metaphors for environmental decision making as a form of practice – hammering as a practice arises as a set of relationships between the hammerer, the hammer and the hammered, whereas a concert gives rise to a performance as an emergent property of a number of interrelated elements.

### Box 5   Metaphors and understanding

Lakoff and Johnson (1980) claim that 'metaphor is pervasive in everyday life, not just in language but in thought and action'. Our ordinary conceptual system, in terms of which we both think and act, is fundamentally metaphorical in nature. It is claimed that metaphors create our realities when acted upon as well as making a range of experiences available (Lakoff and Johnson, 1980; Krippendorff, 1993).

Schön (1979) illustrates the creative, or generative, function of metaphors. He describes the development of a new paintbrush with synthetic bristles that failed to apply an even coat of paint. Somebody observed that 'a paintbrush is a kind of pump'. This was taken as an invitation to start to consider a paintbrush as a pump. Certain aspects of the paintbrush and its performance 'came to the

> foreground'. Attention then focused on the spaces between the bristles, and these were then thought of as channels through which paint could flow. Other ideas followed from thinking of a paintbrush in terms of a pump. A conclusion was that instead of wiping paint onto a surface, a paintbrush could pump the paint. It was not so much the image of a pump that was important, but the invitation to consider a process of pumping.
>
> This example illustrated quite clearly how understandings of one concept (a paintbrush) can be organised, or structured, in terms of a different concept (pump, or pumping). Schön pointed to metaphors as 'seeing as', that is 'seeing X as Y'. In the process of restructuring, perceptions of both X and Y are transformed. 'Seeing X as Y' thus gives a reasonable operational definition of a metaphor.
>
> Structuring understandings of one concept in terms of another concept does not imply that understandings are improved, merely that they are different (Schön, 1979). But what does it mean to structure our understandings? 'Structure' invokes a metaphor of seeing understandings-as-buildings (Lakoff and Johnson, 1980). Terms like develop, build and foundation can then be used to describe aspects of understanding. Indeed the term 'understand' is metaphorical, implying that we 'stand upon' some foundations.
>
> Metaphors may thus be said to structure our understandings because metaphors have entailments through which they highlight and make coherent certain aspects of our experience. Two particularly powerful metaphors arise when we choose to see something as a 'problem' or as an 'opportunity'.
>
> (Source: adapted from McClintock et al., 2004)

There are many metaphors that can be teased out from the images depicted in Figure 15 – the obvious ones are considering environmental decision making in the aviation expansion case (i) as attacking complexity with a blunt instrument or (ii) as a performance. When I think about these images in relation to the case study they evoke other metaphors. I could claim that 'the environment was hammered by the decision-making process'. If this claim were made then I would be using a number of metaphors, e.g. 'the environment as hammerable' and 'the decision-making process as a hammer'. Alternatively I could describe the 'decision-making process as a well-orchestrated performance'. From the perspective of Andrew Cahn, BA Director of Government Affairs (Book 1, Section 5.5), it was a very satisfactory performance. He said: 'I have to say we are pretty delighted'. Other stakeholders were less impressed by the 'performance'!

In Book 1 you were introduced to Dryzek's (1997) ideas about discourse. Discourse and metaphors are related because certain discourses are populated by particular metaphors. Historical events are a common source of metaphor – it is amazing how many metaphors are remnants from the First World War and other military encounters (e.g. setting targets; over the top; being bombarded with information, etc). Figure 16 depicts a particular metaphor which has had many unintended consequences in public administration in recent years. Science (e.g. chaos and complexity science) and theory itself (e.g. systems theory) can also become a source of alternative metaphors.

Figure 16   A depiction of the metaphor 'service users as targets' which has had many unintended consequences (Source: Wadsworth, 1997b)

Metaphors have the capacity to hide or display certain aspects of our thinking. For example, in the UK a common way of describing the countryside is 'as a tapestry' because of the network of fields, hedges and different colours. The metaphor displays, or reveals, all the aspects normally associated with a tapestry but it hides, or conceals, the smells, frequency of farm accidents, noise, etc. that are also a feature of the UK countryside.

### SAQ 16   Using metaphors in your practice

Give one example of how metaphors can be used in a generative sense to reveal new insights and one example of how a metaphor can conceal particular aspects of a situation.

Exploring a metaphor can be built into your own practice – for example you can look at a paper or report and do an analysis of the metaphors in terms of what they reveal and conceal. In my own work, I have found it a very useful way to explore the mental models of authors. In some cases, I have then fed my analysis back in group situations and used it to trigger a discussion about the implications of the metaphors that are being used.

What do the images in Figure 15 reveal and conceal for you as metaphors of environmental decision making in the case study situation? To answer this question look at Reading 2 and then try SAQ 17 followed by Activity 14.

## Reading 2

Read 'Metaphors for reflecting on research practice: researching *with* people' by McClintock et al.

### Study note

Reading 2 is included because a key feature of becoming systemically aware concerns language and how it is used to construct arguments and discourse; metaphors are central to this process. The process of distinguishing metaphors and exploring what they reveal and conceal can be used to explore or re-explore a situation. The paper also addresses issues to do with participation (researching or deciding with) which

I will discuss in a later section of Book 2. When reading this paper please think of the four main metaphors that are discussed in the following terms:

research-as-action → environmental decision making-as-action

research-as-narrative → environmental decision making-as-narrative

research-as-facilitation → environmental decision making-as-facilitation

research-as-responsible → environmental decision making-as-responsible

If you want to be economical in your reading of this paper then concentrate on two of the metaphors that most appeal to you. The material here will also be relevant to later material in Book 3 (e.g. action) and Book 4 (e.g. responsibility).

### SAQ 17  Distinguishing metaphors

What arguments do the authors of Reading 2 make for distinguishing metaphors and how is this connected to the notion that metaphors can both reveal and conceal?

### Activity 14  Exploring a situation through metaphor

Using the ideas in Reading 2 for guidance, explore the images of environmental decision making as a practice of hammering and as a performance. By explore, I mean what does each image (metaphor) make apparent (reveal) and what does it hide from view (conceal)? Relate your answer to the 'Freedom to fly?' case study.

---

Drawing on my own systemic awareness, I recognise in each of the images in Figure 15 a set of elements which, when connected together, give rise to a performance. One performance is that of hammering, in which the main elements are a hammer, a hammerer and something that is hammered. All three of these elements have to be present for hammering to emerge as a form of practice. In the other image, the main elements are players, instruments, a conductor, a score, a stage in a hall and an audience and once again all of these elements are necessary for a public performance to emerge as an outcome. However, the elements are not in themselves sufficient for good performances to emerge in either example – you can reflect on your own experience to think about what is required to be a good hammerer, and certainly most good orchestral performances require a lot of practice and individuals who are skilled in some way. There is also the question of purpose! Those engaged in the practice also need to be aware of the purpose. For example, if the double bass player had no idea of the purpose for the joint activity then they could severely disrupt a performance!

What do these two images have in common? Each has (i) a context in which the performance is enacted, (ii) a person or persons – the practitioner(s) – and (iii) tools and techniques (the hammer, the instruments, the orchestration of the score, etc.). There is also a fourth aspect which is not so apparent because each image is static – each element in these images has a history which can be explored and understood.

There is always a history of the context (the computer, the concert hall), the practitioners (each is a unique individual and thinks and acts differently even though they may come from similar cultures) and the tools and techniques (Box 6). There is also a history of performing in a particular way – what is recognised as good practice in one setting may not be the same in another setting.

When I refer to exploring or re-exploring the situation as part of environmental decision making, then I am aware that all of these elements and their systemic connections are important if a performance that is effective is to ultimately emerge. This claim of course raises the question of what constitutes an effective performance in environmental decision making? This question will be taken up in Book 4 and in your own practice as part of your project.

> ### SAQ 18   Environmental decision making as a practice
>
> What are some of the main elements of environmental decision making as a practice?

In environmental decision making there is (i) always a situation where something is at issue, (ii) there are people and (iii) social technologies involved and each of these (iv) have a history – i.e. the situation/issue, the people and the social technology – which it is possible to know about. Furthermore, I could claim that environmental decision making is an emergent property of these interacting factors – situation, people, social technologies and history (just as a good performance is an emergent property of all the elements associated with an orchestra and its audience).

I have extracted some general elements from the two images in Figure 15 which relate to practice and built them into a model of environmental decision making as systems practice in Figure 17. I want to talk you through this figure, and in the process connect it to your own process of engaging with the case study in Book 1. I have divided Figure 17 into four parts (i–iv) and will explain each in turn.

In Figure 17(i) I have depicted a person who could be a decision maker or could be you engaging with the case study. The bubble with the framework is used to signify that we all have our particular ways of thinking which are unique (earlier I called these traditions of understanding out of which we think and act). These ways of thinking determine what we see – literally what we pay attention to or perceive (hence the eye – see also Figure 18). How we think about a situation, as well as the nature of the situation, affect how we understand it. I have depicted the situation with some people in it – these could be stakeholders in the situation, such as staff of BA, BAA or NGOs, or they could be people who are affected but not actively involved as a stakeholder (e.g. residents in the vicinity of Heathrow Airport who did not respond to any of the public consultations).

In Figure 17(ii) I make the point that each human being has a history which is both biological (we grow and develop) and social (we live in particular families and societies and have different experiences which lead us to think and act differently). And because we can learn, we can change our mind about how we think about

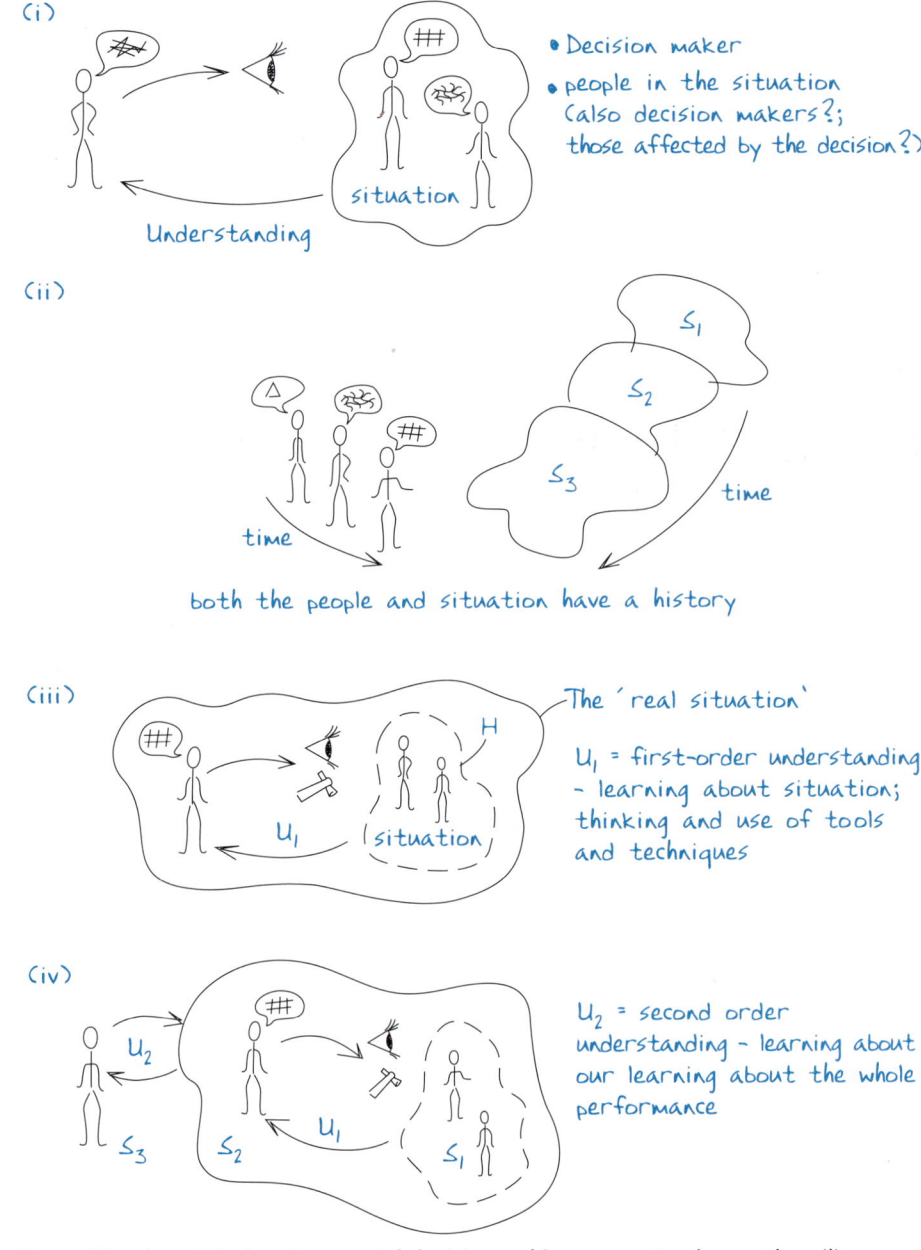

Figure 17 A model of environmental decision making as a systemic practice: (i) a decision maker engages with an environmental decision-making situation; (ii) the decision maker and situation each have a history; (iii) the 'real situation' includes the decision maker – there is no external position; (iv) standing back it is possible to learn about learning in practice (see text for further explanation)

situations – some experiences can have profound effects on how we think and act, others less so. But what will be a profound experience for me might not be so for you – it is biologically impossible to have exactly the same experience as another person. The unique feature we humans have is to use language – we can talk about our experiences, just as some of the different stakeholders in the airport expansion case study have done in taped interviews (but the meaning they intended is not necessarily the meaning that you took from what was said – this will depend on *your*

Figure 18  A metaphorical account of the way theories and ways of thinking (planet on telescope) determine what we see in the world. The mischief makers in this example are the theory makers – their framing of the situation can determine what is experienced and done

history and how much effort *you* have made at listening to, checking out and interpreting what has been said).

Situations also have a history (I have depicted this as S1 → S3 – a changing situation over time) but history must be interpreted by someone at a particular moment in time. The aviation expansion case study was written at a particular moment in time – the history and context of the author, Andrea Berardi, influenced what he did and paid attention to, just as your own experience and context have influenced how you have interpreted the case study situation. Elements in the situation also have a history. Take, for example, the history of using oil and the possibility that the world may be facing a post-oil future. Understanding this history is, in my view, critical to understanding the case study from a systems perspective. Reading 3 is an account of the history of energy use.

## Reading 3

Reading 3 comes from a book called *The End of Oil* by Paul Roberts. It provides an overview of the history of how the world economy has become dependent on oil as the main source of energy.

### SAQ 19  Constructing a timeline

Construct a simple timeline showing the main phases of energy use over human history.

In Figure 17(iii) I have added in history (H) and made the initial situation permeable by use of an incomplete boundary, but I have incorporated all of the elements in a wider boundary and labelled it as the 'real situation'. I have done so because in 'real'

environmental situations in which you have a stake (as is required for your project) there is not really an external position from which to view the situation. Unlike a simulation, as our case study is likely to be for many of you, when you become an active stakeholder in a situation then you are a part of the situation. I say more about stakeholders and stakeholding in Section 4.4. I have added one other feature to this figure symbolised by the hammer – this is the use of tools or techniques or frameworks which also shape how a situation may be engaged with. I could have introduced this in Figure 17(i) but left it to now as I want to say more about how tools and techniques can act as social technologies – which, just like theories, mediate what we do. I describe what I mean by social technologies in Box 6.

> ### Box 6  Social technologies
>
> Examples of social technologies from the case study include 'cost–benefit analysis' (described in more detail in Book 3), 'White Papers', 'public inquiries', 'carbon emission schemes', 'environmental management schemes' and 'regulatory impact assessment' (the last two are discussed in more detail in Part 2). There will have been many more examples which are less obvious such as the format of committee meetings in Whitehall, protocols for ministerial decision making, templates for public consultation, procedures for hiring consultants, etc.
>
> By social technologies, I mean technologies that are often invisible because they are embedded in daily practices, including our language and use of numbers. An example based on numbers is the practice of giving scores as exam marks – this was 'invented' in the late eighteenth century but today it seems unthinkable that we would not quantify scores for exams. Another example is the use of 'an agenda' and 'minutes' as part of regular meetings. At some historical moment, someone invented these practices and they have been conserved as practices over time even though on some occasions our meetings might be more productive and creative if we did not employ an agenda and minutes. Because I am aware of the ways in which an agenda and minute-taking can help or hinder a meeting, I sometimes use other techniques to structure a meeting: for example a SWOT analysis (see 'SWOT analysis and its variants' in the *Techniques* book) can be used as an alternative – it structures discussion and leaves behind a written record.
>
>
>
> Social technologies are distinct from artefacts such as a hammer or a computer considered in isolation, which is what we usually think about when technology is mentioned, and they are characterised by a set of relationships in which the technology plays a mediating role just as the hammer does in Figure 15a.
>
> In my terms management, or decision making, can be a social technology when it is made up of procedures and rules designed to standardise behaviour – or in other words, sets of techniques used routinely without awareness of the origins and implications of the use of such techniques, the role of the practitioner and the need for contextual understanding about the situation.
>
>

My use of the term 'social technologies' is very close to what some economists, particularly institutional economists, refer to as 'institutions' – there are multiple uses and interpretations of the term 'institution'. In English, it is often used interchangeably with 'organisation'. Following North (1990) the term 'institution' describes an 'established law, custom, usage, practice, organisation, or other element in the political or social life of a people'. Institutions can be policies and objectives, laws, rules, regulations, organisations, policy mechanisms; and norms, traditions, practices and customs (SLIM, 2004a). Institutions influence how we think and what we do.

In my use of the term 'social technologies' I wish to draw attention to how 'institutions' are usually named as 'things' independent of the context of practice in which there is always a relationship between the 'thing' (the hammer in Figure 15a), someone (the hammerer) and the context of practice (for example a lot of research funds go to develop tools for decision making without thinking of how the tool will be put into practice – as depicted in Figure 15a). I would go further and claim that social technologies can orchestrate a performance in the sense that hammering can be considered a performance. Figure 15a explains how technology (in this case an artefact), a person and a situation interact to give rise to a practice – the practice of hammering. The practice is an emergent property of the interaction of the hammerer, the hammer and the hammered. Hammering as a form of practice would make little sense without each of these elements interacting and aligning with an espoused purpose, e.g. to destroy the computer, or to vent one's anger. This example enables me to make two other distinctions that are important for system practice – purposeful and purposive behaviour. These are addressed in Section 5.1.

The same logic applies to 'public inquiries' as to hammering (see Box 6 in Book 1). In the UK context, public inquiries are a social technology that institutionalises particular understandings and practices in environmental decision making. It should be possible to explore the history of public inquiries and to ask if the thinking and circumstances that gave rise to them are still valid today, i.e. do they remain a valid social technology?

If you still feel a bit confused about social technologies then try the following SAQ. I have spent some time on this because I consider that understanding social technologies and 'institutional arrangements' will become increasingly important in environmental decision making. If you are particularly interested I have put a specific case study in a reading on the T863 course website – this is not essential reading.

### SAQ 20  What is a social technology?

How is a social technology defined and why is it relevant to environmental decision making?

In Figure 17(iv) I have made a distinction about the nature of the understandings that can arise from different forms of practice – you can claim that you understand the situation or, in addition, you can claim that you understand your understanding of the situation. I call these two situations first- and second-order understanding and each relates to the ways in which we learn about the situation (this is taken up in Books 3 and 4). The move from (iii) to (iv) does not involve another person but is a shift in attitude, or state of mind, of the type associated with moving from the question 'How do I understand the situation?' to 'What is the significance of the thinking and tools I am using in this situation and how do they affect how I understand the situation?'

### SAQ 21   The importance of history

Explain why history is important to environmental decision making based on your understanding of Figure 17.

By now you may have noted that Figure 17 does not capture all aspects of the complexity of the case study. I have not accounted for multiple decision makers, in the sense depicted in the image of the orchestra (Figure 15b), in which there are multiple decision makers who give rise to a performance. Nor have I depicted how these dynamic situations change over time. For example will the decisions that were agreed upon in the aviation expansion case study stick in the light of:

1   The changing price of oil?

2   The growing awareness of the amount of subsidy received by the airline industry?

3   The audience – possibly UK citizens?

I have also said little about how using a systems approach connects with Figure 17. My response to this question is in the form of Activity 15.

### Activity 15   Factors that influence decision-making practices

In Book 1 you were introduced to seven factors that influence decisions. These were the decision makers, the decision situation, thinking in terms of problems or opportunities, decision criteria, time, people affected by the decision and decision support – tools and techniques. In this activity I want you to re-cast these factors in terms of influencing environmental decision making as a form of practice. Can you think of other factors to add to these seven? What, in your view, would differentiate systemic environmental decision making from just environmental decision making? Draw on your own experience of engaging with the case study, the images in Figure 15 and the models depicted in Figure 17 to devise your answers.

In this section I have referred to the idea of performance as an emergent property of a set of dynamics. I have related this to the case study by claiming that from the perspective of some stakeholders, the decision-making performance was very satisfying but for others it was not. This raises the question of whether a better performance could have been orchestrated (to extend the metaphor) which was more satisfying to a greater range of stakeholders. What might have happened had the decision-making process started and been managed differently?

I have also provided certain images (metaphors) and models of practice with which to explore the case study situation. My aim was to show how an appreciation of metaphors can be used as part of an exploring or re-exploring process and especially as a means to break out of traps in thinking. My model of practice moves beyond just understanding the case study situation to encompass you as someone with a history engaged in a process of understanding. Changes in understanding are necessary but not sufficient – there is also a need to change practices. The main practices we are concerned with developing are systems practices for environmental decision making.

## 4.3 The relationship between understanding and practice

How would you characterise your engagement with the 'Freedom to fly?' case study at this stage of the course? Would you say it has some or all of the features depicted in Figure 19? Can you add other features of your own?

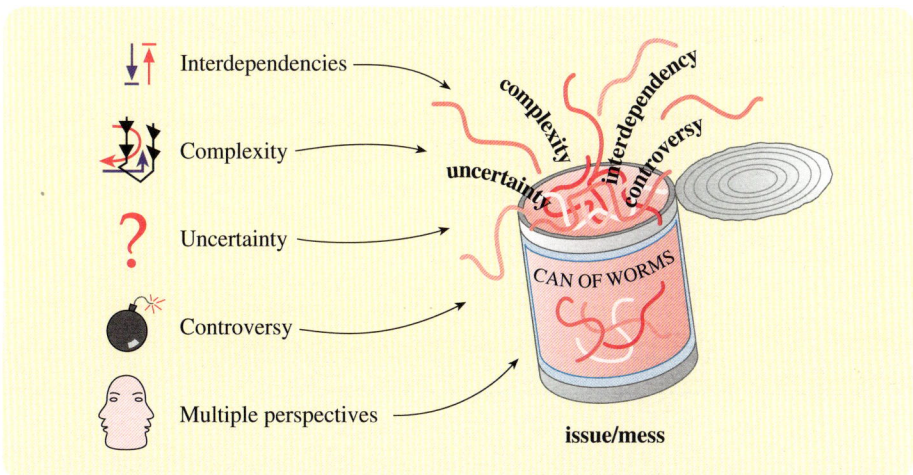

Figure 19  What is at issue? Some of the characteristics of the case study and most environmental decision-making situations (Source: adapted from SLIM, 2004)

I want to start this section by introducing some of the basic elements of a heuristic device (something that can be used to aid learning). This heuristic device (Figure 20) starts by acknowledging that all situations have a history – as explained in the previous section – and that what we seek to do in environmental decision making is to transform situations in which something, or many things, are at issue into an improved situation (S1 → S2). It also suggests that one of the main dynamics that can aid this transformation process is the interplay between understandings and practices (these are depicted on the X and Y axes respectively and imply a change for the better, but better is always situation-sensitive). The interaction of understandings and practices will determine the direction and rate of the transformation process.

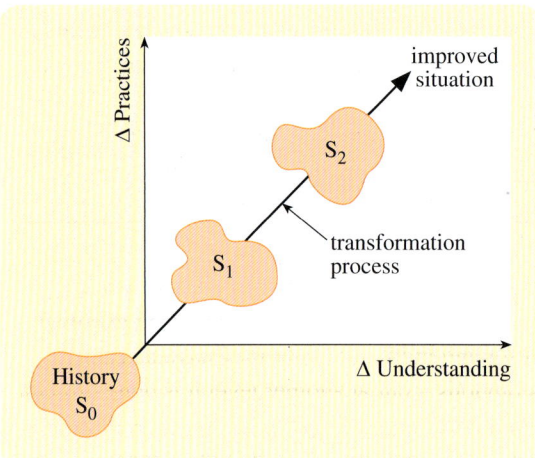

Figure 20  A heuristic device which relates changes in understanding and practices to the transformation of situations of complexity, uncertainty, interdependence, controversy and multiple perspectives towards some improved situation (Source: adapted from SLIM, 2004b)

In the remaining part of this section, I provide systems 'tools' to aid both your understanding and practice in situations of complexity. Used appropriately they may enhance your understanding and practices, and thus the transformation of situations in which you are involved.

At this stage I will orientate each of these to understanding the case study (exploring and re-exploring) but I expect that as the course goes on you will incorporate them into your own practices as and when they are relevant.

### 4.3.1  Traps

The clearest evidence of being stuck is when you find yourself in a situation that you have faced before, and all you can think of doing is what you did before even though you know that did not work.

Sir Geoffrey Vickers wrote in the 1960s and 1970s with great insight and simplicity about the whole business of how we think about ourselves and our institutions. He had an illuminating analogy about traps:

> Lobster pots are designed to catch lobsters. A man entering a lobster pot would become suspicious of the narrowing tunnel, he would shrink from the drop at the end: and if he fell in, he would recognise the entrance as a possible exit and climb out again – even if he were the shape of a lobster.
>
> A trap is a trap only for the creatures which cannot solve the problems it sets. Man traps are dangerous only in relation to the limitations of what men can see and value and do.

(Vickers, 1972, p. 15)

We all have problems which we meet and struggle with but never really solve; they are the problems which are somehow beyond the limits of what we can 'see and value and do'. Many of them have deep roots in our experience and upbringing and in the society in which we live. For example, for almost the whole of the twentieth century the problem of increasing demand for energy was met by increasing the supply. However, in the 1980s, a few people saw the problem differently and argued that it would be better solved by energy conservation. Whatever the particular advantages or disadvantages of this, it is clear that it is an alternative. More interestingly, it is one that was genuinely not apparent to all those concerned with energy supply over a very long period. This is because people who defined the problem as one of increasing supply, and devoted their efforts to doing this, simply did not see or value ways of reducing demand.

Another idea that will run through the course is that it is possible to think differently about our issues of concern. I specify 'our' quite deliberately because I want to convey the notion that a problem does not exist for any individual until they have taken some responsibility for it. At one level this is obvious – but at another level it is quite difficult to grasp. Throughout school, and throughout training for a particular job, we are all taught facts and concepts as if there is only one right way of putting them together to get a result. There *are* ways of putting them together which have been shown to be useful in the past and these are worth learning about, but in doing so, there is always a risk that we ignore many other ways to think about, and agree, an issue.

It is thinking in a certain way that leads people to act as they do, and gets them into a trap. Hence, carrying on thinking in exactly the same way is unlikely to get them out of the trap. The way out must be through thinking differently. Sir Geoffrey Vickers, immediately after his lobster analogy, wrote 'We, the trapped, tend to take our own state of mind for granted – which is partly why we are trapped'.

Thus when I emphasise the need to 'stand back' to explore the context of environmental issues I am also inviting you to stop taking your own state of mind, your own thinking, for granted and to critically appreciate other states of mind, other perspectives, other ways of thinking.

### SAQ 22   What is a trap?

Describe what a trap is and provide one example.

There are different perspectives on whether commitment to economic growth (as currently defined) is a trap or not, as outlined in Book 1 in reference to concepts of sustainable development. Box 7 contains a short article written by the then chair of the UK's Sustainable Development Commission in 2003 in which he raises questions about the ongoing commitment to economic growth. When you have finished reading Box 7, answer Activity 16 in which you can articulate your own perspective.

### Box 7   Odd couple

*We are richer but no happier, says Jonathon Porritt, so why still pursue economic growth when its environmental costs are so high?*

So, what makes a politician take on the impossible? If politics really is 'the art of the possible', what makes Tony Blair dedicate himself to trying to sort out the problems of Africa or persuading his fellow world leaders that climate change is for real, needing attention right now rather than next century?

In the same spirit of inquiry, when do you suppose any world leader will summon up the courage to initiate a proper public debate about economic growth and the degree to which it achieves, or not, its stated aim – namely, to make us all happier? There are very few genuinely off-limits issues in politics, but this is the biggest of them all.

Ignoring it will not make it go away. So the sustainable development commission is urging the prime minister and the chancellor to be much bolder in engaging the British public in a more mature debate about economic growth and its contribution to people's prosperity. Should we continue to depend on our growth-obsessed model of progress to generate the improvements in quality of life and personal wellbeing for which people so hunger?

Even to ask this question opens one up to all sorts of risks. 'Sustainable development commission launches campaign against economic growth' was how one broadsheet responded to the launch of our publication in this area, Redefining Prosperity. How wrong. This is not a question of 'growth at all costs' versus 'no growth'. No one wants to go back to the sterile debate of the early 1970s, which was framed in exactly those polarised terms.

But no one – not even the most rabid free-market ideologue – now denies that securing the benefits that economic growth brings also simultaneously generates social and environmental costs. If those costs are large enough, they can outweigh the welfare gains.

Environmentalists argue that these costs are indeed so grave (in terms of impact on eco-systems, resource depletion, climate change, species extinction and so on) as to threaten nature's capacity for self-regeneration and, in the process, threaten humankind's capacity to improve our quality of life.

In broad policy terms, the government's favoured strategy – its only strategy – for squaring this circle is improving productivity while using fewer natural resources. That is, getting more economic value from each unit of production, thereby decoupling economic growth from increased resource use.

This aim of extra resource productivity lies at the heart of the government's forthcoming sustainable consumption and production strategy, and featured prominently in the three big environment speeches that the prime minister gave in 2001 and his sustainable development speech in February this year.

There is no doubt that 'more from less' is a very seductive strategy. It appears to offer an almost pain-free route to a 'cleaner environment' without jeopardising normal economic priorities. It is far easier to concentrate efforts on seeking technological changes that improve efficiency of resource use than it is to confront problems of reducing demand for ever-increasing consumption.

But taking this issue seriously – systematically driving down resource and energy consumption across the entire economy – is not as pain free as it first appears. A mountain of problems has been created by decades of subsidising industries that heavily use natural resources while, at the same time, keeping prices low by letting those industries pollute the environment without paying clean-up costs.

We have become used to low prices paid for by unacceptable damage to the environment and resent having this taken away. The fuel tax protests of 2000 are etched in the memory of civil servants and ministers alike as an example of what happens when an environmentally-friendly policy is used insensitively or punitively.

No one in government could summon up the courage to defend the fuel tax escalator as a key policy measure in the government's overall transport and climate-change strategies. This was both deeply regrettable and an important reminder that something as seemingly 'simple' as resource productivity demands consistent and inspirational political leadership. On that occasion, there was none.

And there is an even bigger problem looming. It is by no means clear that economic growth is delivering the goods. The relationship between economic growth and our quality of life, or 'life satisfaction', has been seized on recently by senior government advisers.

In a paper published by the Cabinet Office's strategy unit in December 2002 (Life Satisfaction: the state of knowledge and implications for government), Nick Donovan and David Halpern highlight the basic problem: in the past three decades in the UK, average individual prosperity has increased by 80 percentage points while the life satisfaction index has remained roughly constant.

If people are not getting happier, why is our economic strategy still dedicated to delivering more of the same kind of growth? The challenge is a tough one: how do we decouple people's real quality of life (measured by how good they feel about life) from ever higher levels of personal consumption? How can we recouple economic growth with improved personal wellbeing and a better quality of life? After all, that is supposed to be the point of such growth.

It took the best part of 20 years to demonstrate that economic growth and increased energy consumption need not be inextricably wed, and that it was perfectly possible to achieve high levels of economic growth without increases in energy consumption. But will it take another 20 years to persuade politicians that we can separate improved wellbeing and individual happiness from ever higher levels of consumption? If it does, real sustainable development is pretty much a dead duck.

*Jonathon Porritt is chairman of the UK sustainable development commission and programme director of Forum for the Future. ...*

(Source: *The Guardian,* Wednesday 9 July 2003)

> **Activity 16  Do you recognise 'traps' in thinking in the case study?**

What traps in thinking do you recognise from your own engagement with the case study? Do you recognise any traps in the thinking of Jonathon Porritt in his article? Make some notes on these, and at the same time consider the analogy of the lobster pot in relation to your own traditions of understanding out of which you think and act. Have you become aware, or more aware, of these?

### 4.3.2 Messes and difficulties

Russell Ackoff first gave the term 'mess' a specific meaning in the context of decision making in 1974 (Ackoff, 1974a, b). He did so in response to the insights of two eminent American philosophers, William James and John Dewey, who recognised that problems are taken up by, not given to, decision makers and that problems are extracted from unstructured states of confusion – an issue. Ackoff argues that

> What decision makers deal with, I maintain, are messes not problems. This is hardly illuminating, however, unless I make more explicit what I mean by a 'mess'. A mess is a set of external conditions that produces dissatisfaction. It can be conceptualised as a system of problems in the same sense in which a physical body can be conceptualised as a system of atoms.
>
> (Ackoff, 1974b)

From this definition of mess, Ackoff recognised a number of implications for decision makers:

1. A problem is an ultimate element abstracted from a mess. Ultimate elements are necessarily abstractions which cannot be observed (I would add to Ackoff's definition at this point by including opportunities as well as problems).

2. Problems, even as abstract mental constructs, do not exist in isolation, although it is possible to isolate them conceptually.

3. The 'solution' to a mess – whatever it may be – is not the simple sum of the solutions to the problems which are or can be extracted from it. No mess can be resolved by solving each of its component problems independently of the others, because no mess can be decomposed into independent problems.

4. Simple situations do exist which can be improved by extracting one problem from them and solving it. These are called difficulties and they are seen as exceptions rather than the norm in terms of decisions that are needed in environmental, organisational and social contexts.

5. The attempt to deal with a system of problems as a system – synthetically, as a whole – is an essential property of planning in contrast to problem solving.

### Difficulties

Recognising a situation as a difficulty has advantages when it is clear to those involved what the problem is, and what would constitute a solution; also when it is fairly clear how many people are involved in both the problem and its solution, and the timescale to act is limited.

### Messes

In contrast, recognising a situation as a mess has advantages when it is not at all clear what is wrong, nor what would constitute a solution, or there is uncertainty about the number of people involved or the timescale of the set of interacting possible problems, and their potential solutions and opportunities are uncertain.

In general, situations in which messes are recognised are more worrying because of the large degree of uncertainty surrounding the nature of the problems and opportunities – it is not known what the consequences of 'failure' or 'success' might be, it is not clear what has to be known in order to understand the issue better, and there are usually no guidelines to indicate whether a course of action will make things better or worse.

The difference between seeing a situation as a difficulty or a mess can be summed up by saying that difficulties are problems where the boundary has been agreed (i.e. they are 'bounded' problems) whereas messes are a set of interacting potential problems and opportunities in which there is no, or little, agreement about the boundaries to any one problem or opportunity. By classifying problems or opportunities as bounded it is implied that they are limited and it is reasonably well known where the limits are. In contrast, unbounded problems and opportunities may be completely open-ended – and often appear to be so for longer than those involved in it would wish. In reality, you will find that problems and opportunities do not fall easily into one category or the other. This means that you need to consider just how 'problems' come to be 'problems' – that is, how they are formulated and how they differ from opportunities. Approaching problem formulation through a systemic analysis involves iteration and altering what you see as the problem or opportunity. Recognising a situation as a mess or difficulty is a choice you can make.

### SAQ 23   Mess and difficulty

Describe three features a practitioner might use to distinguish a mess from a difficulty. Is any one of these distinguishing features more significant than the others?

### Activity 17   Treating situations as messes

In the case study, can you recognise circumstances in the overall decision-making process where considering the situation as a mess may have been advantageous or led to a different decision-making process?

---

By introducing the distinctions between messes and difficulties, I am inviting you to step back from the common understanding that all situations have 'objective' features which are knowable in the same way by everyone. Treating complex situations as difficulties tends not to improve the situation except perhaps in the very short term.

### 4.3.3 Boundaries and levels

The concept 'boundary' and the process of conceptualising a boundary around a system of interest are important elements in a systemic approach to environmental decision making (see Figure 12). Asking boundary-setting questions is a powerful means to explore or re-explore a situation and to move towards formulating systems of interest.

Identifying boundaries is a familiar activity for most of us. The boundary of a country, for example, separates one area of national government from another; the boundary of a field might demarcate different ways of managing land or producing crops. A dictionary sets out the boundaries between the meanings of different words. There are also boundaries to activities, such as washing dishes or organising a meeting, and boundaries to systems (in the everyday sense of the word), such as a digestive system, a heating system or an educational system. In this latter case, however, we would rarely find agreement on where the 'system' started and finished because we would all have different perspectives on what was in or outside the 'education system' and what its purpose was.

Drawing boundaries is relevant to decision makers in many different contexts. They help to separate and to simplify, and to focus on what is important in a particular situation and what is less important and can be ignored. For example:

1. identifying the geographical location of boundaries within which new development activity might take place under a policy, project or programme
2. identifying the people who are involved in an activity who might need to participate in decision making
3. separating your own professional responsibilities from those of a colleague – identifying the boundaries of your role
4. working out the expected effects of a technology or an intervention (e.g. forming a lobby group)
5. defining where responsibility and accountability might reside.

In some situations, it might be difficult to place boundaries – not all situations are easily bounded, or they may be fiercely contested – but thinking through where the limits lie can help in planning, challenging, negotiating and evaluating many different activities.

Whilst some boundaries are physical and can be easily seen, others are more abstract – they are constructs used to develop and communicate our understanding and to define and negotiate limits. We shall define boundaries in abstract terms and in relation to the concept of a 'system'. Thus a boundary is determined by stakeholders and relevant actors when they differentiate a 'system' from its 'environment', a 'sub-system' from the 'system' and a 'system' from a 'supra-system', establishing a set of systemic levels as in Figure 21. As outlined earlier, the act of formulating a system of interest gives rise to (i) a system of interest, (ii) an environment (of the system of interest) and (iii) a boundary, which establishes a system–environment relationship.

When you formulate a system of interest, as you do when doing a systems map, then a number of levels are also recognised (environment, system, sub-system and so on). It is sometimes claimed that the most important skill in systems thinking is being able to move across different levels of abstraction. This idea is captured in Figure 21 which expresses levels in terms of 'why', 'what', 'how'.

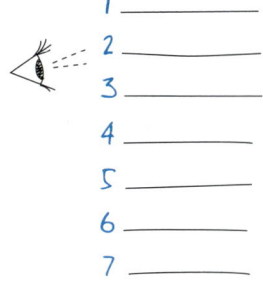

- 'System,' 'subsystem,' 'wider system' are relative terms. Choice is made by an observer: if level 3 is 'system' then for that observer 2 is wider system and 4 is sub-system level.

- 'System' is the level of T (transformation). Activities contributing to doing T are then sub-systems. The wider system level is that of O (owner) in CATWOE, who could stop T.

- This systems thinking ensures thinking at three levels: What? (system)
  How? (sub-system)
  Why? (wider system)

- 'Do P by Q in order to contribute to achieving R' covers the three levels.

But the choice of level is always observer-dependent:

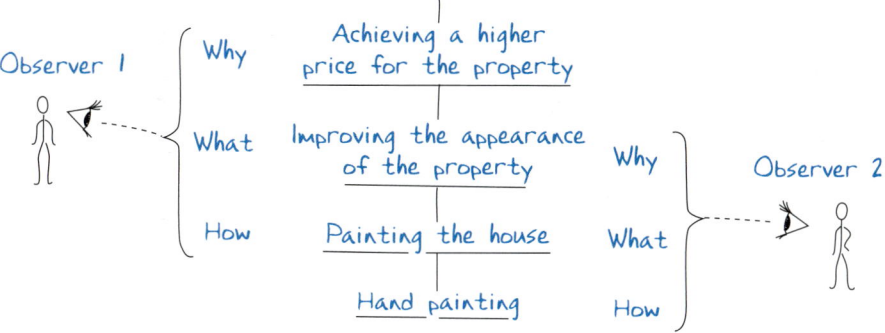

Figure 21    Choice of level is observer dependent (from Checkland 2000)

## Study note

The mnemonic CATWOE and the PQR expression, referred to in Figure 21, are used in soft systems methodology (SSM), which will be explained in Section 6.

Checkland (1999) claims that 'the idea of level, or layers (or hierarchy, though the word tends to carry connotations of authoritarianism which are not relevant) is absolutely fundamental to systems thinking' (p. S28). He suggests that human conversation is dogged by the confusion which follows from a common inability to organise thoughts and expression consciously in several layers. One of the best ways of doing this is to separate out consciously *why, what* and *how* as depicted in Figure 21. Figure 21 also makes the point that different people might make different judgements about which level to take as that of the system of interest. What and how, system and sub-system are relative, not absolute, concepts.

### SAQ 24    Relationship between boundary and levels

In what ways are boundary and levels connected when thinking systemically?

### Activity 18  Levels you recognise in the case study

In your engagement with the case study, what levels have you become aware of? My response follows in the text below.

---

From my own engagement with the case study I have conceptualised the following levels:

- local level (e.g. Stansted/Heathrow airports and surrounding communities)
- regional level (airports in the south east of England)
- national level (UK airline policy)
- European level (European policies and practices – especially cheap flights; carbon trading)
- international or global level (international airline policy; international organisations).

I can relate my five levels (above) to policy implications – airport expansion has different implications at different levels. I can also recognise different stakeholders at different levels (I return to this in the next section). When I started thinking about levels, I became aware that I could include different sets of elements at each level – different policies; different social technologies; different stakeholders; different issues or problems, etc. So for me this technique is one way of depicting:

1. how different environmental issues appear at different levels (e.g. noise at a local level)
2. the relationships between levels
3. the emergent properties that only appear at higher levels – e.g. global warming as a phenomenon emerges out of activities operating at lower levels (the same could be said for what we call the 'global economy').

Some of the complexity is also revealed, especially if I reintroduce history. One can conceptualise each level as resting on a particular history. Because I think the relationship between levels and history is important to exploring an environmental decision-making situation systemically, I introduced Reading 3 earlier about the history of global energy use.

Upham et al. (2003) identify a range of issues associated with airport expansion in England which appear at each of the five levels identified earlier (local; regional; national; European; international or global level). I have summarised Upham et al.'s (2003) main issues as I perceive them across levels in the following table (Table 4). Some issues went across all levels – particularly their observation that differing perspectives on economy and environment give rise to policy and planning conflicts, which in turn present problem for regulation. One potential trap that they identify, from my perspective, would be to use monetarised values as the only basis for environmental decision making.

Table 4  A summary of issues associated with airport expansion in the south east of England identified at different levels

| Level | Issue |
|---|---|
| Local | Aircraft and airport operations generate noise from take-offs and landings, engine testing, surface transport and construction making noise the most serious local problem. Contaminated land, ground and surface water from jet fuels, aircraft de-icing, waste generation and land-take. |
| Regional | Eco-efficiency only has narrow geographical focus? |
| National | At what point do advantages of extra air capacity outweigh the disadvantages? How should sufficiency be determined and by whom? Limits to growth could be achieved through regulations on noise or by placing an upper cap on tradeable $CO_2$ emissions permits. The UK's objectives for sustainable development are neither commensurate nor compatible (i.e. they are not systemically desirable). When total economic impacts are excessive it is necessary to know not only how transport modes compare but how best to reduce total impacts absolutely. The Government's first question in its consultation exercise about aviation expansion in 2000 implies decision making on the basis of monetarised costs and benefits (see Book 3) as a means of informing decisions on the extent and distribution of UK air traffic. Intra-national political negotiations on meeting climate change targets are needed (i.e. joining-up actions across the organisational and policy silos of government). |
| European | Some moves have been made towards charges at airports for gaseous emissions as a means to influence noise and emissions. Recognition that efficiencies must be achieved through the life cycles of a wide range of products and services and that growth in material usage necessary for growth in the physical economy should not exceed efficiency gains. Participation and consultation on expansion plans for major airport infrastructure are already required under EC Environmental Impact Assessment law (see Part 2) yet development consultation can often be a cursory and unsatisfactory affair for affected residents. |
| International or global level | Passenger traffic has grown at 9% per year since 1960 and freight traffic has also grown – air activity grows as GDP grows. Total $CO_2$ emissions from air travel are equivalent to emissions from Canada and the UK. Measuring the flows of masses mobilised by the human economy through the biosphere implies that growth in the physical scale of aviation will generally entail movement away from conditions of environmental sustainability. A healthy environment should arguably be sought for its own sake and for the benefits this brings, not on the condition that its monetarised benefits exceed monetarised costs. |

(based on Upham et al. 2003)

In my experience, thinking in terms of levels can be illuminating and give insights into where it might be best to intervene, or to appreciate the limits to proposals because of the systemic implications at a higher level.

The issues associated with aviation expansion need to be set in the broader context of international energy futures. What goes on at this level will influence, but not control, what goes on at other levels – opportunities for change can emerge at any level but constraints and possibilities will differ across levels. There are always opportunities for situation improvement at different levels but being aware of the systemic implications of any proposed change will help to avoid unintended consequences.

I anticipate that by now you will have a perspective on the future of aviation expansion that you can articulate. I wonder if in arriving at your position, you imagine projecting into the future based on the current situation or do you imagine some future situation that you see as desirable to move towards? These are two quite different ways of moving into the future, i.e. forecasting and backcasting. Please remember that as human beings, our living happens every moment of every day (i.e. we live in an unfolding present just like a ripple on a pond) and consequently the past and the present are actually just different manners of living in the present. Thus backcasting and the alternative, forecasting, can realise different futures! Backcasting leads to different policy choices, and thus decisions, than those based on forecasting, or decision making based on projections from the present; I also feel backcasting is better able to deal with the systemic practice of thinking and acting across levels. One could well ask, in relation to aviation, and the broader issues of sustainability, whether we wish to be a product of the past or a cause of the future (Figure 22)!

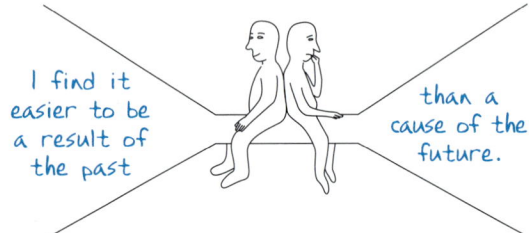

Figure 22   Do we wish to be a product of the past or a cause of the future?

## Study note

Before doing SAQ 25 go to the *Techniques* book section on Backcasting and read through it.

### SAQ 25   How does backcasting differ from forecasting?

Describe how backcasting differs from forecasting and then outline the first step to be taken when doing backcasting.

### 4.3.4   Transformation processes

The word 'transformation' has several meanings such as 'the action of changing in form, shape or appearance' and 'a complete change in character or nature'. When I discussed Figure 20, I used the word transformation in both these senses. Within systems thinking it is generally recognised that a core concept is that of the transformation process (T) by means of which defined inputs (I) are transformed into defined outputs (O) by the operations or activities of a system. This can be modelled by means of an input–output diagram of the sort shown in Figure 23. In this example,

# 4 SYSTEMS THINKING FOR EXPLORING AND RE-EXPLORING

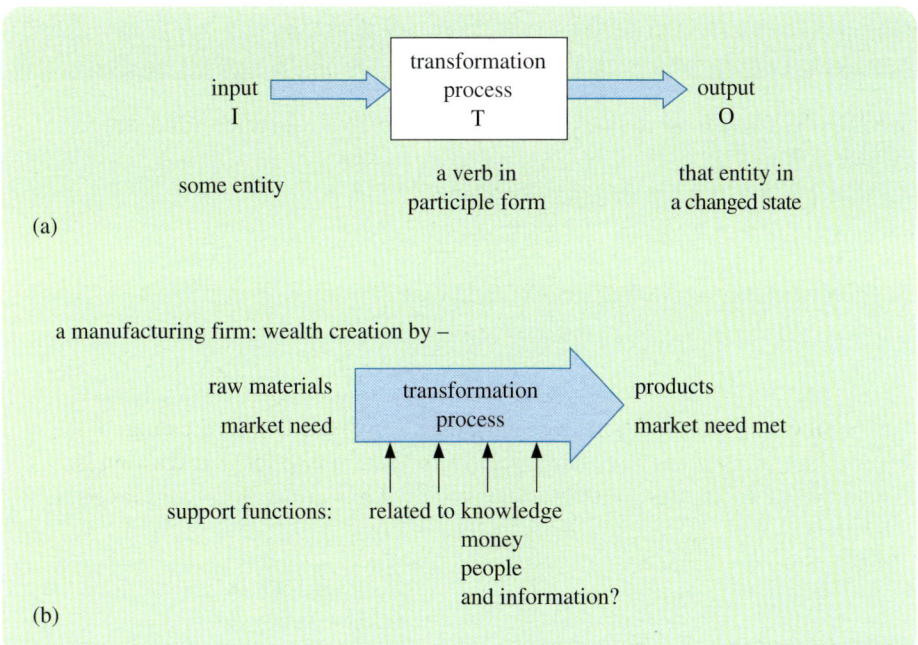

Figure 23 Two models of the transformation process as understood in systems thinking: (a) an input–output model in which inputs are transformed by the system (as seen in the *Techniques* book); (b) a transformation process involving physical products (raw materials) and an abstract concept (market needs)

an entity I is transformed by activities or processes in the system into an output of the form I in a changed state. In this model it is suggested that the transformation process is best described by a verb in participle form.

Any purposeful activity can be expressed as an input–output process of transformation. For example the aviation expansion case study could be considered as the following transformation:

decision about airport expansion not made → decision about expansion made

In this case the transformation, expressed as a verb, would be 'making a decision'.

## Study note

It is possible to construct an activity model based on verbs – read the sections in the *Techniques* book on Activity sequence diagrams (see Diagramming) and Conceptual modelling (see Modelling) and then answer the following SAQs.

### SAQ 26  Activity modelling

Outline the similarities and differences in conventions for developing activity sequence diagrams and conceptual models.

As indicated in Figure 23b, transformations can be physical or abstract. Try SAQ 27 to see if you can appreciate the differences.

> ### SAQ 27  Transformation types
>
> Which of the following is an example of a physical transformation and which an abstract?
>
> (i) unpainted fence → painted fence
>
> (ii) need for painted fence → need for painted fence met
>
> Suggest what the transformation is in each case.

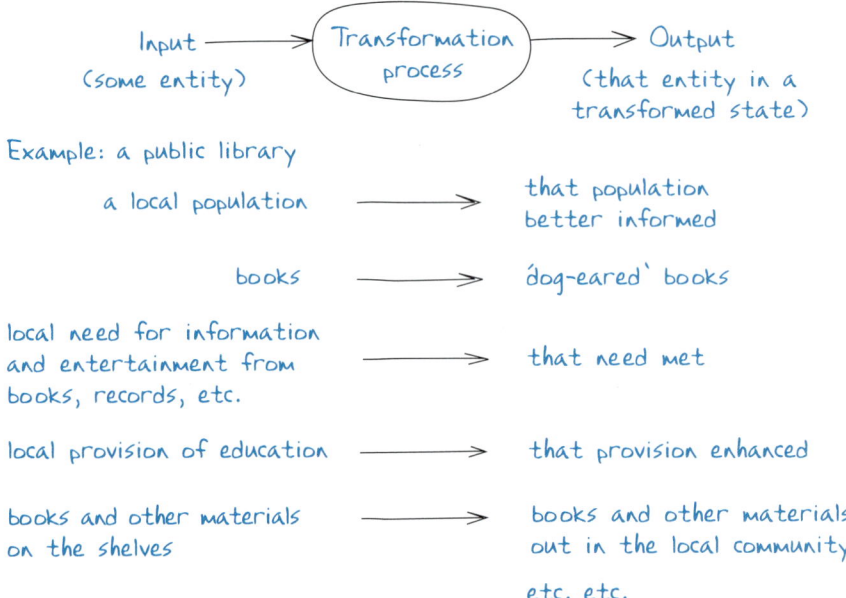

Figure 24  Some examples of transformation processes that can be associated with a situation such as a public library (Source: P. Checkland, personal communication)

It is important to note that all inputs and outputs are expressed as entities and NOT as activities (see Figure 24), and the concept 'input' is not to be confused with the concept 'resources' needed to carry out the transformation (e.g. money, people, information as depicted in Figure 23b). A classic error is the sort:

need for a decision → decision

One way of checking if you have the transformation right is to ask what the arrow means (or does) when you use this notation. It is easy to read the arrow above as 'leads to' but this is not the same as a transformation. For example, in relation to Figure 20, an appropriate transformation would be:

situation as a mess (not improved) → situation improved

And an appropriate transformation might be 'situation improving' which enables me to conclude this section by re-stating that what we are interested in developing is your systems practice by engaging in situation-improving transformations through systemic environmental decision making!

### Activity 19    Thinking in terms of transformations

Using what you have just learned about transformation processes, and following the logic of Figure 24, list some examples of transformation processes that you would associate with a White Paper.

I will return to transformation processes in Section 5, where I explain more about formulating systems of interest. In this section I have introduced a series of tools for understanding and practice in relation to exploring and re-exploring environmental decision-making situations. So far, however, I have said relatively little about who is in the situation – the stakeholders and the processes associated with stakeholding.

## 4.4   Stakeholders and stakeholding

To know fully about a situation, one has to know who the people are. In Book 1, two types of people were identified as influencing decisions – the decision maker(s) and people affected by the decision. The images presented in Figure 15 provide some further insights into the question: who are the people? In recent times the word stakeholder has entered common usage meaning a person who has an interest or concern in something. As was mentioned briefly in Book 1, there are a number of perspectives on what is meant by 'stakeholder' and 'stakeholding'. Reading 4 gives an overview of some of these concepts in relation to a particular environmental issue: water management at catchment scale.

### Reading 4

Read 'Stakeholders and stakeholding in integrated catchment management and sustainable use of water'. This reading comes from a six country European research project called SLIM. It is one of several Policy Briefings prepared collaboratively by members of the project. When you have finished this short reading complete the SAQ and following activity.

### SAQ 28    Stakeholder and stakeholding

How are stakeholder and stakeholding described in Reading 4?

### SAQ 29    Stakeholder analysis

What are the steps in stakeholder analysis (SA) described in Reading 4?

In Activity 2 you were asked to do a rich picture of the case study situation. A protocol for rich pictures is to include yourself as I have done (Figure 4). Look at your answer to this activity and see to what extent your stakeholding in aviation or airport expansion is captured in your rich picture. I depicted myself as a 'concerned' user of cheap air travel but I have no immediate stakeholding in airport expansion in that I do not live close to an airport or depend on the industry for my livelihood (I am, however, concerned about the systemic implications of expansion). Your rich picture may also be a useful starting point to do an audit of other stakeholders – how many have you included in your rich picture?

Stakeholders may have common or different interests. When stakeholders have different interests then certain stakeholder interests may be overridden by the decision-making process; conflict can arise or, alternatively, facilitation might be used to move towards accommodations between different interests (this process is discussed in more detail in Book 3). It is possible that, with appropriate facilitation in complex environmental decision-making situations, networks of individuals and groups can come together with a common system of interest (e.g. a business, a campaign, a voluntary organisation, a project) which is characterised by trust, cooperation, commitment and responsibility. Some examples are given in Reading 4, but, as described, 'the notion of "stakeholding" and "stake-holders" requires some recognition and acceptance by policy makers of the diversity of stakeholders' perspectives, knowledges and contexts. This diversity means that stakeholders do not necessarily agree on what the objective of action is, nor on how to achieve it. But divergent ideas about purpose and objectives cannot be reconciled only by more or better data'.

### Activity 20  Stakeholder analysis using a systems map

Read the section entitled 'Stakeholder analysis' in the *Techniques* book and then, drawing on any relevant earlier work, use a systems map to construct a stakeholder analysis of the airport expansion decision-making process. Use your understanding of boundaries and levels to help you with this. When you have finished your map, record any insights you gained in your learning journal or blog.

---

Mark Sagoff (1989) provides another perspective on stakeholding. He argues that a political process is a process of debate and compromise and is supposed to be creative in ways that cause individuals to change their values and to rise above self-interest. However, the economic analyses, particularly cost–benefit approaches, that are pervasive in environmental decision making merely gratify existing desires rather than educating and elevating public opinion. From Sagoff's perspective, economic analyses do this because they limit conflict to those who have something at stake for which they are prepared to pay. This prevents the socialisation of conflict, which he sees as crucial to the functioning of democracy.

An example cited by Sagoff (1989) is:

> Suppose a corporation proposes and an environmentalist group opposes the building of a shopping centre in a rural area just outside of town. An economist might make a recommendation based on prices assigned to the various wants and preferences of relevant interest groups. This would effectively limit conflict to the immediate parties who know about and are affected by the project. The genius of democracy, however, is to let the conflict spread to a larger audience.
>
> (Sagoff, 1989, p. 96)

Thus Sagoff is arguing that a stakeholder is someone with more than merely an economic interest in a system of interest.

Sagoff goes on to say that when the conflict is spread to a larger audience then the 'decision-making process ... may become a kind of public good, since it allows everyone who participates in it the feeling of relevance, importance, and community consciousness flowing from that participation'. He acknowledges that this may seem inefficient but justifies it by claiming that this is what democratic government is all about. The alternative – technocracy – quarantines or localises conflict so that it can be resolved by the application of some mechanical rule or decision procedure.

Did you do your SA by yourself or with others? Think about what might have happened if you had done it with others. The way it is done will reflect your own thinking and values, time and circumstances, and as outlined in the *Techniques* book, what tools or techniques you use to do it. The question of who participates in any process associated with environmental decision making is a critical one because the answer will determine what perspectives are taken into account, whose knowledge will count, and thus the overall trajectory of the decision-making process. These points are the subject of attention in Section 5, but before moving on try Activity 21 which relates to the case study.

### Activity 21 Possible contribution of stakeholder analysis

Consider the consultation processes carried out in the lead up to the release of the Aviation White Paper in the case study. Based on your own experience and your reading of Section 4.4, what assessment would you make about (i) the possible contribution stakeholder analysis did make, or could have made to the design of the consultation process and (ii) how, if at all, the consultation process built stakeholding in the environmental decision?

# 5 Perspectives on a situation

## 5.1 Valuing multiple perspectives

In the case study in Book 1 we were told that 'the overwhelming message from the consultation [exercise] was of opposition to airport expansion on the grounds of noise, air pollution, road congestion, loss of land and impact on the environment, wildlife and local community'. Despite this result the Government in its final White Paper committed itself to airport expansion. Why did this happen? What claims can be made about the capacity of the airport expansion decision-making process to deal with different perspectives?

Let me explore this a little further by posing a number of questions.

1. What do you think the problem was to which airport expansion was the answer?
2. Have I phrased the first question in the wrong way – was it an opportunity rather than a problem?
3. What, from your perspective, is the main purpose of aviation?
4. What other purposes can you suggest?
5. What opportunities have been forgone by framing the problem and the proposed solution in the way they were?
6. If you were to describe the whole environmental decision-making process as 'a system to ...' how would you complete the sentence using the logic 'do P by Q in order to achieve R'?

You may find question 6 a bit cryptic at this stage, so let me give you an example of what I mean. I could choose to describe the whole environmental decision-making process in the aviation expansion case study as: 'a system to meet Treasury demands to expand the aviation sector of the economy by enhancing economic growth'. This description of a system of interest contains the following elements: do P = meet Treasury demands, by Q = expand aviation sector, in order to achieve R = economic growth. Please note I am not saying this is or was the system, but I can choose to look at it as if it were this system with a view to learning about the situation.

In my questions, I have used two terms that have particular meanings within systems thinking. These are 'purpose' and 'perspective'.

### 5.1.1 Purposeful and purposive

It is possible to ascribe a purpose to what we or others do, the actions we take. How particular actions, or activities are construed will differ from person to person because of their different perspectives, which arise from their traditions of understanding. For example, I have implicitly (if not explicitly) attributed the purpose of 'maintaining economic growth' to the decision-making process associated with aviation expansion in the UK. In truth, however, I have not spoken with those responsible for the design and conduct of the White Paper process and it could well be that they attributed other purposes to what they were doing.

Even if we do not ascribe purposes to our own actions, another observer may infer our purposes by observing our actions and their outcomes, so that in their eyes we implicitly have a purpose to our actions. Ascribing purpose is an important process in taking a systems approach to managing complexity.

Two forms of behaviour in relation to purpose have been distinguished. One is *purposeful* behaviour, which Checkland (1993) describes as behaviour that is willed – there is thus some sense of voluntary action. The other is *purposive* behaviour – behaviour to which an observer can attribute purpose. Thus, in the case study situation, if I described the purpose of the Minister responsible for the White Paper as 'meeting some political imperative', I would be attributing purpose to him and describing purposive behaviour. I might possibly say his intention was to control the issue for political reasons. Of course, if I were to talk with him I might find out this was not the case at all. He might have been acting in a purposeful manner which was not evident to me.

Within systems thinking, purpose is a contested notion. However purpose is always attributed to a system by someone. Within systems practice the attribution of purpose can be a creative, learning process.

For me there is a risk in reducing the notion of purpose to mean an objective or goal that can be achieved, and in some cases optimised. I make this distinction because the important aspect of systemic practice, compared with systematic practice, is exploring or inquiring of a situation: 'What would I learn from attributing purpose to this situation?' Alternatively the question might be posed as 'In reflection, what purpose do I attribute to my own actions in this situation?'

### SAQ 30 Purposeful and purposive – examples

Decide which of the following scenarios best exemplify purposefulness or purposiveness.

(a) A group of friends who drink together regularly at the local pub are enthusiastic about football and decide rather than just watching and talking about it they will form their own team. This they do.

(b) Sophie noticed a group of youths running down the street and immediately thought they were responsible for the vandalised telephone kiosk nearby.

(c) My company has adopted the internationally recognised set of environmental management standards, but after a year of working with them we find they are not helpful in our particular circumstances. However, we feel we have to stick with the international standards to maintain credibility.

(d) We learned our customers were dissatisfied with our after-sales support. As a result, we changed our ways of operating; this has had positive effects right through the business.

### 5.1.2 Perspective

Systems thinker C. West Churchman (1971) once claimed that systems thinking begins when you can put yourself in the mind of another. Of course this is not possible in the literal sense, but metaphorically it conveys a key aspect of systems practice – appreciating multiple perspectives! outline how I understand the concept of 'perspective' in Box 8.

### Box 8  A story about perspective

Figure 25   Images of soil erosion – an environmental issue in many parts of the world

In the fertile wheat-growing area of the Darling Downs in Queensland, Australia, researchers were concerned for many years that the farming practices were leading to excessive soil erosion. However the farmers had a different perspective. After considerable time, some particularly smart agricultural extension staff realised that all of the images of erosion that the research services used in their publications were of very deep gullies and that for farmers this was what they considered erosion to be. Within this perception they were right – they did not have erosion. This realisation led them to build a rainfall simulator which could be set up in the field in a way that enabled the farmers to choose

> a range of treatments relating to soil surface cover (bare soil, surface mulch, different types of crop residue, etc.), run a particular rainfall event (amount, intensity and duration) and collect the soil, if any, that was eroded in another part of the simulator. Using this device, the imperceptible but significant erosion under certain cropping regimes was made visible to the farmers. They had experienced it themselves.
>
> The bottom image in Figure 25 shows sheet erosion on cropping land – which is not really perceptible – and a classic image of soil erosion (Figure 25, top image).

I define perspective as 'a way of experiencing where experiencing is a cognitive act'. But what do I mean by 'experience'? For me experience arises in the act of making a distinction in relation to ourselves. The act of making a distinction is quite basic to what it is to be human. When we make a distinction, we split the world into two parts: this and that. We separate the thing distinguished from its background. We do that when we distinguish a system from its environment, often forgetting that the word system is actually shorthand for specifying a system in relation to an environment. In process terms, this is the same as drawing a circle on a sheet of paper. When the circle is closed, three different elements are brought forth at the same time: an inside, an outside and a border (in systems terminology, a boundary). In daily life, we have developed all sorts of perceptual shortcuts that cause us to forget this is what we do – we live, most of the time, with our focus on one of these three elements: the inside, the outside or the border.

## Activity 22  Multiple perspectives in the case study situation

Readings 3 to 7 for Book 1 and the audio programme titled *Consultation within the White Paper* include various responses to the SERAS consultation. In Activity 20 in Book 1 you were asked to read and listen to these responses and then make notes. I now want to extend this activity in three ways:

(i) Look at your notes about these readings from the Book 1 activity in the light of the six questions I posed at the beginning of this section. Map out, using a spray diagram, the different perspectives of these stakeholder groups. (You may need to quickly scan through the readings again to refresh your memory but it should not be necessary to read these again in detail to complete the activity.)

Note: you can choose to develop one, two or three diagrams to answer this question – whichever best helps you to differentiate between the different perspectives.

(ii) The programme *Consultation within the White Paper* included interviews with a selection of stakeholders made during this consultation phase. Listen to the various reactions to the information contained within the consultation document. Add to your spray diagram as you listen to the interviews, keeping in mind my six questions posed at the beginning of Section 5.1.

(iii) The views of stakeholders outside the UK were not considered in the case study, even though planes must land somewhere. Listen once again to the views from the perspective of some Ugandans involved in aviation in the programme *Perspectives from Uganda*. Add these perspectives to your spray diagram.

After having listened to the interviews and completed your spray diagram, make some notes on how, if at all, your own perspective has changed about the case study situation and the decision-making process, as a result of doing this activity.

You may care to return to your answer to Activity 20 (in Book 2), your stakeholder map, and see if your spray diagram accounts for all perspectives.

### Study note

If you want more practice in exploring stakeholder perspectives, there is an activity you can do on the following website:

http://open2.net/systems/thinking/per.html

This is optional. When you find this site you will see that it is part of a larger site developed with the BBC about systems thinking and practice for managing complexity. On this particular page is an exercise about perspectives. The online activity asks you to write an account of the perspectives you perceive each stakeholder to have.

I hope by now that you have begun to appreciate that stakeholders have different perspectives and that each one of us only has a partial view of any situation. Another way of saying this is that different people can attribute different purposes to the same situation. In systems terms, achievement of purpose is the same thing as asking 'Has the transformation been achieved?' (see Section 4.3.4). In my example above, it was:

Treasury need not met → Treasury need met.

Clashes of perspective and purpose can lead to conflict or inaction (passive aggressive behaviour) often because there is no agreement on the nature of the problem or opportunity (*what*) nor agreement about *how* to proceed or what would constitute success (*why*). This can lead to debate, or at worst stand-offs, about what constitutes desirable and feasible change. In these situations negotiation is important. These matters are taken up in Book 3.

If one accepts that we each have unique histories that give rise to different perspectives, then it is easier to appreciate why so many meetings and decision-making processes can be experienced as frustrating. Based on my experience some of what occurs is:

1. arguing about 'how' to do something before all present have a clear understanding about 'what' is being discussed
2. failure to be listened to – to have your perspective heard and valued
3. procedures and structures (e.g. design of room or seating arrangements formalised procedures such as planning appeals) which interfere with meaningful dialogue, limit the breadth of perspective and/or their relevance
4. failure to have useful data to inform what is being discussed or decided
5. failure to acknowledge that the emotional climate needs to be managed as much as 'formal' processes – this requires 'emotional intelligence'.

Another common trap is the trap of discipline-based expertise (see below). No doubt you can think of more.

### Disciplinary boundaries in professional practice

In our society experts, particularly those with a scientific, or other professional backgrounds, are frequently called upon to give evidence on matters affecting particular decisions. There is also a tendency for experts from one discipline to be called on to give, or offer, expert advice in areas beyond their experience. This is common not only in the legal process but also in policy development and political decision making. The evidence of scientists can be very influential in shaping particular decisions. Brown et al. (1995) make the claim that 'early attempts at intervention [in environmental issues] by single profession experts [does] nothing to resolve the issues' and that there needs to be a move towards multi-interest, multiscale and multidisciplinary cooperation in exploring and resolving environmental issues. 'Stepping back' in this case means becoming aware that there are institutionalised disciplines of thought which are potential traps and that a number of practical challenges must be faced by environmental decision makers (see Box 9).

> **Box 9  Practical challenges arising from disciplinary and professional perspectives**
>
> The Western cultural set of identifying the elements of a dilemma as in opposition to one another serves environmental management very badly. This is true at whatever level we discuss: local, national or global. Until the mid-eighties, the management of the industrialised world's natural resources was dominated by single profession organisations. Water boards were advised by engineers, mining councils by geologists and so on. The training of the wide range of professions involved in environment management was almost exclusively technical and specialised. The training of professions perceived as having no direct connection with environmental management included no mention of environmental issues, even as these became all-pervading. This put individuals in a poor position to cope with multi-faceted issues, and increased the likelihood of a them-and-us mentality
>
> The custom of adopting expert advice on each separate facet of an issue is so deep-seated as to be the cultural norm. To change the system of unchallenged supremacy in one area is, in the first instance, to increase the degree of conflict. When different groups work together on a particular issue, they bring different languages, terms of reference, professional loyalties and basic understanding of the problem. What different professions see as the problem varies enormously.
>
> (Source: Brown et al., 1995, pp. 27–8)

Another way of viewing the dilemma raised by Brown et al. (1995) is captured in Figure 26. This shows that in a given context, there is a tendency for individuals from a particular background, discipline or culture to 'see' the world only in a particular way – to formulate different systems of interest. A group of people who are brought together to explore an environmental issue and who retain their individual ways of seeing the world would be taking what I call a multidisciplinary approach. There are many examples of so-called multidisciplinary teams, but in practice they often work in both practical and theoretical isolation. Taking an interdisciplinary approach involves doing more work and making an attempt either (i) to gain some form of synthesis of perspectives and understanding from individuals with different backgrounds or (ii) to appreciate and learn from the different perspectives because of the different insights they provide on a phenomenon or situation of common concern. Both involve listening to others and acknowledging that they have a perspective, even if you do not agree with it. This is not always easy.

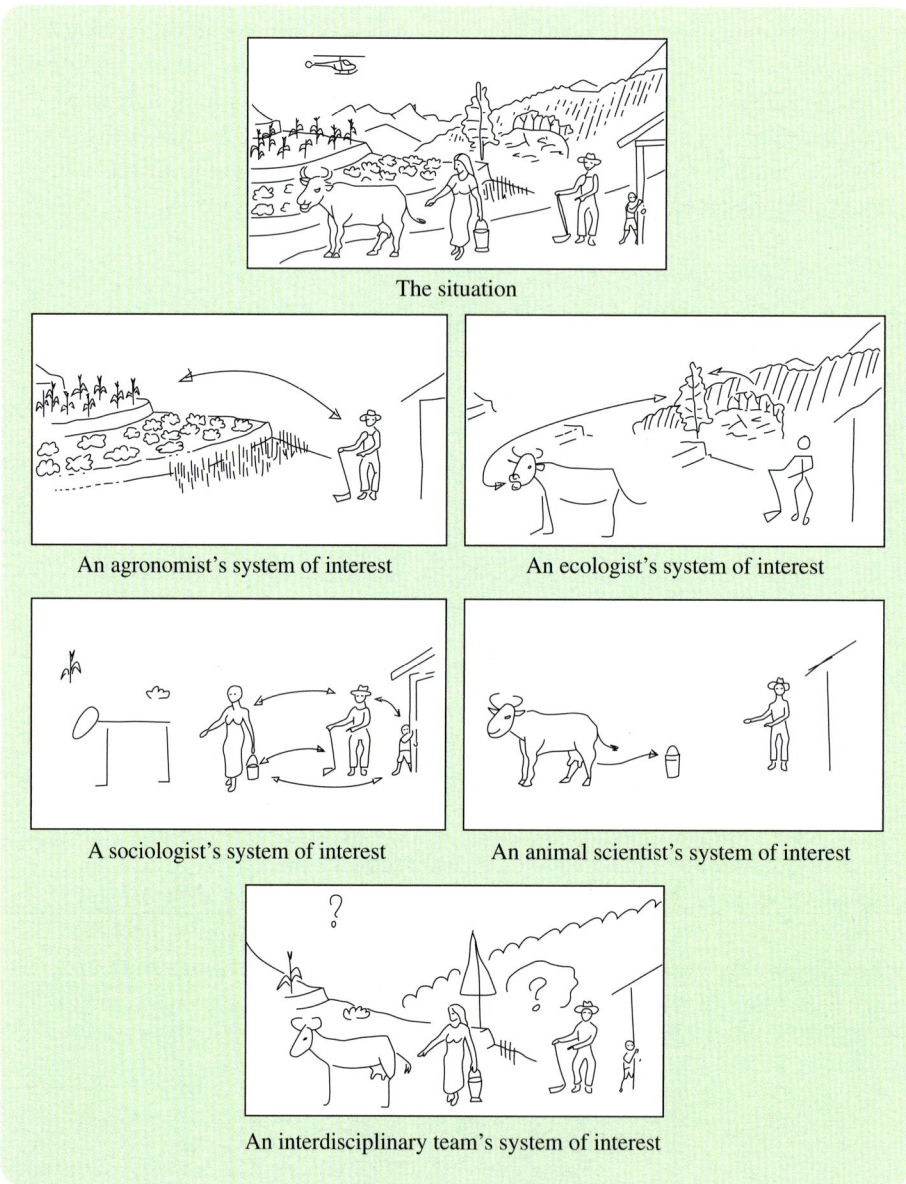

Figure 26    Perspectives taken by disciplinary experts differ from that taken by an effective interdisciplinary team with the result that different systems of interest are formulated

Figure 26 depicts how a 'real situation' is seen by professionals of different disciplinary backgrounds. It is based on the experience that many of us are trained to see only some things. Sometimes this is referred to as the theory dependency of facts (i.e. particular theories shape what we see and interpret, as depicted by Figure 18).

What implications does this appreciation of 'perspective' have for environmental decision making? To answer this question, I will consider how environmental issues arise and how they come to be named as problems or opportunities. I also suggest that being aware of the nature and role of different perspectives is central to environmental decision making; in the process of stepping back and exploring and re-exploring a situation we become aware that the process leads to changes in understandings and practices as well as a modified situation (Figure 20).

Figure 27   A group of stakeholders in a situation engaged in conversation mapping and the output, a conversation map

Before moving on, I want to introduce one particular technique, conversation mapping, that I have found useful for surfacing multiple perspectives and building stakeholding in a complex situation. Figure 27 shows a group of people engaged in conversation mapping and the output, a conversation map. I am introducing this here for your possible future use in your own practice. I am not suggesting it as a technique to use in relation to the case study at this time – but it could have been used. If we were in a face-to-face situation I could have asked you to develop a conversation map in groups of four to six to explore your perspectives of the case study situation. It may be possible to gauge many perspectives on the case study by looking at the postings on the T863 computer conference.

### Study note

If you have not done so you might like to take some time to read about Conversation maps (see Diagramming) in the *Techniques* book. As you read you could jot any ideas down that you have about how it might be used.

## 5.2 Knowing what the problem or opportunity is

From the 'Freedom to fly?' case study you will know that from the start of the process, the British Government saw the issue as an attempt to 'maximise the significant social and economic benefits that growth in aviation would bring' whilst minimising or 'paying for' the environmental impacts of such development. In subsequent consultations on airport expansion the following three 'fundamental questions' were posed:

1. How much extra airport capacity (defined as the number of passengers embarking on a flight per annum) will be needed over the next 30 years?
2. How will the environmental impacts be mitigated or paid for?
3. Based on the forecasted passenger number, where should the new airport capacity be located?

I suggest that from the start the UK Government framed the issue (named what it was) and reduced the possible range of 'hows' by using language based on particular understandings, which in turn led them to articulate particular questions. Together these 'frame' the situation in a particular way. But it is possible to explore such framings and examine what the framing reveals and conceals. For example, I have already referred to the Government's commitment to particular understandings of economic growth; earlier I referred to 'backcasting' as a particular technique which is fundamentally different from 'forecasting'. I have also referred to the role metaphor plays in relation to our understandings and practices. Some of the respondents to the White Paper consultation recognised this 'framing' issue and labelled it 'predict and provide'. In the arena of environmental decision making two metaphors are common – the problem and opportunity metaphors.

### Activity 23  What was the problem/opportunity?

Having engaged with the case study what assessment have you made of how the 'problem/opportunity' was framed in the environmental decision-making process? How, if at all, would you choose to name the problem or opportunity?

What limitations, if any, can you see for a process of environmental decision making from accepting your 'naming' of the problem or opportunity?

## 5.2.1 The 'problem' and 'opportunity' metaphors

In environmental decision making it is very easy to ignore the nature of the situation, and for individuals and groups to fall into the trap of thinking that they recognise what the problem or opportunity is and that they know how to proceed to generate the solution. Associated with this, there is the belief that problems and opportunities can be readily 'named' or 'identified'. The notion that problems and opportunities can be easily identified is the same as equating them with difficulties. Individuals or groups who pursue this approach are soon likely to encounter:

- other people with different perspectives who disagree about what the problem or opportunity is as well as how to proceed, as in the case study;
- particular technologies which people use and understand differently and which circumscribe our behaviours – they may be artefacts such as a computer or a 'social technology' such as legislation, forecasting, cost–benefit analysis (CBA – see Book 3) or some of the common environmental management approaches (e.g. EIA; EMAS – see Part 2 of this book);
- different cultural traditions both within and between organisations and nationalities.

I want to suggest that problems and opportunities are formulated in our language through social and cultural processes, which include how we use technologies, rather than having any independent existence. For example, our awareness of climate change has come about because of our ability to make particular types of measurement. What is contested, however, is whether the levels measured are part of some long term natural fluctuation, whether the primary cause is human activity (anthropogenic) and whether the effects will be positive or negative or both. Collectively, over the last 20 years or so, we have been engaged in a process of deciding whether human induced climate change is a 'real problem'. Modelling is a form of practice which has played an important role; it is intimately associated with the process of 'problem' and 'opportunity' generating.

Issues arise when enough people have a sense of concern or unease. This is usually before there is any clear statement about the nature of a problem or opportunity. Issues emerge from messes through social, often contested, processes (Figure 19). When something becomes an issue, it is an important topic for discussion. The transition of human-caused global warming from 'issue' to 'problem' is a good example (although the USA's response to the Kyoto Protocol, adopted in 1997, after President Bush's election in 2000 and 2004 suggests it is still contested).

A contrasting position to the one I am proposing is the belief that problems and opportunities exist independently of the processes by which we formulate them – that they exist 'out there' in nature. These distinctions have important implications because how we think about problems and opportunities determines our actions. This point was raised in Table 1 in Book 1. I expand on the possible forms of behaviour associated with differing interpretations of the problem metaphor in Table 5.

Table 5  Possible forms of behaviour associated with differing interpretations of the problem metaphor

| Behaviour associated with a belief that problems exist independently of us | Behaviour associated with a belief that problems are formulated through social processes |
|---|---|
| Energy and resources are devoted to research and technology development so as to discover solutions, which in turn generate new problems | Effort is devoted to understanding how we formulate problems – i.e. what history do they have? What facts are said to inform them? Who has been involved? |
| Particular experts or forms of expertise may be privileged and given credit for identifying the problem | The contested nature of problems is recognised, as is the meaning we give to data; attention is given to processes which involve communication and interpretation |
| Tendency to become enmeshed in the negative connotations of problems | Recognition that a person/group's problem may be another's opportunity |
| Because the words 'problem' and 'opportunity' are nouns, it is easy to see them as 'things' rather than as descriptors of situations (e.g. 'it is a problem' compared with 'I find the situation problematic') | It is possible to ask what the problem or opportunity metaphor reveals or conceals. |

### Activity 24   Exploring your own perspective on problems and opportunities

Drawing on the distinctions between messes and difficulties and the material in Table 5 make some notes on how you have dealt with the problem/opportunity metaphor in the past. What implications does your perspective have for your own practice?

What constitutes an environmental problem or opportunity is open to interpretation and very much depends on individual, group, disciplinary and social perspectives; the same is true of what constitutes effective environmental decision making. The following two definitions typify the main divide: Glasbergen and Cörvers (1995) define environmental problems as 'those instances in which people's behaviour affects their physical environment in such a way as to place their own health, other people's health, the built environment or natural systems in jeopardy'. In contrast, Beck (1992) claims that 'environmental problems are not problems of our surroundings, but – in their origins and through their consequences – are thoroughly social problems, problems of people, their history, their living conditions, their relation to the world and reality, their social, cultural and living conditions. At the end of the twentieth century nature is society and society is also nature'. In inviting you to stand back from naming 'a problem' or ' an opportunity' by exploring and re-exploring and valuing multiple perspectives on environmental issues, and in suggesting that problems and opportunities emerge from environmental issues, I am asking you to consider another perspective, a systems perspective, which is a synthesis of a natural science and a social science perspective. This is one of the main ways to break out of traps in thinking and acting.

From my perspective, there are three potential traps, which may be avoided by standing back and exploring the situation, that all relate in some way to the problem and opportunity metaphor. These are:

1. the question of knowing how we know – the basis on which knowledge claims can be made
2. the historical divide between humans and nature, or the biophysical and social worlds
3. the question of sensitivity to initial starting conditions, which has been made more popular in recent times in discourses about chaos and complexity science.

These three points are the subject of the next sections. Some of the implications that arise from these three factors are that particular understandings and practices become reified in social technologies (e.g. EIA; EMAS, public inquiries; white papers, directives, etc.) and in the practices of disciplinary-based experts as well as the structures of organisations (e.g. departments, divisions, etc.) which can sometimes give rise to what is referred to as a 'silo mentality' or a failure to work effectively across organisational boundaries (Figure 28).

Figure 28   A depiction of 'over the fence' engineering, an example of 'silo working'

## 5.3   Knowing how we know

How environmental managing is practised very much depends on how we answer the question 'How do we know what we know?' Let's start from a global perspective. Consider the understandings which arise from Australian Aboriginal culture or that from research in Botswana by Louise Fortmann (Box 10).

### Box 10 Different ways of knowing and some implications

#### Vignette 1

Ethnographer Deborah Bird Rose (cited in Knudtson and Suzuki, 1992) articulated four transcendent rules which shaped the 'ways of knowing' of the Yarralin Aboriginal community in Australia. These were:

1. Balance – a system cannot be life enhancing if it is out of kilter, and each part shares in the responsibility of sustaining itself and balancing others.
2. Response – communication is reciprocal. There is a moral obligation here: to learn to understand, to pay attention and to respond.
3. Symmetry – in opposing and balancing each other, parts must be equivalent because the purpose is not to 'win' or to dominate, but to block thereby producing further balance.
4. Autonomy – no species, no group or country is 'boss' for another; each adheres to its own Law. Authority and dependence are necessary within parts, but not between parts.

#### Vignette 2

Louise Fortmann's (1989) case study of 50 years of rangeland use in Botswana provides a wonderful illustration of what might happen when the context of environmental issues is not adequately explored and appreciated. Official policy developed by researchers and bureaucrats consistently defined the major problem of the pastoral regions as overstocking, which they predicted would lead to certain ecological disaster. To them, the problem was clear, as was the technical solution (de-stocking). The local experience of the pastoralists, on the other hand, defined the problem as too little land. The local solution was also very different: renting, or simply using an enormous concession of land previously given to a European mining company. The local experience was that the local range could and did carry an increased cattle population and that, apart from localised problems, the dire official predictions did not materialise. While there is general agreement that the quality of the environment (as indicated by the quality of the grazing, the number of trees and the extent of erosion) is deteriorating, there is clearly no agreement on causes or solutions. Of particular significance is that each story was consistently told by both 'worldviews' and held for a period of 50 years, showing how different and how unconnected traditions of understanding can be.

The situation in Botswana arose in part because of particular aspects of the disciplinary trap. Range science is now a recognised discipline and is taught in many universities in both rich and poorer countries. Its twin goals of the protection of the environment through the concept of sustainable yield (economic and biological) and the improvement of the productivity of ranges, particularly of forage and animals, had their origin in North America and were rapidly adopted in Australia. Since range science and range management developed in North America, its approach was necessarily adapted to the social and ecological milieu of North American rangelands. A central feature of this history is that range management has evolved to meet the needs of a system based on either privately owned land or, as is largely the case in Australia, land owned by the state and leased to individual livestock producers on a long term basis, i.e. managed much as private property would be. So pervasive is this history, which constitutes this particular 'tradition of understanding', that it is difficult for those involved in it to see range management in any way other than their own way. This becomes very obvious when it is advocated that the privatisation of rangelands is considered to be a precondition for the protection of natural resources (Baden and Stroup, 1977; Hopcraft, 1981). It is additionally apparent when the techniques of range management that have been developed in the West are applied – and consistently fail (Gilles, 1985) – in poorer countries. The thinking that they could possibly be effective in the first place is indicative of the continued blindness to seeing that such knowledge is socially constructed and is thus only applicable to its place of origin.

(Source: Russell and Ison, 2000)

These two vignettes reflect contrasting epistemologies – what we accept as a basis for valid knowledge. Stories about differences in epistemology are often highlighted in contrasting cultural situations but they also apply within and between groups in most societies and organisations, even in families and between professions (e.g. Figure 26).

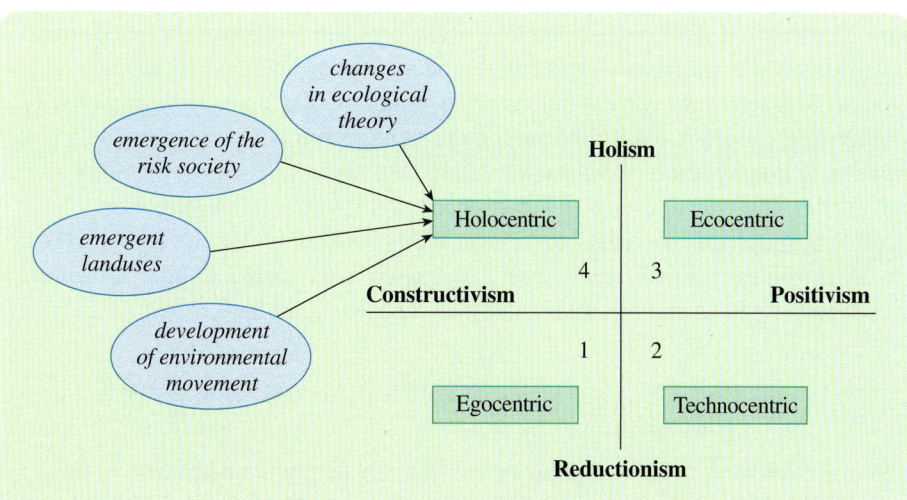

Figure 29  Four ways of knowing in relation to environmental decision making and natural resources management (Source: SLIM, 2004c)

Practices used in natural resource management can be placed in one of four quartiles relating to different ways of knowing, as conceived by Miller (1983, 1985) and Bawden (1998) and outlined in Figure 29. Miller used the figure to characterise the paradigms (ways of thinking and acting) favoured by his colleagues involved in the battle against the spruce budworm in Canada. Technocentric thinking (Quadrant 2) is characterised by a reductionist and positivist perspective. Colleagues with this perspective recommended spraying. Ecocentric thinking (Quadrant 3) represents a positivist but also holistic perspective – in terms used in this course, a systematic perspective. Colleagues with this perspective focused on natural controls and the management of the ecosystem as a whole. A few of Miller's colleagues had developed a holocentric perspective (Quadrant 4), that is, a holistic and constructivist, systemic perspective. They focused on the problem as the outcome of human activity and on critical learning (with some reason because the spruce budworm became a pest as a result of the human decision to manage enormous tracts of land with a monoculture). To take another example, in the case of microbial pollution of drinking water from an area of land: technocentric thinkers might recommend chemical water treatment; ecocentric thinkers might recommend alteration of vegetation cover to reduce water runoff; and holocentric thinkers might focus on changing human behaviour to bring about changes in vegetation and other measures. Each thinking scenario can and should encompass the one numbered 'below' it (SLIM, 2004c).

Today, most problems of natural resource management and environmental decision making probably lie in Quadrant 4, partly due to societal trends such as those noted in Figure 29. Water management at the catchment scale and many problems of the sustainable use of water at other scales are in this category. As outlined in Figure 19, such situations are characterised by certain features. They are complex and not simply complicated. The results of stakeholders' interventions are uncertain. The varying, often conflicting, interests of a wide range of stakeholders must be accommodated, and the range of knowledge involved in managing them is extremely broad. In complex natural resource situations, capacity is needed to operate with awareness in and across all four quadrants.

Different ways of knowing (epistemologies) give rise to different perspectives which in turn give rise to differing interpretations of the problem and opportunity metaphors. In a world in which we have to increasingly manage 'one planet living' we face choices as to whether we value different perspectives or face increasing homogeneity (like high street shops in the UK becoming the same in every city) through the narrowing or politicisation of discourse. Social diversity is surely as desirable as biodiversity? 'One planet living' is a metaphor I prefer to that of globalisation, because it suggests that we must take responsibility for how we live on earth and with each other, whereas 'globalisation', as it is discussed in the media, implies something that is happening to us and in relation to which we have no agency.

### Activity 25   Ways of knowing

Do the different ways of knowing shown in Figure 29 help you make sense of the perspectives held by those interviewed about airport expansion? Is it helpful in making sense of your own way, or ways, of knowing? Make notes on your insights and questions. Suggest some implications of your insights for designing or managing environmental decision-making processes.

The material in this section has implications for the education and training of environmental managers, planners, policy makers, etc. in particular (SLIM, 2004c). There are strong links between our ways of knowing and how different cultures, professionals, etc. understand the relationship between the social and the biophysical.

## 5.4  Relating the social and the biophysical

Reading 1 introduced you to the carbon cycle (if you were not already aware of it) and the idea that many aspects of the biophysical world can be understood in interconnected, systemic terms. These are sometimes summarised in terms of nutrient cycles (e.g. nitrogen cycle, sulphur cycle) recognising that any one cycle interacts with others (Figure 2). Systemic understandings are increasingly informing how many scientists think about the so-called natural world. For example, in the area of earth sciences, understandings from the study of plate tectonics show that the surface of the earth is in process, i.e. constantly moving. Because the rate of movement is often imperceptible to us on a daily, or even generational, basis we are often not aware of this and see the earth as something 'solid' and 'unmoving'. Of course, the science of ecology has also contributed to changing perceptions about the dynamics of the biophysical world. Unfortunately in both of these areas of science, earth science and ecology, scientists often exclude humans from consideration as if they were outside nature.

A common trap is to assume that science can provide 'objective' answers for particular courses of action in environmental decision making. In my experience, this is rarely the case. I am not saying that science does not have an important contribution to make but I am questioning the bases on which scientific understandings are used for decision making – as Reading 5 explains, science may contribute to increased uncertainty.

### Reading 5

Now read the paper on ecological constraints from SLIM and then answer the SAQ.

> ### SAQ 31   Ecosystems and ecological constraints
>
> How do the authors of Reading 5 understand ecosystems and the notion of ecological constraints, and how does this contrast with the prevailing positivist view?

My answer to SAQ 31 follows in the text. The authors of Reading 5 argue against the prevailing assumption that a river catchment ecosystem is an autonomous entity that can be identified as having an agreed geographical or biological boundary and the associated positivist view that science is ultimately able to describe this objective, agreed reality. Within this positivist view, people involved in a catchment are then expected to undertake appropriate actions, to ensure that the system's properties remain within the specified limits. Actions are defined by policy and enacted in regulations or through fiscal incentives, supported through research and dissemination of results to practitioners. Also within this view, ecosystems are assumed to change over time towards a natural climax state, depending on climate and geology, that represents 'good ecological status'. These authors hold a contrasting view which is that ecosystems can exhibit many different patterns of behaviour, including succession to a climax, cyclical change between different states or chaotic change. Many factors change continually as a result either of processes inherent in ecosystem function or of human activities. There are fundamental constraints on mass balances and energy flow in any biophysical system such as a catchment, however – the choice of the boundary on the ecosystem considered to be of interest, and of its desirable state, are purely human decisions. Human demands on catchments and learning about the function of living systems develop, along with changes in the biophysical system. It is therefore difficult, or inappropriate, to expect science alone to determine a set of single-valued indicators of ecological status.

### Activity 26 Perspective on science and environmental decision making

Before starting this course, what was your own perspective on how science could contribute to environmental decision making? How, if at all, has it changed due to your study of the course so far, including your engagement with the arguments put forward in Reading 5?

The outcomes or trajectory of an environmental decision-making process are often locked in from the start. The perspectives, positions with respect to the problem and opportunity metaphors, ways of knowing and understandings of the social–biophysical relationship of those involved – they all impact on the initial starting conditions. Environmental legislation and schemes, discussed in Part 2, often encompass all of these factors and thus can be a strong influence on initial starting conditions.

## 5.5 Initial starting conditions

I have already referred to the importance of history – the history of how we know, practice and employ social technologies, and characterise situations. This is depicted in Figure 20 as an important factor or variable in how issues are socially constructed. It is not possible to escape history, but the initial starting conditions for any purposeful human activity such as a project, an environmental decision-making process, etc. can be shaped and influenced even if ultimately the outcomes cannot be influenced deterministically. The factors described in Sections 5.1 to 5.4 are also influential.

I have already pointed out that we have a choice as to how we characterise situations – we can choose to see them as messes or difficulties. Or we can choose to see them as systems (recognising that all systems are formulated by someone). In Table 6, I describe three ways we can choose to characterise systems – simple, complex and complex adaptive. These are additional to the archetypes that were described in Section 4.2. Each choice has different implications for the trajectory of environmental decision making.

Table 6  Three systems-based classifications of situations

| Simple systems | Complex systems | Complex adaptive systems |
| --- | --- | --- |
| Have predictable behaviour, e.g. a fixed interest bank account. | Generate counterintuitive, seemingly acausal behaviour that is full of surprises, e.g. lower taxes and interest rates leading to higher unemployment. | The elements of a system can change themselves – this relates to notions of autonomy. |
| Few interactions and feedback or feedforward loops, e.g. a simple barter economy with few goods and services. | A large array of variables with many interactions, lags, feedback loops and feedforward loops, which create the possibility that new, self-organising behaviours will emerge, e.g. most large organisations, life itself. | Complex outcomes can emerge from a few simple rules (this relates to initial starting conditions and the idea that complicated targets and plans may stifle creative and adaptive ability). |
| Centralised decision making, e.g. power is concentrated among a few decision makers. | Decentralised decision making – because power is more diffuse, the numerous components generate the actual system behaviour. | Small changes can have big effects and large changes may have no effect – i.e. non-linearity operates (e.g. in the UK a small band of lorry drivers interconnected by mobile phones almost brought the country to a standstill by blocking petrol deliveries to service stations). |
| Are decomposable because of weak interactions, i.e. it is possible to look at components without losing properties of the whole. | Are irreducible – neglecting any part of the process or severing any of the connections linking its parts usually destroys essential aspects of the system behaviour or structure. | Thrive on tension and paradox. (It is argued that healthy organisations exist on the edge of chaos – a region of moderate certainty and agreement.) |
| | There are dynamic changes in the system and the environment. | Are embedded within larger complex systems, and are made up of smaller complex systems. |

(After Casti, 1994, pp. 271–3 and Plsek, 2001)

I do not regard the categories in Table 6 as being descriptions of different types of 'real' systems – instead I see them more as questions of the sort 'what would be revealed or concealed about the situation of interest if I were to regard it as a simple system', etc. Asking such questions at the start will realise different outcomes.

From my perspective the factors that most affect the trajectory of any decision revolve around the questions: (i) 'who was involved?' and (ii) 'what was the quality of their involvement?' In the case study, most stakeholders were involved through processes of consultation. There were no real examples of starting off participatively. I expand on these points in Section 6 and they are taken up again in Book 3. Consultation and participation constitute different starting conditions which determine the range of possible trajectories of an environmental decision-making process.

In Section 5, I have explored how and why multiple perspectives come to exist and influence the nature of issues, problems and opportunities in complex situations or messes. I have suggested that initial starting conditions, which include how we think and act (our knowing), as well as framing issues, determine how a process of environmental decision making will unfold. As I outlined at the beginning, there is no clear boundary between the first and second stages of the T863 framework, but in the following Section 6, attention moves more towards the second than the first.

# 6 Formulating problems, opportunities and systems of interest in environmental decision-making situations

In this section, I discuss the move from divergent to convergent thinking that characterises the shift from the first to the second stage of the T863 framework. But whose thinking is converging? When confronted with messes, there is a strong case for moving beyond consultation to participation in environmental decision making so as to value multiple perspectives, but the emerging evidence suggests that participation is necessary but not sufficient for effective and systemic environmental decision making.

## 6.1 From exploring to formulating

My approach in Book 2 started by asking you to re-explore the case study situation. I suggested that it was useful to consider the case study as an example of a mess – a situation which was complex, contested, uncertain and where differing stakeholders perceived different problems and hence likely solutions. I also invited you to broaden the boundary of the situation by considering airport expansion in the context of climate change and the history of our use of oil as the world's main source of energy.

### 6.1.1 Divergent and convergent thinking

Another way of thinking about the move from exploring to formulating (and perhaps later to re-exploring and re-formulating) is in terms of cycles of divergent and convergent thinking. Divergent thinking involves being open and spontaneous and reluctant to eliminate alternative scenarios or to restrict a diversity of viewpoints or perspectives. In contrast, convergent thinking selects and classifies, combining competing representations until it encapsulates them in a single acceptable form on which those involved can agree. Moscovici and Doise (1994) argue that in the decision-making process divergent and convergent thinking are held in a tension – they are not opposites but constitute a duality or unity. However, it is helpful at any particular point to know which type of thinking you are using and at what stage it is likely to be more helpful to use divergent or convergent thinking in an environmental decision-making process.

An example to hand is the sort of thinking required in the process of writing this course. As an author, I go through cycles or phases of finding out (divergent thinking) but ultimately I, and the course team, have to decide what to include in and exclude from the course material (convergent thinking). Some of us find it easier to do one than the other. Being aware of this can sometimes be helpful in understanding our own role in an environmental decision-making process.

Whenever we iterate and re-explore or re-formulate we are also progressing through the experiential learning cycle discussed in Section 4.3 of Book 1. The very act of deciding to re-explore or to re-formulate is an act of reflection on our prior experience. As such, it shows a preparedness to monitor the process(es) we are engaged in and to evaluate them. I raise this here to make the point that monitoring and evaluation start at the beginning of any process of environmental decision making; they are not something to add on at the end. However, as text, by its very nature, must be linear, I am forced to leave the main discussion of monitoring and evaluation until later. At this stage, it is sufficient to note that when any system of interest is recognised then a key question will be 'what are the measures of performance of that system against which monitoring and evaluation judgements might be made?'

I introduced the key elements of systems practice in Section 4, but so far I have said very little about how to formulate systems of interest in situations of complexity. I now want to remedy that situation, but before doing that I need to clarify some of the differences between consultation and participation. Like environmental decision making, systems practice can be done consultatively or participatively.

## 6.2 Consultation or participation?

To answer the question 'Consultation or participation?' means being aware of the differences and similarities, and the implications of choosing one or other or both in an environmental decision-making situation. Table 7 describes a typology of participation.

> ### SAQ 32 Participation and levels of power
>
> Table 7 contains within it the distinctions Heron (1989) has made about power which were described in Book 1 (Section 3.2), i.e. (i) hierarchical with 'power over' leading to 'deciding for'; (ii) cooperative, or 'power with', leading to 'deciding with'; (iii) autonomous, or 'power to', leading to 'delegating deciding to'. Read Table 7 carefully and then match, as best you can, Heron's classes of power with the different forms of participation.

The forms of participation identified in Table 7 differ not only in the way power is used, but also in the extent to which stakeholders in any environmental issue can take ownership of, and learn about, the issue (you might like to compare the processes underpinning the categories in Table 7 with the processes associated with building stakeholding that were discussed in Reading 4). Ackoff (1980) made a similar point when he identified a set of three operating principles for interactive (or proactive) planning.

1. *The participative principle*: rejects the approach to planning which believes that the principal benefit of planning comes from the consumption of the plan it produces. This principle accepts that the main benefit of planning comes from engaging in the process of planning. (This implies that no one can plan effectively for someone else and it is better to plan for oneself, no matter how badly, than to be planned for by someone else, no matter how well.) Ackoff (1980) suggests that professional planners should be 'facilitators of the planning of others for themselves' and that the main advantage of this strategy is that implementation of the plan does not become an issue because there is widespread ownership of the plan by those involved (see 'Planning for Real' introduced later in this section).

Table 7  A typology of participation: how people participate in environmental decision making based on projects and programmes

| Typology | Characteristics |
| --- | --- |
| 1 Passive participation | People participate by being told what is going to happen or has already happened. It is a unilateral announcement by an administration or project management without any listening to people's responses. The information being shared belongs only to external professionals. |
| 2 Participation in information giving | People participate by answering questions posed by extractive researchers using questionnaire surveys or similar approaches. People do not have the opportunity to influence proceedings, as the findings are neither shared nor checked for accuracy. |
| 3 Participation by consultation | People participate by being consulted and external agents listen to views. These external agents define both problems and solutions, and may modify these in the light of people's responses. Such a consultative process does not concede any share in decision making and professionals are under no obligation to take on board people's views. The public inquiry and government round tables fit within this category. |
| 4 Participation for material incentives | People participate by providing resources, e.g. labour, in return for food, cash or other material incentives. Much on-farm research falls in this category, as farmers provide the fields but are not involved in experimentation or the process of learning. It is very common to see this called participation, yet people have no stake in prolonging activities when the incentives end. |
| 5 Functional participation | People participate by forming groups to meet predetermined objectives related to the project, which can involve the development or promotion of externally initiated social organisation. Such involvement does not tend to be at early stages of project cycles or planning, but rather after major decisions have been made. These institutions tend to be dependent on external initiators and facilitators, but may become self-dependent. |
| 6 Interactive participation | People participate in joint analysis, which leads to action plans and the formation of new local institutions or the strengthening of existing ones. It tends to involve interdisciplinary methodologies that seek multiple perspectives, and make use of systemic and structured learning processes. These groups take control over local decisions and so people have a stake in maintaining structures or practices. |
| 7 Self-mobilisation | People participate by taking initiatives independent of external institutions to change situations. They develop contacts with external institutions for resources and technical advice they need, but retain control over how resources are used. Such self-initiated mobilisation and collective action may or may not challenge existing inequitable distributions of wealth and power. |

(Source: adapted from Pretty, 1994 and Adnan et al., 1992)

2  *The principle of continuity*: rejects the notion of cyclical planning and advocates continuous planning. Plans should be continuously revised, says Ackoff (1980), 'in the light of their performance; unexpected problems and opportunities that arise, and the latest understanding, much of which arises during implementation'. Furthermore 'since the principal benefit of planning derives from engaging in it, why should it be discontinued?' (This claim can be related to the idea of adaptive management.)

3  *The holistic principle*: asserts that all units at the same level of an organisation or issue should be planned for simultaneously and interdependently and that no level of a multilevel system can be planned for effectively without involving every level of that system. Ackoff equates this to: 'every part of a system and every level of it should be planned for simultaneously and interdependently'. This stands in opposition to the prevailing practices of top-down and bottom-up planning.

### Activity 27  Different forms of participation used in the case study

Using the seven types of participation described in Table 7, and your understanding of the aviation expansion case study, suggest how, if at all, these different types of participation were incorporated into the environmental decision-making process.

### Activity 28  Perspectives on planning

Ackoff (1980) outlines a particular approach to planning which focuses on the process rather than the plan. Thinking in this way can result in a different approach to environmental decision making. Think about how you have experienced the planning process in your own life. You might like to answer this question from a number of perspectives, e.g. as a professional responsible for designing or carrying out planning; as a participant in a planning process; as a householder/citizen subject to planning regulations from your local government authority and associated planning acts; as a member of an organisation (e.g. work, local community, school, NGO, family, etc.); as a resident of, or visitor to, the countryside. Do not use more than three different perspectives.

From my perspective the typology presented in Table 7 has some limitations. The main one is that it suggests that there is continuity between the different types (sometimes called a ladder of participation). This is misleading, as consultation and participation are quite distinct – they need different understandings and practices and have a different ethical basis. Some examples of particular consultative and participative techniques which can be used to start the process of environmental decision making are now presented (though the boundary between starting off and other stages of our framework is not always clear, especially when talking about participatory processes). There will be more about this subject in Book 3. Before moving on, go to the DVD and watch *Participating in Environmental Decision Making* which provides an overview of the issues associated with starting out participatively. Before starting, read through the following SAQ.

## Study note

The *Participating in Environmental Decision Making* video on the DVD is relevant to several different parts of the course and raises issues that will be further discussed in Books 3 and 4. This video focuses on participatory techniques for environmental decision making and some of the issues of facilitating environmental decision-making processes. In particular, it shows how different perspectives on environmental issues can be taken into account so that there is participation by stakeholders in decision making. It will take about 30 minutes to watch the video. I suggest you use a rich picture or spray diagram to help you summarise some of the main points. You may also like to record your reactions to the video in your learning journal or discuss it with others on the T863 computer conference.

There are many ways of encouraging people to participate in decision making and several are explored in T863. The video focuses on two particular examples – 'Participatory Rural Appraisal' (PRA) and 'Planning for Real' (PfR). Both the PRA and PfR approaches use a set of methods and techniques to enable local people to explore their knowledge of life and conditions, to plan and to act. These methods and techniques are not used exclusively for environmental decision making but they do provide ways of taking a whole range of environmental factors into account in decision making alongside other considerations.

The PRA example comes from a workshop run in Kyrgyzstan in Central Asia by the Oxford-based International Non-Governmental Training Research Centre. The video shows PRA facilitators being trained and then trying out the techniques with local people in the field. The Planning for Real activities were run by the Neighbourhood Initiatives Foundation in the English village of Drinkstone and in North Bransholme, a large council estate on the outskirts of Hull in the UK. Planning for Real has four stages: (i) training in use of the techniques; (ii) 'pounding the street' to encourage participation; (iii) Planning for Real events; and (iv) prioritisation. Both Drinkstone and North Bransholme provide examples of real decision-making processes – not simulations – but they are at very different stages and on different scales. The early stages of decision making are shown at Drinkstone and the training stage of Planning for Real. At North Bransholme, the video shows the later stages of decision making using Planning for Real – the stages of pounding the street, PfR events and prioritisation. You will see various snapshots of Planning for Real in the video, but it is worth noting that there was a lot more going on than it was possible to show, particularly in North Bransholme, because of the scale of the activity.

Interviews with local residents and facilitators are shown on the DVD. Other perspectives are also offered, not just on PRA and PfR but on some of the underlying principles of participating in environmental decision making.

### SAQ 33  Handing over the stick

What does the metaphor of 'handing over the stick' as used in the video mean in relation to participatory decision making?

I hope the video will have given you some insights into why I am addressing issues of consultation and participation here. I could have linked them more strongly to the first stage of the T863 framework (exploring and re-exploring) where they are certainly relevant (e.g. how different perspectives are taken into account). My rationale for addressing them here is that the question of who is involved is critical to how a problem, opportunity or system of interest becomes expressed, stabilised and agreed upon. That does not necessarily mean they become static and reified but there is always a risk that this can happen. The best way to avoid unhelpful reification of problems or opportunities is to maintain stakeholder involvement in a process of decision making.

Consultation features very strongly in the aviation expansion case study (see Table 4 in Book 1) but not at the starting out stage – timing is critical! For this reason, I have drawn on other examples for both consultation and participation (see below) to show how they could be used in the starting off phase.

### 6.2.1 Starting with consultation

Consultation can take many forms. The example developed here is round tables which come from the idea of everyone being equal around the table (i.e. there is no head) and that those present offer multiple perspectives on the subjects under deliberation. Round tables were a particular consultative approach popular amongst some governments as a means to respond to the commitments made to sustainable development in the 1992 Earth Summit. The concept of a round table had its origins in Canada, but they were subsequently set up in the UK, USA, France and China. Over 100 countries have set up national, multistakeholder bodies to take forward sustainable development but only those mentioned above have opted specifically for round tables.

The UK Round Table was established in January 1995 as part of the Government's strategy for sustainable development. It initially operated with a core group of not more than 25 members drawn from different sectors. The core membership was reduced in the second year of operation and its mandate extended to 1999. The Government was expected to consult the round table in developing and implementing its sustainable development strategy. The extent to which this has occurred is unclear; it is not specifically mentioned in the 1997 Annual Report of the UK round table in terms of how, if at all, the Government has responded to the activities and recommendations of the round table.

When thinking about the case study, perhaps you may have already spotted some potential weaknesses of round tables as a consultative device? The most obvious is that the UK round table appears not to have played a role in setting the framing conditions for the White Paper, which they could have been asked to do. This raises questions about whether government 'joined up' the activities of the round table with other policy initiatives. The round table did, however, address significant issues: for example in 1997, recommendations were made on five topics: making connections (seamless passenger and freight journeys); getting around town (concerned with sustainable transport policies); housing and urban capacity; fresh water; and energy and planning. It is not clear what, if any, impact these recommendations had.

The UK round table published its fifth and final Annual Report in July 2000. In May 1999, the Government published its sustainable development White Paper *A Better Quality of Life* and subsumed the round table into a new Sustainable Development Commission, labelled as the government's independent watchdog on sustainable development. In its new guise, it has been closely associated with producing 'Securing the future – UK Government sustainable development strategy' which the UK Government launched in conjunction with a Strategic Framework on 7 March 2005.

A copy of the Executive Summary of the strategy can be seen on the T863 course website.

It is unclear how a 'commission' differs from a round table. Many of the same, or similar, people now sit as 'commissioners' as formerly sat around the round table. In both cases government appointed the members; the website says that 'commissioners are selected to provide a wide range of expertise and experience, and are drawn from commerce, youth work, academia, trade unions, politics and government, non-profit, and grassroots action. [...] When making the appointments, Government takes into account the need to draw expertise from across the UK; from business, local government and non-government sectors; and to reflect the diversity of the UK population' (http://www.sd-commission.org.uk/pages/commissioners.html).

It is difficult to judge how successful, nationally and internationally, 'round tabling' has been as a consultative process. I am not overly convinced of their usefulness; to be able to judge I would want to know whether they were joined up in policy development and how they worked in practice, i.e. how was the conversation managed, were differences valued and listened to, did individuals speak as representatives of a sector, or as individuals open to their own understandings? If you are not from the UK you might like to explore whether there are similar bodies in your own country.

The examples of a 'round table' and a 'commission' seem to me to be qualitatively different forms of consultation than that carried out in the 'Freedom to fly?' case study. In the case study situation, there seemed to be little consultation and no participation in formulating the questions – the naming of the issue or problem (or opportunity) – that were subsequently included in the consultation documents. A technique called the 'Delphi technique' is described in the *Techniques* book – have a look at it now and consider whether something like this could be used as a means to involve more stakeholders in formulating questions that could then be put out for wider consultation. Its purpose is to elicit information and opinions from participants to assist planning and decision making. Typically, it involves a panel of people who participate in the process at a distance, usually by post or email. In my experience, it is better to use a Delphi process than to have a process, or questions, decided by a narrow interest group, but it has significant limitations compared to other, more participatory processes.

As an institution (as defined in Box 6 on social technologies), at least the commission has a range of perspectives represented on it and has taken some challenging positions with respect to government policy. However, it also suffers from being a consultative body – government is not bound to its advice or to the issues, problems or opportunities as perceived by members of the commission.

There are other examples of change in the consultation process in relation to White Paper development. The following example refers to the National Health Service (NHS) in England, which is one of the largest employers in the world and is experienced by most as a highly complex organisation. A Citizens' Summit – held in October 2005 as part of the Your Health, Your Care, Your Say initiative – was described to me by one participant as an extraordinary exercise in democratic consultation, designed to find out what people want from community health and social care services. The culmination of several regional meetings, the national event brought together 1000 people from around England to debate the issues and help shape future policy on community health and social care services. In a first for government, the Citizens' Summit, including facilitated round table discussions with members of the public, was webcast live on the NHS website. The day's events were also made available to view on demand, providing the opportunity to compare the outcome from the day with the resulting White Paper when it is published (early 2006).

## Study note

If you are interested in finding out more, the home page of the event, with more information and video clips from the day, can be found, at the time of writing, at: http://www.dh.gov.uk/NewsHome/YourHealthYourCareYourSay/fs/en.

If you go to this page, then click on Citizen summit, this will take you to a new window with more background to the event and an overview of the process. The web page also has details of the questions discussed and results from the live voting undertaken throughout the day.

In terms of the differences between starting off through consultation or participation the Citizens' Summit was built around pre-formed questions (i.e. the participants did not formulate the questions) which, according to one participant, were not seemingly connected in a systemic manner. The main questions, and therefore the answers, were discussed independently of each other during the course of the event. Despite this, 98% of participants enjoyed the day, 94% agreed that they had had their say, 40% thought it would be influential, 56% were not sure and only 4% did not think the results would be influential. 96% agreed that events like it should be conducted on other topics in the future!

## 6.2.2 Starting off participatively

A great diversity of participative techniques and methodologies are potentially available to start off the process of environmental decision making. Table 8 provides an example of how a range of participatory tools and techniques were used in starting off a health project in Kenya which took into account features of the agro-ecosystem. This particular example is of an initial workshop which ran over five days. Please do not worry if you are unsure about some of these techniques – some are in the *Techniques* book and some are not. If you are really interested you can use the techniques listed as a source of keywords and descriptors for a search of an online bibliographic database or on the web.

Most examples of starting off participatively share six common characteristics depending on how they are implemented (after Pretty, 1995).

1. They have a defined methodology and systemic learning process. The focus is on cumulative learning by all the participants and, given the nature of these approaches as systems of inquiry and interaction, their use has to be participative.
2. They draw on multiple perspectives. A central objective is to seek diversity, rather than characterise complexity in terms of average values.
3. They involve group learning processes. This recognises that the complexity of the world will only be revealed through group inquiry and interaction.
4. They are context specific. The approaches are flexible enough to be adapted to suit each new set of conditions and actors, and so there are multiple variants.
5. They involve facilitating experts and stakeholders. The methodologies are concerned with the transformation of existing activities to try to bring about decisions which people in the situation regard as leading to improvements. The role of the 'expert' is best thought of as helping people in their situation to carry out their own study and so to achieve something. These facilitating experts may be stakeholders themselves.
6. They lead to sustained action. The learning process leads to debate and dialogue about change and debate changes the perceptions of the actors and their readiness to contemplate action. Action is agreed and implementable changes will therefore represent an accommodation between the different conflicting views. Action here includes local institution building, so increasing the capacity for people to initiate action of their own.

Many of these points were raised in the *Participating in Environmental Decision Making* video on the DVD.

Table 8  Participatory tools to start off an environmental decision-making process in Kenya

| Activities | Tools | Data to be captured |
|---|---|---|
| **Day 1** | | |
| 1 Introduction | Ice-breakers<br>Self-introduction<br>Logistics (meals, groups/teams)<br>Social maps | • Develop rapport, social structure of the village |
| 2 Knowing the village (geographical/administrative units) | Resource maps | • Physical structure of village<br>• Natural resource inventory<br>• Land use patterns, problem identification |
| 3 Historical background | Historical profile | • Historical background<br>• Major events and their impact on community<br>• Problem identification and coping strategies |
| 4 Trend and time lines | Trend lines* | • Resource availability and distribution over time and space<br>• Disease and pests dynamics<br>• Infrastructure |
| 5 Seasonal activities and trends | Seasonal calendars | • Yearly schedules<br>• Agricultural activities<br>• Effects of climate on agriculture |
| 6 Mapping out route for transect walk and evaluation | Maps | |
| **Day 2** | | |
| | Transect walk | • Natural resource inventories<br>• Topography, village structure, farming systems |
| 7a) Triangulation and field observation<br>b) Drawing the transect profile<br>c) Livelihoods | Semi-structural interviews<br><br>Profile<br>Livelihood analysis<br><br>Mobility chart | • Land use, layout<br><br>• Sources, incomes, expenditure<br>• Sources of goods and services, and market quantities of goods and services<br>• Institutions and relations/linkages<br>• Roles/responsibilities |
| **Day 3** | | |
| | Venn diagram (chapati)† | • Sources of information/information flow<br>• Problems related to institutions and linkages |
| 8 Identification and analysis of institution | Information flow<br>Map/charts<br>Activity profile/daily calendar | • Inventory of activities by gender and age<br>• Labour distribution<br>• Health concerns by age and gender<br>• Impact on their productivity<br>• Coping strategies |
| 9 Health analysis | Health analysis | • Inventory of resource ownership, access and control by gender and age |
| 10 Analysis of major gender concerns in agro-ecosystem health | Access and control profile/matrix | • Problems related to access and control of resources |

| Activities | Tools | Data to be captured |
|---|---|---|
| **Day 4** | | |
| | Decision-making matrix | • Causes and effects of the problems |
| | | • List of major problems in order of priority |
| 11 Problem identification and analysis | Scoring matrix<br>Pairwise ranking | • Lists of opportunities<br>• Means and ends of the opportunities |
| 12 Needs identification and assessment | Problem tree | • Resources/inputs<br>• Responsibilities time-frame |
| **Day 5** | | |
| | Scoring matrix<br>Pairwise ranking | • Description of the problems, objectives, beneficiary community, detailed budget strategy of implementation |
| 13 Action planning | Objectives tree<br>Community action plans<br>Proposal write-up | |

(Source: Walther-Toews, 2005)

*Notes*:
\* In a trend line, a group of older villagers draws one large graph showing, for instance, changes in population, disease rates, water availability – i.e. any variables they deem to be important. The vertical axis is qualitative (when a line goes up it means more); the horizontal axis is time, often marked off by key historical events (military coups, earthquakes, wars, famines).
† Villagers list all the organisations working in their village (government, non-government, unofficial, ad hoc, etc.). They then assign a large, medium or small 'chapatti' to each, according to how important they deem them to be. Finally, they lay them out on the ground and show how organisations cooperate or not on various activities by overlapping them to various degrees. These informal Venn diagrams, become, among other things, a means of identifying the organisations one should work with in order to achieve programmatic aims.

Five phases are key to participatory development and decision making each with their own challenges (Guijt and RBU, 1996); these include:

1. Preparation: laying the groundwork means identifying and negotiating roles of stakeholders as well as managing up-front investment – which brings later rewards.
2. Field immersion: situation analysis that ensures multiple perspectives are equally represented.
3. Analysis of inter- and intra-communal difference: group-based analysis to identify shared/group specific concerns and possible solutions requires careful negotiation to overcome power differences.
4. Planning of community or group action plan: final decision about community/group priority requires careful negotiation about group responsibilities/inputs/sanctions.
5. Implementation and monitoring and evaluation: implementing community/group plans requires continual monitoring of progress from the start and adjustment to sustain improvements, plus efforts to decrease dependency on external support.

The length of each phase will vary, depending on the history of the situation and the stage in the development or decision-making process. Roles and responsibilities of the different parties will vary from phase to phase.

Issues associated with consultation and participation will be picked up again in Part 2 as well as in Book 3 where social learning will be introduced. Whilst there are many advocates of starting out participatively (e.g. Chambers, 2005) there are also many critics. Some of the critique is built on the misapplication of techniques, inadequate understanding of participatory practices, the failure to deal adequately with issues of power and also the failure to adequately institutionalise the gains from participation.

## 6.3 Generating systems of interest for environmental decision making

As I outlined at the beginning of this book, systems approaches are concerned with understanding cycles, managing for counterintuitive effects and avoiding unintended consequences. A key aspect of doing this is to allow for multiple, partial perspectives to inform a decision-making process around an issue of concern. Multiple perspectives can be generated in a number of ways so as to approach the initial phases of environmental decision making systemically. These include:

1   doing a stakeholder analysis
2   using consultative and participative processes with or without the help of formal techniques
3   asking boundary-setting questions, as a precursor to ...
4   ... formulating and re-formulating systems of interest as part of a learning-based inquiry.

Each of these approaches is a means to:

1   enhance the creativity of the process of exploring situations and problem or opportunity formulation
2   encourage social learning and ownership of the issues at hand (discussed in Book 3)
3   develop criteria against which you might subsequently judge or evaluate the environmental decision-making process (see Part 3)
4   avoid narrow, and ultimately impractical or unsustainable, decisions and allow local and non-local (or insider/outsider) perspectives to be considered.

All these approaches require certain personal skills, particularly facilitation and group-working (SLIM, 2004c).

In this section, I am going to introduce some new techniques to aid your systems practice for environmental decision making. My focus is on formulating systems of interest as a device for learning about a situation so as to move towards improvement.

> **Activity 29 Using boundary judgements as a technique**
>
> Read the section on Boundary judgement in the *Techniques* book jotting down as you read any points that you do not follow. Start your reading by asking the question: When and how could I use this technique?

### 6.3.1 Asking boundary-setting questions

People with different perspectives will recognise different systems of interest in the same context or, put another way, they will choose to bound their system of interest differently. Anyone engaged in facilitating or designing an environmental decision-making process is ultimately interested in action for some purpose(s) in a given context. But this can mask a whole set of complex questions: What theories inform the process? Who are or should be the actors? Who specifies the purpose(s)? What is the context and how is it understood and by whom? These are all boundary-setting questions. As Ulrich notes:

> we cannot conceive of systems without assuming some kind of systems boundaries. If we are not interested in understanding boundary judgements, i.e. in critical reflection and debate on what are and what ought to be boundaries of the system in question, systems thinking makes no sense; if we are, systems thinking becomes a form of critique.
>
> (Ulrich, 1996)

Ulrich (2000) developed a set of questions that can be used as a form of boundary critique in the process of formulating a system of interest. They are worthy of consideration at the beginning of any process of environmental decision making, i.e. they can be used either as part of an exploring or re-exploring process or as a means to formulate particular systems of interest (i.e. they can be used for both diverging and converging).

Two features of Table 1 in the *Techniques* book require elaboration (Reynolds, 2006):

1.  The three questions associated with each source of influence address parallel issues: the first question in each group (1, 4, 7 and 10) addresses issues of social role; the second question (2, 5, 8 and 11) addresses issues of role specific concerns; and the third question (3, 6, 9 and 12) relates to key problems associated with roles and role specific concerns. In more contemporary language, these terms are best associated with 'stakeholders', 'stakes' and 'stakeholdings' respectively.

2.  Each question is asked in two modes, thereby generating 24 questions in total. In critical systems heuristics (CSH), the area of systems thinking developed by Ulrich, all questions need to be asked in a normative, ideal mode (i.e. what 'ought' to be ...) as well as in the descriptive mode (what 'is' the situation). Contrasting the two modes provides the source of critique necessary to make an evaluation.

I take up evaluation in Part 3; the following activity asks you to use the questions in the normative 'ought' mode (from your perspective).

### Activity 30  Using CSH in 'ought' mode

Based on your understandings of the consultation process and the role that participation did or did not play in the aviation expansion decision-making process, devise answers to each of Ulrich's 12 questions in an 'ought' mode. It is advisable to start with Question 2 – What ought to be the purpose of the consultation process thought of as a system (S)? – and then address questions of who ought to be the beneficiary and what ought to be the measures of success, continuing with the subsequent nine CSH questions.

Record in your learning journal, or on your blog, the insights and questions that arose for you as you did this activity.

---

I do not expect you to have found Activity 30 particularly easy, but by attempting it I would expect you to gain some clarity and insights into the aviation expansion decision-making situation. Once you had settled on your answers (I would have expected considerable iteration) then you would be well equipped to begin exploring further aspects of the system of interest which you had settled upon. It should be clear what you thought the purpose of the consultation process ought to be and how effectiveness ought to have been judged. In systems thinking this is referred to as a *measure of performance*, and is expressed in relation to the purpose. Other measures of performance include efficiency, efficacy, elegance, ethicality and no doubt more that you can think of. I will say more about these below. I hope the activity also prompted you to begin thinking about comparisons between what you felt 'ought' to have been with what actually happened (as best you can tell), i.e. the 'is' mode. A follow-up activity where you will be using your 'ought mode' findings will appear in Book 3.

### 6.3.2  Mini case study based on using soft systems methodology

I have already introduced various aspects of soft systems methodology (SSM), developed by Peter Checkland and his colleagues in a 30-year action research project. Examples include the material on transformation processes and the idea of formulating systems in terms of do P by Q because of R. In this section you will be introduced to more aspects of SSM, as well as seeing how different elements can be put together. I am not planning to introduce the formal methodology as such – those interested are referred to the thirty year retrospective on Checkland's work (Checkland, 1999) which is on the T863 course website.

To prepare for Reading 6 first turn to the *Techniques* book and read the section on 'Root definition and its formulation'. Pay particular attention to the CATWOE mnemonic – note that there are variations of it – and the relationship of CATWOE to a 'root definition'. I want you to use CATWOE as a device to help you conduct a systemic inquiry into Reading 6. This is not as difficult as it might sound. You will discover that in Reading 6, Martin Bunch describes how he used CATWOE, which is also part of soft systems methodology.

Read Activity 31 now and then Reading 6, the paper by Martin Bunch. Use your first reading of the paper to answer Activity 31. To do this you might find it helpful to experiment with the metaphor of 'putting yourself in the author's shoes'.

# 6 FORMULATING PROBLEMS, OPPORTUNITIES AND SYSTEMS OF INTEREST IN ENVIRONMENTAL DECISION-MAKING SITUATIONS

Figure 30  A metaphor for doing the mini case study (Activity 31) – practice at different levels of abstraction, in this case how we understand our understandings of complex situations (Source: adapted from Leunig, 1985)

## Activity 31   A critical assessment of systems practice for environmental decision making

In this activity, which relates to Reading 6, I would like you to undertake a critical assessment of the author's systems practice with a view to enhancing your own practice. Please use diagrams to do this wherever they are relevant.

I suggest you start by doing an audit of the author's systems practice – this would cover use of systems concepts, tools or techniques (a systems map could be used for this purpose).

Make notes on how you find the problem/opportunity metaphor being dealt with.

What does your stakeholder mapping reveal about the range of perspectives contributing to the decision making?

What boundary judgements have been made? By whom?

Are you able to see examples of how his practice contributes to negotiating?

How, if at all, have issues of power been addressed?

Consider how, if at all, monitoring and evaluation are built into practice.

## Reading 6

Read the paper 'Soft systems methodology and the ecosystem approach: a system study of the Cooum River and environs in Chennai, India' by Martin Bunch.

Whilst I consider the case study in Reading 6 an excellent example of how systemic thinking can be applied to environmental decision making, I am not sure what practical lessons you will be able to take from it to apply in your own situation (your work, your T863 project, etc.). To help you I provide a simple set of conceptual models in Box 11 which are at the core of SSM.

### Box 11  Some of the key elements of SSM

Root Definition: A system to communicate with Mum by writing and posting letters to her in order to maintain good relations with her

Do P by Q in order to achieve R.

P: communicate (WHAT)
Q: writing and posting letters (HOW)
R: maintaining good relations (WHY)

$E_1$: letters being received by Mum
$E_2$: minimum time spent on this communication
$E_3$: state of relations with Mum

C   Mum
A   Mum's son or daughter
T   need to communicate with Mum – need met by letter writing
W   this is a good means of communicating
O   Mum's son or daughter
E   a postal service which delivers posted letters

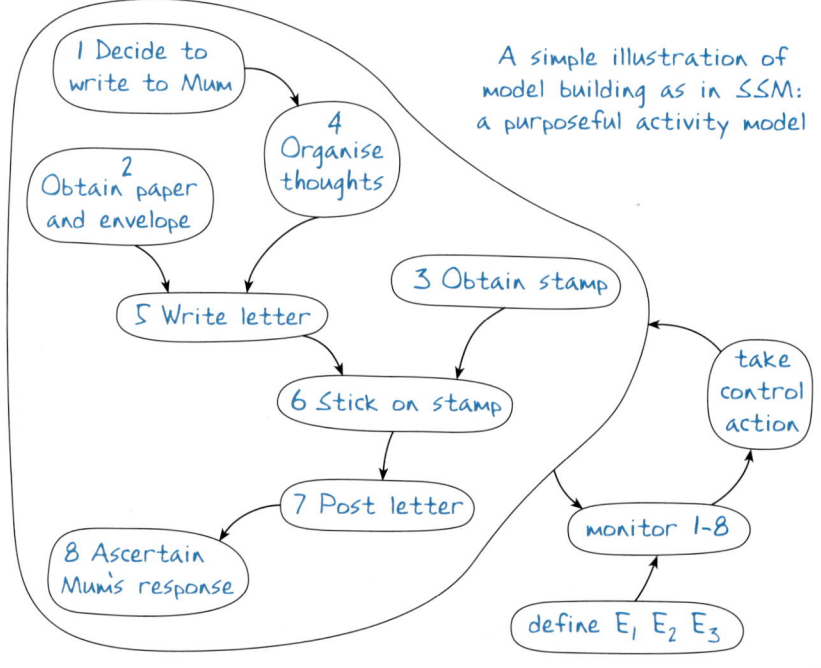

A simple illustration of model building as in SSM: a purposeful activity model

Figure 31   (Source: Peter Checkland, personal communication)

This simple example (Box 11) contains the most important elements of Checkland's soft systems methodology, namely a root definition (a description of a system of interest), a CATWOE analysis, measures of performance (the three Es: $E_1$ = efficacy or does the system function; $E_2$ = efficiency or how well does it work; and $E_3$ = effectiveness or does it achieve its overall purpose) and a conceptual model using verbs and comprising a linked set of sub-systems each responsible for a transformation.

### SAQ 34  Stages and principles of SSM

In Reading 6 what are the main stages in the inquiring/learning system that is SSM and what are the five principles that relate to this model?

### SAQ 35  PQR and a root definition

In Box 11 what are P, Q and R in relation to the root definition?

### SAQ 36  Blobs in a conceptual model

What do each of the blobs in the conceptual model in Box 11 have in common?

### SAQ 37  Worldviews

Why does SSM make a point about being explicit about worldviews?

How did you make out with the logic of the material in Box 11? Remember that this type of modelling is not trying to model a 'real world' system, but to build conceptual models of purposeful systems (systems of interest) using verbs as the modelling language and based on explicit worldviews, as part of an inquiry process designed to aid changes in understanding and practices of the sort described in Figure 20.

In Box 12 and Figure 32 I have depicted how I and some of my colleagues have used systemic inquiry as a process to facilitate changes in understanding and practices within a large government agency, as they attempted to implement river-basin planning and management. This was part of their implementation of the European Water Framework Directive. I do not have space to dwell on the detail other than to say that systemic inquiry is a higher-level way of managing projects than most current project management activities enable.

Figure 32  A schema depicting various stages and activities associated with conducting a systemic inquiry with stakeholders in river-basin planning (Source: Collins et al., 2005)

### Box 12  Conducting a systemic inquiry for social learning using aspects of SSM

The schema set out in Figure 32 is built around a central model for enacting a systemic inquiry (based on SSM) developed by Checkland (2002). You will also detect a replica of Figure 20 – the heuristic device for exploring understandings and practices. A systemic inquiry commences by setting up a structured exploration of a situation characterised by uncertainty. This was the situation we found during our first event with key stakeholders in the Water Framework Directive (WFD) implementation. We used rich pictures (1) to initiate a dialogue, surface mental models (different perspectives), reveal connectivity and begin to converge on the nature of the issue(s). In other events conversation mapping (2) was used to similar effect.

In some, but not all workshops, systems models as devices were used. The example shown here (3) is of developing a root definition of river basin management planning as a 'system to do ...'. Doing this participatively with key internal stakeholders (4) in part dealt with the politics and cultural context and facilitated moves towards concerted action that were seen as feasible, as for example the definition of the PoMs (Programme of Measures) project (5). Within the River Basin Management Planning team their understandings and practices clearly changed such that the situation was progressed as depicted within the SLIM heuristic (6). The Project Steering Group as part of Workstream 4 monitored the overall inquiry and took control action when required. Measures of performance have been developed as we progressed and continue to be articulated based on our reflections on the overall process and articulated in a related 'workstream' (7). We have also built capacity to use some of these tools.

### SAQ 38    Activities in conducting a systemic inquiry

Using Figure 32 and Box 12 list the activities that comprise a systemic inquiry as modelled in that example.

So how might you start to use these ideas in your own work? Have a look at the material in Box 13 – which we call 'Snappy Systems'. Figure 33 shows a model of the overall process of doing SSM as it was originally conceived. Read the material in the box in the light of that model and Figure 3 in Reading 6. When you have finished, have a go at Activity 32.

### Box 13    'Snappy Systems'

Figure 33 depicts SSM as it was originally conceived in the early 1980s as a seven stage model. As a methodology it began with creating a rich picture of a situation considered 'problematical'. In the terms of the T863 framework the starting point was to explore and re-explore the situation (e.g. rich pictures were done at the start as well as throughout an SSM inquiry recognising that the situation was always changing and that a series of rich pictures was also an effective way of monitoring what was happening in the situation). Remember that one of the outputs of a rich picture is themes for further inquiry. Another important feature of the early model was that it made a distinction between the 'real world' and the conceptual world. I made this point earlier when I said that systems practice involved moving between different levels of abstraction just like the move from understanding to understanding understanding.

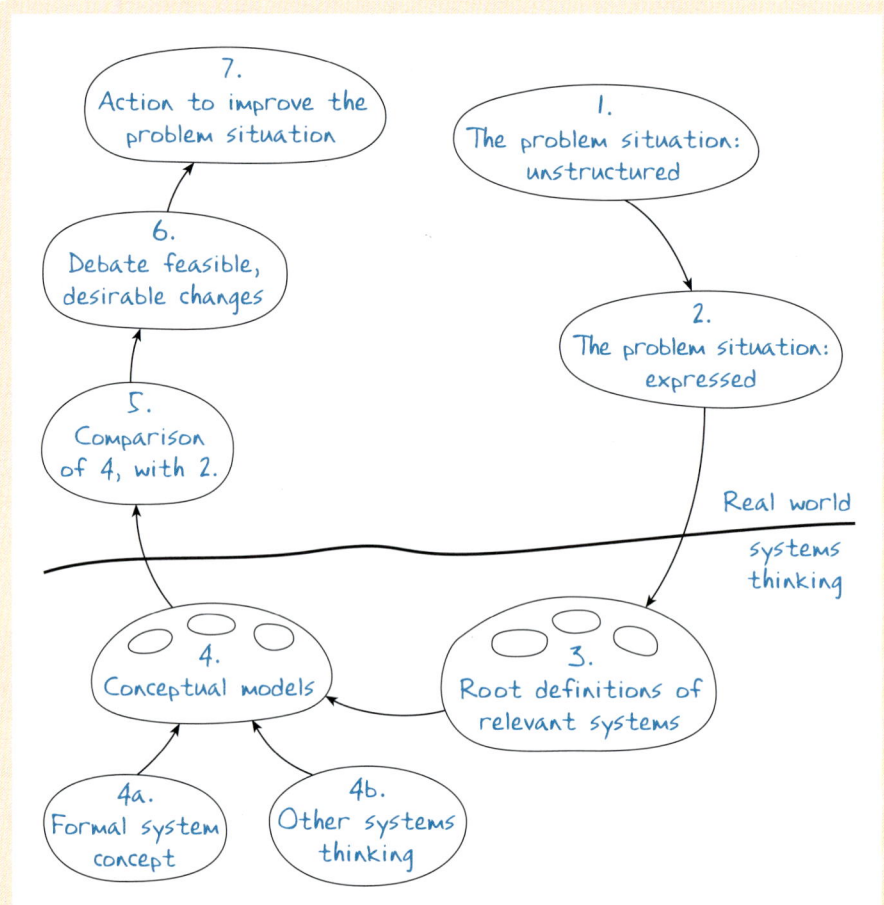

Figure 33  The original seven step model for doing an SSM inquiry

When following the original seven step model it can be quite tricky in practice to find one's way from a rich picture to a root definition, even if one identifies themes as a way of getting started. 'Snappy Systems' is another intermediate step that can help. It was developed by the Open University Systems Department to help students in the early stages of learning Checkland's SSM. Like the identification of themes in the rich picture, Snappy Systems is not part of the 'official' version of SSM but it has the advantage of enabling you to generate a number of different perspectives, and thus stay as holistic as possible in your thinking.

Snappy Systems can be applied in a number of ways. A starting point is to address the question: 'What kind of system would help to address the theme I have chosen from my rich picture (or reading of a text, or imagining possible transformations, etc.)?' It is a means to formulate systems of interest as a device for inquiring into and changing a complex situation.

### Ideas generation: Round 1

First write down the theme at the top of a large sheet of paper. Another person, even if they know relatively little about the task you're undertaking, is an enormous help.

The ideas-generation phase works best if you simply write down every idea that comes up without any evaluation at all. It will take discipline at first but this uncritical approach becomes easier with practice. Each idea should be in the form 'a system to ...' although it helps to keep up the speed if you don't write this down every time (see also Brainstorming in the *Techniques* book.

Keep it snappy: a high-energy approach will enable the ideas to come quickly, and reduce the temptation to censor. Don't discard any ideas without writing them down – even absurd ideas can help generate more useful ideas.

If the ideas slow down, take a 30 second breather and start again.

## Stakeholders

When you feel you have exhausted all the possible ideas, make a list of all the possible stakeholders in the theme you are addressing. These may not be the intended beneficiaries of the improvement you are trying to achieve – indeed you should try and include stakeholders beyond those whose stakeholding is obvious.

## Ideas generation: Round 2

Now adopt the role of one of the stakeholders you have identified and resume the task of listing possible systems to address your theme. Again, keep it snappy.

This phase of the process brings in alternative perspectives and will increase the range of possible systems that become visible to you.

Aim to generate between 25 and 30 ideas. Although sometimes it can be a struggle, it becomes much easier if you can think your way into the perspective of one or more of the stakeholders. Here is an example:

Theme: colour-matching dyes (in the process of dyeing fabrics).

> A system to:
>> change the lighting
>>
>> bring more daylight into the studio
>>
>> change our supplier
>>
>> use coloured light in the showroom
>>
>> overdye everything in dark blue
>>
>> improve QA at the suppliers
>
> (from the perspective of a colour mixer at the suppliers).
>
> A system to:
>> make colour mixing less boring
>>
>> meet the customer

discuss the customer's needs

improve the lighting

improve the labelling of base-colour supplies

improve the labelling of delivered colour mixes

clean the light fixtures regularly (and at customer's studio)

clean the windows

measure and control lighting quality on a daily basis

use better quality materials.

### Selecting a system

The next task is to select one or more of these system names and develop a root definition from it. There is no rational basis for this selection, so rely on some sort of intuition that one of these can be developed into a useful root definition. Sometimes this is the one that looks most sensible, but more usually it is the one that seems to capture the spirit of a significant number of the ideas that have been generated. It will get to the heart of the theme you are working with. Sometimes there is a potential system that stands out because it is intriguing in some way or it energises your imagination. In some ways, the choice doesn't matter too much because a root definition, once fully developed, will be a powerful device for inquiring into how the situation can be improved, whatever its origin.

### Starting with a transformation

I have already introduced the idea of starting with a transformation in Section 4.3.4. This can be used in conjunction with PQR.

### Employing PQR

I introduced PQR in Section 5, i.e. a means to describe a system to do P by Q because of R (when completed this gives all of the elements of a root definition).

### CATWOE and variations

These are discussed in the *Techniques* book under 'Root definition and its formulation'. Activity 32 will ask you to engage with this material.

The process of doing Snappy Systems is helpful because it allows ideas to generate further ideas and to manage the creative movement between ideas or themes and a root definition of a possible system of interest. Being critical, filtering ideas for what is realistic and what is not can come later. But perhaps the most useful aspect of Snappy Systems is the access to alternative perspectives. Accessing other perspectives allows consideration of a wider range of options and keeps your thinking holistic enough to find an eventual outcome that will be capable of being perceived as an improvement.

### Activity 32  Conducting a systemic 'meta-inquiry'

Reading 6 describes the use of SSM and an ecosystem approach to attempt situation improvement in the Cooum River environs of Chennai, India. As it is unlikely that you will have had first-hand experience of this particular situation we are forced to accept the author's account of his actions. As with all readings and accounts of practice one should not accept them uncritically. Undertake an inquiry into this case study based on what the author has said and claimed, using some of the systems techniques that he has used himself, i.e. CATWOE and root definitions.

To complete this activity:

1. Read through Reading 6 again and generate a set of transformations (T) for possible systems of interest (of the form 'a system to do P by Q to achieve R') which, from your perspective, you can relate to the overall purpose of the author in his case study situation.

2. Select one of the systems of interest you have identified and use CATWOE to iterate between your original system description and a refined one based on your CATWOE analysis, i.e. provide an answer to who you would regard as fulfilling the categories Client and Owner and what you regard as the Transformation, Worldview and Environment in relation to your system description.

3. Using one of the modified root definitions that you have formulated (after iteration) brainstorm a set of 7 +/− 2 activities (verbs) that would have to happen if the system were to function as a system (the end result of doing this should look like the example given in Box 11). This stage is called building a conceptual model which is a model based on verbs (See Modelling: conceptual modelling in the *Techniques* book).

4. Consider how the idea of levels has, or hasn't, influenced the way you have answered this activity;

5. Make notes in your learning journal or on your blog about what you have gained from this activity and what, if any, difficulties you have had or which remain for you.

I have not addressed the later stages of the original seven step model in SSM (Figure 32). These stages concern a comparison between a conceptual mode of a root definition of a system of interest and the 'real world' situation. This is also a stage many find difficult because it involves moving between different levels of abstraction (i.e. from the conceptual to the real worlds). Effective practice begins when you are able to engage with this approach and always be clear to yourself and others as to when you are operating in the conceptual world and when you are operating in the 'real world'. This comparison stage is concerned with reaching or identifying accommodations about desirable and feasible change which is the next stage of the framework and one of the subjects of Book 3.

## 6.4 Review – moving on

At the beginning of Part 1, I said that systemic awareness was concerned with:

1. cycles – seeing and understanding the implications of connectedness and feedback processes
2. counterintuitive effects
3. avoiding unintended consequences by starting out systemically and attempting to appreciate, in advance, some of the systemic features of a situation.

Modelling is a key skill and technique which we have argued you need to understand and at least have some competence in doing – but we define modelling very broadly.

I have also pointed out how methods and techniques can become displaced, either because they have been superseded or because those who used them failed to adapt them to the changing context, e.g. they may form the basis of new methods even though the original rationale for them no longer exists. In Part 2 you will be referred to a review of environmental impact assessment (EIA) practice in the EU which is an example of what I mean.

These traps are of failing to learn from using a method or technique and adapting it to new contexts. There are a number of ways in which this form of learning can be inhibited. They include unquestioning adherence to tradition; enshrining particular methods in legislation or rigid regulations; and putting particular methods into systematic practice before considering the systemic.

Enshrining particular approaches to environmental decision making in White Papers, legislation or regulations, such as EIA, or the 'public inquiry' process can exacerbate our tendency to think that these are the only approaches that are relevant and can lead to traps in thinking and practice. This is because there is a risk that they will be implemented uncritically or in ways that subvert what was originally intended by their proponents. The act of enshrining methods and techniques in legislation may lead to prescriptive and routinised practices, which are then pursued regardless of circumstances. A similar trap may also arise through codes of behaviour or professional practice, prescriptive terms of reference and a lack of awareness of the theory, or epistemology, behind a particular approach.

One of the negative features of approaches formalised in regulations, policy or legislation is that they may not be adaptable to changing circumstances or contexts. This results in imposing something onto a situation – for which it may no longer be suited. An alternative to imposing a process onto a situation is to allow the process to arise from the usually unique features of the context. In any process of environmental decision making, whether enshrined in legislation or not, there is rarely any way in which all of the factors relevant to that decision can be known with certainty. In some cases it may seem that there is very strong agreement about the problem and the solution. For example, this seems to be the case in legislating for emission levels, where certain limits are prescribed. However, to those intimately involved, the boundaries of the problem and the extent to which control is possible can still appear fuzzy because not all is known about the behaviour of particular compounds in all contexts (temperatures and wind patterns; effects on people of different age groups, etc.). There may also be a tendency to equate quantitative data with certainty. My reading of the 'Freedom to fly?' case study suggests that quantitative data and the understandings embedded in the SERAS approach held sway at the expense of other, alternative understandings. For example, a more flexible and adaptive public inquiry process, that included more of the different stakeholders at the outset, may lead to more effective environmental decision making than the current systematic and proceduralised approach.

In Part 2 a range of different approaches to environmental decision making that have become formalised, often by means of legislation or because they have been increasingly taken up by environmental managers due to regulations or compulsory or voluntary schemes, will be examined. How they rate in terms of the rigidity with which they have been applied and their relevance to the contexts in which they have been used, particularly in relation to the first two stages of our environmental decision-making framework, will be considered.

# Part Two  Exploring and formulating through environmental legislation and schemes

## 7  Exploring and formulating what? The scope of Part Two

This part focuses on environmental legislation and formalised schemes (such as ISO 14001) and how they are or can be used in exploring and re-exploring situations and formulating problems, opportunities and systems of interest of relevance to environmental decision making. In some cases, brief overviews of the legislation and schemes are given, by way of introduction, which may also be relevant to other parts of the T863 framework. I will therefore introduce the legislation and schemes in broad terms but will concentrate on those stages that are most relevant to this book. You may find it useful to make notes in your journal of aspects of the legislation and schemes that raise broader environmental decision-making issues, for you to return to when studying the later books. As environmental legislation and schemes have become a significant part of many people's environmental decision making, and are relevant to all stages of the T863 framework, later books will consider some further aspects of them.

Many people come to environmental decision making through their use of or engagement with legislation or schemes. They are therefore very powerful devices (institutional arrangements) which shape practices and even how we think about environmental issues. They all contain certain perspectives on the nature of 'the environment', how it can be understood, managed, changed and the activities of individuals guided or regulated. Legislation and schemes are thus very influential features of environmental decision-making situations, creating initial starting conditions, and affecting how we see, or do not see, problems and opportunities.

### 7.1  The overall trajectory of environmental legislation and schemes – past, present and future

#### Study note

The language of environmental legislation and schemes is quite specialised and can tend towards jargon. Efforts have been made by the author to explain all terms when they are first introduced, though some may have slipped through unexplained! Make a note of terms unfamiliar to you in your journal for later use. If further explanations of terms are needed they can usually be found online e.g. through using a search engine such as Google (http://www.google.co.uk).

Environmental legislation has been around for a long time in some countries and is in evidence today in nearly all parts of the world. The earliest environmental legislation can probably be traced back to Roman times when, for instance, laws concerning reasonable use of water were developed. One of the earliest records of air pollution control, according to the UK Environment Agency (2003), was in 1306 when a royal

Figure 34

proclamation banned the burning of coal in London. Legislation aimed at controlling atmospheric emissions from the caustic-soda industry in the United Kingdom dates as far back as 1863. Other early examples include the 1872 legislation passed by the United States Congress to make Yellowstone the world's first national park. Regulations for implementation of environmental laws and statutes (written laws) evolved alongside this primary legislation. Precedents that influenced current environmental legislation also occurred a long time ago. For instance, as early as 1868 there was a landmark case, 'Rylands v. Fletcher', still frequently referred to in law, where the principle of 'strict liability' was established. In this case, in 1860–61, water from a reservoir built for Mr Rylands' mill flooded a mine run by Mr Fletcher. Mr Rylands was made responsible for damages even though he couldn't avert the damage. Strict liability for environmental contamination has become a key concept in environmental law. The court in 'Rylands v. Fletcher' ruled:

> We think that the true rule of law is, that the person who for his own purposes brings on his lands and collects and keeps there anything likely to do mischief if it escapes, must keep it in at his peril, and if he does not do so, is prima facie answerable for all the damage which is the natural consequence of its escape ...
>
> (Rylands v. Fletcher 1868, LR 3 HL 330, 339–340)

Strict liability is still a part of environmental law, guiding the application of 'the polluter pays' principle, which is a key environmental principle in many parts of the world (e.g. it appears in the EC Treaty – the treaty that established the European Community). Following various cases, it is no longer interpreted quite as strongly as it once was, but the European Commission's White Paper on environmental liability (COM (2000) 66 final), adopted on 9 February 2000, still proposed to base the liability regime on 'strict liability' (CEC, 2000; WWF, 2000).

Figure 35  The 'Rylands v. Fletcher' situation

Legislative and regulatory requirements for business, industry, local authorities and governments to improve their environmental management policies and practices have arisen from increased recognition of the needs for environmental protection, pollution control and the efficient and equitable use of natural resources. These needs have been formulated both as problems and opportunities. The requirement for compliance with environmental legislation to avoid potential problems of prosecution and adverse publicity has been influential in encouraging organisations to improve their environmental management practices. The business opportunities of such improvements, such as cost savings and good publicity, have also become influential.

Figure 36  Increasing legislative and regulatory requirements in many sectors

Voluntary initiatives and agreements have also become increasingly important in improving environmental management practices in many parts of the world. These initiatives and agreements differ from legislation in that they are not mandatory, but they do sometimes contribute to compliance with legislation, e.g. in providing processes for helping to manage some environmental aspects. A range of formalised environmental 'schemes' fall in this category, including environmental management systems and standards (such as EMAS and ISO 14001 – see 'Environmental management systems' in the *Techniques* book) and corporate social and environmental responsibility schemes.

There are several different levels at which legislation takes place: international, regional (e.g. Europe), national and local. Both levels and laws are interrelated. For instance, the Climate Change Convention and Protocol at international level has parallel regional and national initiatives. When considering how environmental decision-making situations are explored or re-explored and problems, opportunities and systems of interest are formulated it is important to recognise these interrelationships. Brady (2005) is among those who have commented on the cascading nature of environmental law, with regional and national initiatives following the international level. Given the high number of agreements and declarations that have been negotiated at international level, this implies there are potentially a great many legislative initiatives to explore as part of the context of any environmental decision-making situation. But the relevance of this legislation to any particular system of interest will vary. As far as the early stages of the T863 framework are concerned, awareness that there is a wide range of initiatives, some of which may need to be considered selectively in more detail, is more important than understanding in depth how they have all been developed or implemented. Hence only a summary of some key international environmental legislation is given here (after Brady, 2005), in Box 14, followed later by examples from regional and national levels.

> ### Box 14   Key international environmental legislation
>
> **UN Convention on the Law of the Sea (UNCLOS) 1982.** To establish a legal order for the seas and oceans that will facilitate international communication and promote the peaceful uses of the seas and oceans, the equitable and efficient utilisation of their resources, the conservation of their living resources and the study, protection and preservation of the marine environment.
>
> **Convention for the Protection of the Ozone Layer 1985 (the Vienna Convention).** Requires signatory parties to take measures, including the adoption of legislation and administrative controls, to protect human health and the environment against adverse effects resulting, or likely to result, from human activities that modify or are likely to modify the ozone layer.
>
> **Protocol on Substances that Deplete the Ozone Layer 1987 (the Montreal Protocol).** Sets targets for reducing and eliminating the production and consumption of ozone-depleting substances, makes financial provision for developing countries in terms of alternatives to ozone-depleting chemicals and bans trade of ozone-depleting substances with non-signatory parties.
>
>

**Convention on the Control of Transboundary Movements of Hazardous Wastes and Their Disposal 1989 (the Basel Convention).** To control the export of hazardous/toxic waste and dumping by industrial nations in developing countries, and to reduce the amount of hazardous waste generated.

**Convention on Environmental Impact Assessment in a Transboundary Context 1991 (the Espoo Convention).** To reduce and control significant adverse transboundary environmental impacts from proposed activities, for example crude oil refineries, thermal power stations and reprocessing plants.

**Declaration of the UN Conference on Environment and Development 1992 (the Rio Declaration).** Statement of 27 key principles for sustainable development and international law including the precautionary principle, the polluter pays principle, public participation, risk communication and support for environmental assessment. It updated and consolidated earlier law including the Stockholm Convention 1972.

**Framework Convention on Climate Change 1992 (the Climate Change Convention).** To stabilise atmospheric greenhouse gas concentrations at a level that would prevent dangerous anthropogenic interference with the climate system.

**Convention on Biological Diversity 1992.** To secure the conservation of biodiversity, the sustainable use of its components and the equitable sharing of the benefits of genetic resources.

**Convention on the Transboundary Effects of Industrial Accidents 1992.** Recognised the importance and urgency of preventing the serious adverse effects of industrial accidents on human beings and the environment, and of promoting all measures that stimulate the rational, economic and efficient use of preventative, preparedness and response measures.

**Convention on the Protection and Use of Transboundary Watercourses and International Lakes 1993 (the Helsinki Convention).** To strengthen national measures for protection and ecologically sound management of transboundary surface waters and groundwaters.

**Protocol to the Framework Convention on Climate Change 1997 (the Kyoto Protocol).** Sets targets to deliver commitments under the Climate Change Convention, providing joint implementation, carbon trading and clean development mechanisms.

**Convention on Access to Information, Public Participation in Decision Making and Access to Justice in Environmental Matters 1998 (the Aarhus Convention).** To secure public rights of access to environmental information, public participation in decision making and the right of access to review environmental decision making (Europe-wide only).

**Convention on the Prior Informed Consent Procedure for Certain Hazardous Chemicals and Pesticides in International Trade 1998 (the Rotterdam Convention).** To promote a shared responsibility between countries to protect human health and the environment from the harmful effects of pesticides and other toxic and hazardous chemicals.

**Protocol on Biosafety 2000 (the Cartagena Protocol).** To meet requirements under the Convention on Biological Diversity for the adoption of a protocol on international aspects of biotechnology that may adversely affect human health and conservation and sustainable use of biological diversity.

**Convention on Persistent Organic Pollutants 2001 (the Stockholm Convention).** To protect human health and the environment from persistent organic pollutants (POPs) by restricting and ultimately prohibiting their use and trade.

(Source: Brady, 2005, pp. 58–9)

## Activity 33  Selecting relevant legislation

Select three of the items of international environmental legislation listed in Box 14 that seem to you as if they might be relevant to the aviation expansion case study. For each, explain why they appear to be relevant.

A cascade from international level is, however, not the only way of thinking of environmental legislation and schemes. Examples of both legislation and schemes can be traced back to highly influential initiatives at national levels. For instance, the United States National Environmental Policy Act 1969 introduced the requirement for environmental impact assessment and in doing so set a precedent later followed in other parts of the world. Similarly the role of the British Standards Institute is well recognised in pioneering standards, including environmental standards, later taken up at other levels.

A series of parallel initiatives regarding environmental management systems has been developed at national, regional and international levels. Perhaps partly because they are voluntary initiatives rather than mandatory, they provide what could be interpreted as a third model of development that is neither a cascade nor precedent model but associated with parallel development of schemes. Over time initiatives such as ISO 14001 (the international environmental management systems standard), EMAS (the European Union's (EU) Eco-Management and Audit Scheme) and BS7750 (the 1992 British Standard specification for an environmental management system – now phased out) have been blended together and have proved to be synergistic. I will say more about environmental management systems in Section 8.5.

In formulating a system of interest from an environmental decision-making situation, exploring and recognising what legislation falls within a system boundary and what

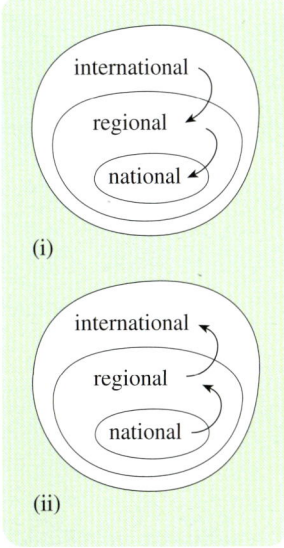

Figure 37  Patterns of (i) cascades and (ii) precedents working between levels in environmental legislation and schemes

lies outside it – in the system's environment – may affect how you approach other stages of decision making such as taking action (which will be discussed in Book 3). If a legislative process, or part of it, falls within your system boundary you may, for instance, consider the perspectives of a specific group of stakeholders involved in that process, whereas if legislation were a factor in the environment of your system of interest you might not consider those perspectives in as much detail. But even if you decide that legislation is not directly within, say, your national level system of interest it can be important to keep broader, international perspectives in mind. You may need to prepare for impending legislation, cascading from international level, and you may also have opportunities to participate in wider decision-making processes concerning new legislation, to ensure that national perspectives are taken into account at regional or international levels. The relationship between European and European member states' environmental legislation provides many examples of legislation where regional and national levels are linked and stakeholders have taken part in decision-making processes at both levels, such as in the process of developing the European Water Framework Directive and Environmental Impact Assessment Directives.

Overall, the number of schemes, standards, regulations, policies and laws for environmental management and decision making has grown rapidly over the past 30 years. In the European Union alone there are several hundred current environmentally related directives and voluntary agreements. A few examples are:

- European Union's (EU) Eco-Management and Audit Scheme (EMAS) (regulation 18346/93), replaced in 2001 by EMAS2 (Council regulation 761/01)
- EU's environmental policy, which takes the form of the sixth Environment Action Programme – Environment 2010: Our Future, Our Choice
- Water Framework Directive (2000/60/EC)
- Integrated Pollution Prevention and Control Directive (96/61/EC)
- Directives on restriction of the use of certain hazardous substances in Electrical and Electronic Equipment (2002/95/EC) and Waste Electrical and Electronic Equipment (2002/96/EC)
- Directive on High Activity Sealed Sources (2003/122/Euratom) and a new regulatory regime for the security of radioactive source implemented from the end of 2005 award at Member State level.
- Environmental Impact Assessment Directive (85/337/EEC) and amending Directive (97/11/EC)
- Strategic Environmental Assessment Directive (2001/42/EC).

### Activity 34  Your own environmental legislation

Each nation has different environmental legislation and schemes, even if aligned with some common regional and national initiatives. Spend a little time familiarising yourself with your own national and regional environmental legislation and schemes. Develop a list of examples of legislation for your own country and region, preferably with a brief (one or two sentence) description of the purpose of each item of legislation.

### Study note

You should be able to do this activity by searching online and looking at articles in national and international environmental magazines and journals. If you have difficulty completing this activity now, make a space for it in your journal that you can easily return to when you come across examples over your next few weeks of study. I have not provided a response as my examples are included in the main text.

While the emphasis in these initiatives is on environmental 'management', they all include guidelines for decision making and taking action. Decision making, action and management are of course interrelated. Exactly how they are related though depends on how the terms are conceptualised by those involved. I will not go into this further here but it may be a question to note in your journal to consider at the end of the course.

I am now coming to the end of the past and present aspects of this introductory section but what of the future? Looking back over the history of environmental schemes, regulation and legislation and how they have been used, it is possible to see what has worked well and less well for different purposes. This can give some indications of ways forward.

### Reading 7

Read 'Where next for EU environment policy?' which has come from the ENDS (2005) report, and answer the following questions.

> **SAQ 39  Where next for EU environmental policy?**
>
> According to the ENDS article:
> (i) what factors have led to a 'reduced appetite' for further environmental lawmaking?
> (ii) at what levels of organisation is responsibility taken for addressing environmental issues?
> (iii) what thematic areas are being addressed by the strategies included in the EU's sixth environmental action?
> (iv) what did Environmental Commissioner Stavros Dimas mean by 'better regulation'?
> (v) what different forms can environmental policy initiatives take?
> (vi) what are some of the advantages and disadvantages of voluntary agreements?
> (vii) what are some of the issues of integration mentioned in this article?

In Part 1, we considered what is involved in using systems approaches and examined how systemic thinking can be used to explore a situation and formulate problems, opportunities and systems of interest. In the rest of this part, I will review some aspects of environmental legislation and schemes that have the potential to support environmental decision making and consider how they are used in practice. While systemic thinking and action can certainly be used in complying with legislation or in designing and implementing schemes, these processes are often interpreted primarily in systematic terms. I will argue that some of the processes involved in environmental legislation and schemes could be more effective if more systemic thinking and action were used, particularly in their early stages or where there is scope for iteration. However, both systemic and systematic approaches have a lot to offer when used at appropriate stages of environmental decision making.

## 7.2 Auditing experiences of environmental legislation and schemes

The technique of an 'audit' is often referred to in environmental decision making. Reference to it can be found in two places in the *Techniques* book – as part of Environmental management systems: EMAS and in Evaluation: audit review evaluation.

In both these cases 'audit' refers to a systematic checking process, usually against aims, objectives or targets. In this section you will carry out an audit of your own and some other people's experiences of environmental legislation and schemes and consider how these experiences contribute to environmental decision making.

Before doing that, however, I want to consider briefly some aspects of environmental auditing that sometimes contribute to environmental legislation and schemes. These aspects are also relevant to whether environmental decision making does or can start off systemically, and if so how.

The Confederation of British Industry (CBI, 1990), based on prior work of International Chamber of Commerce (ICC, 1989) defined an 'environmental audit' as:

> the systematic examination of the interactions between any business operation and its surroundings. This includes all emissions to air, land, and water; legal constraints; the effects on the neighbouring community, landscape and ecology; and the public's perception of the operating company in the local area. ... Environmental audit does not stop at compliance with legislation. Nor is it a 'green-washing' public relations exercise. ... Rather it is a total strategic approach to the organization's activities.
>
> (Source: cited in Gray, 1993, p. 79)

This definition describes a systematic technique that could be used in different ways, depending on purpose. The focus on interactions and a 'total strategic approach' suggests to me an approach that could be both systematic and systemic, depending on how it is interpreted. Negotiating a boundary for an audit depends on what system of interest is identified and, as with any boundary negotiation process, requires iteration. In the CBI/ICC definition, 'the business operation' is implied as the system of interest. But where the boundary lies around that operation and what lies within it or in its surroundings will depend on both the nature of the business and the interpretation of those who perceive the business operation. For instance, in our Book 1 case study the aviation industry's needs to take account of noise, emissions, water quality and waste were highlighted as interactions to focus on between the aviation industry's business operation and its surroundings. This is also an example of where legislation and schemes and auditing meet.

There is legislation to cover all of the impacts of an airport and its associated activities, both on the ground and in the air, as shown in Figure 38. Exploring relevant legislation and procedures may be part of an audit, and doing an audit or review may also contribute towards the process of legislation or a scheme. An environmental legislation matrix accompanied Figure 38 in the report where it was presented. This matrix contained details of ten existing and three proposed European directives applying mainly to air quality or noise, and two further communications regarding soil protection and sustainable development. A range of additional standards and recommendations was also included. Each item of legislation, standard or recommendation was listed systematically with date, status and ACI Europe's position or action. Although this document was not (as far as I am aware) prepared as part of an audit, it gives an idea of what is involved in a systematic process of checking details of legislation and schemes that may be relevant when considering interactions between a particular business operation and its surroundings.

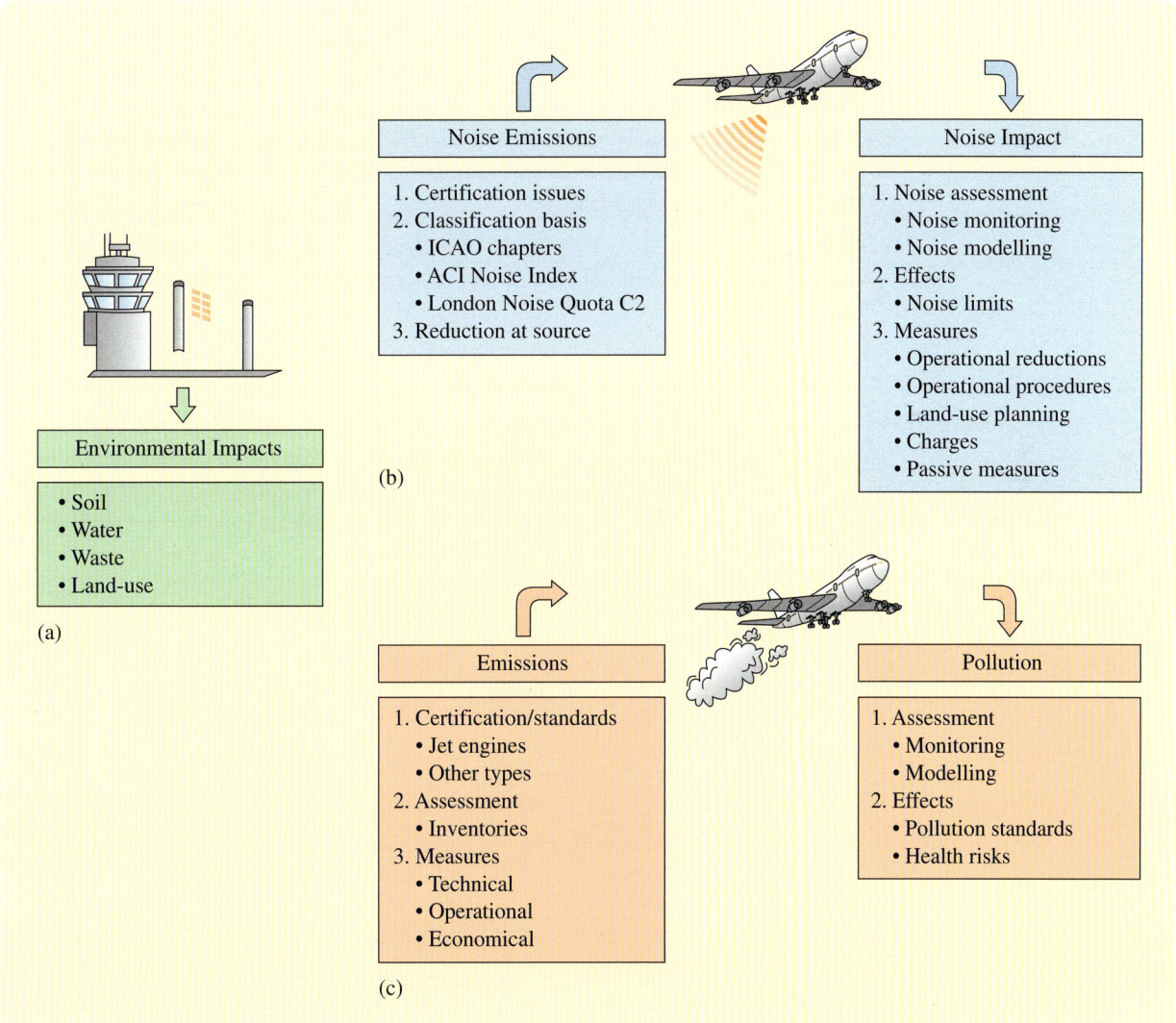

Figure 38    (a) Airport and land/ground-centric environmental impacts;(b) airport and noise impacts; (c) airport and emissions impacts (Source: adapted from ACI Europe Airports Council International, 2004, p. 6)

Many different kinds of environmental audit are carried out by those involved in environmental management and decision making in government, business and industry. They can focus on different processes, e.g. compliance with legislation and regulation and audits of environmental management systems and of environmental performance.

An audit of employees' or other stakeholders' experience of environmental legislation and schemes could well form a part of an environmental audit, depending on the purpose of the audit.

Having looked at what is intended in some processes of environmental auditing, I now want you to have a go at conducting your own audit, initially of your experiences rather than of a wider environmental decision-making situation.

### Activity 35    Start an audit of your experience of environmental legislation and schemes

(i) Choose some categories for checking your experience of environmental legislation and schemes.

(ii) Using your chosen categories, systematically list examples of environmentally related voluntary initiatives and/or mandatory legislation of which you are aware through your own experience.

(iii) Has your experience of environmental legislation and schemes affected your environmental decision making? If so, explain why and how. If not, explain why not.

(iv) Set yourself some objectives regarding gaining future experience of environmental legislation and schemes.

(v) Draw up a form that could be filled in by you in six months' time to complete a second stage of the audit to check your progress towards your objectives. (Don't forget to leave a space for aspects you may not anticipate!)

### Study note

For part (i) your categories could be time, types of environmental issues such as air, water, land, etc. or phases of your experience that only you may recognise, e.g. Company X phase, Membership of Y phase, Home-based phase.

For part (ii) if you do not know the names of specific acts and initiatives, note down the areas of activity where you think they apply.

## 7.3 Some questions of purpose of environmental legislation and schemes

Understanding different people's perceptions of purpose can give you both an indication of their systems of interest and insights into whether or not they are taking a systemic or systematic approach to environmental decision making.

Three possible purposes for conducting an environmental audit were given in the last section in the 'definition' quote from the CBI/ICC. They were compliance with legislation, a 'green-washing' public relations exercise and a total strategic approach to an organisation's activities. (The first two purposes sound to me mainly systematic but the third sounds more systemic.) In Part 1 of this book you considered some questions of purpose in relation to the aviation case study. There is probably insufficient detail in the case study for you to be able to fully understand the purposes of stakeholders in using environmental legislation and schemes. But you will be able to consider some of these questions in your own project, if appropriate to your chosen situation.

### Activity 36  Exploring the purpose of legislation and schemes

Read the following three short abstracts, which come from the Institute of Environmental Management and Assessment's (IEMA) 'e-briefings', and for each note down the declared purposes of legislation or scheme described by the author.

1  **What is the Water Framework Directive**
   **by Andy Bailey, Technical Adviser, Centre for Environmental Assessment and Management (CEAM)**

   Requiring all inland and coastal waters to reach 'good status' by 2015 the EU Water Framework Directive 2000/60/EC (WFD) has been described as 'the most significant piece of water legislation for a generation' (Environment Agency, 2004). The Water Framework Directive provides a holistic approach to the management of Europe's water bodies. For the first time plans (River Basin Management Plans) are to be made to provide a coordinated framework for the sustainable management of water resources which belong to the same ecological, hydrological and hydrogeological system (river-basin district).

2  **Environmental Management Systems**
   **by Martin Baxter, Technical Director, IEMA**

   An environmental management system (EMS) is a structured framework for managing an organisation's significant environmental impacts. Some organisations have adopted the framework specified in national or international standards, which set out the requirements of an EMS, and have had their systems externally assessed and certified against these; others have developed their EMS in a more informal way. Whatever approach has been adopted, the elements of the EMS framework will largely be the same.

3  **What is Strategic environmental assessment (SEA)?**
   **by Karl Fuller, Director of CEAM, IEMA**

   Strategic environmental assessment is a tool used to consider the potential impact of proposed plans, policies and programmes on the environment. By taking into account the environmental issues, as well as the social and economic factors at the strategic decision-making level, SEA can also be used to contribute to sustainable development. It has long been recognised that policies, plans and programmes, examined for their economic and social implications, but not their environmental impacts, have resulted in significant environmental damage. SEA enables an assessment with a specific focus on the environment. For example an SEA of a national energy policy would take account of the environmental impacts associated with coal fired production as against other alternatives.

---

All three of these examples are relevant to potential aviation expansion, though not part of the Aviation White Paper process described in Book 1. The Water Framework Directive deals with protection of all waters, surface and groundwater and river basin management. This tends to be a 'ground-centric' perspective as far as airports are concerned, and they will have to comply with relevant standards concerning disposal of wastes and use of water. Environmental management systems are being used in many airports around Europe (Upham et al., 2003, pp. 123–4) and SEA applies to proposed plans, policies and programmes regarding aviation development and expansion.

In practice, policymakers or designers of environmental legislation and schemes may have specific purposes in mind, but there is considerable variation in the ways in which legislation and schemes are interpreted and used. This is partly because there is a very wide range of environmental legislation and schemes, and intended purposes do vary. In addition it depends on how and what stakeholders negotiate with each other regarding development and use of the legislation or scheme (a topic that will be discussed in Book 3). It is also partly because the legislation and schemes become part of different systems of interest. Consider for instance part of Karl Fuller's account of SEA and its application in Box 15.

> ### Box 15 SEA and its application
>
> SEA is a broad concept that can be interpreted differently in terms of scope, role and purpose.
>
> The use of SEA varies between and within countries, and is applied through different systems and models.
>
> > EIA-based: SEA carried out under EIA legislation (Netherlands) or procedures (Canada)
> >
> > Environmental appraisal: SEA provision is made through a comparable, less formalised process of policy and plan appraisal (UK)
> >
> > Dual-track system: SEA arrangements are differentiated and implemented as separate processes (e.g. the Netherlands' e-test (or appraisal) of legislation and strategic EIA of specified plans and programmes)
>
>

> Integrated policy and planning system: SEA elements are part of effects-based policy and plan making (New Zealand)
>
> Sustainability appraisal: SEA is replaced by integrated (social, economic and environmental) assessment and review of major policy and planning issues (e.g. UK sustainability plans)
>
> Current SEA practice focuses mainly at the plan and programme level, on sectors identified as being likely to have significant environmental effects, e.g. transport and energy. SEA has also been applied to regional level development programmes and spatial plans. Prime areas for application of SEA include any plans or programmes that concern land use and natural resources, extraction of raw materials, and waste and pollution generating activities. World Bank development programmes and lending are subject to environmental assessment; however comprehensive SEA systems are very few and far between. In general there needs to be a shift towards SEA of policies, although this may take some time and thought to get to grips with.
>
> (Source: Fuller, 2004)

### SAQ 40  SEA and its application

From Karl Fuller's perspective:
(i) in what respects can SEA be interpreted differently?
(ii) give an example of the way use of SEA varies between countries.
(iii) give an example of the way use of SEA varies within a country.

### Activity 37  Identifying systems of interest

Identify two potential systems of interest in Karl Fuller's account, indicating:
(i) who the systems seem to be of interest to;
(ii) where the system boundaries appear to lie.

Note terms or ideas in Box 15 that are unfamiliar to you to return to when you consider SEA in more depth in Section 8.3.

#### Study note

You may choose to do part (ii) of this activity in words or with systems maps

# 8 How specific environmental legislation and schemes frame a situation and our practices

I will now briefly introduce some specific environmental legislation and schemes and will go on to look at examples of how environmental decision making has been framed or supported through use of these legislation and schemes. In particular, as Book 2 is dealing with just part of the T863 framework, I will try to draw out how environmental decision-making situations have been explored and how problems, opportunities and systems of interest have been formulated in the process of legislation and schemes.

I have chosen to look at six areas:

1. The Aarhus Convention on access to information, public participation in decision making and access to justice in environmental matters
2. Environmental impact assessment and its broader evolution
3. Strategic environmental assessment
4. Regulatory impact assessment
5. Schemes associated with environmental management systems and standards, specifically ISO 14001 and EMAS and
6. Corporate social and environmental responsibility schemes.

My reasons for selecting these six areas are firstly, that they have all become either 'mainstream' or popular in environmental decision making for a variety of reasons and secondly, because, in my view, they all have the potential to be illuminated by the T863 framework. I could instead have selected wastes or water legislation or different schemes and you may go on to consider some alternative legislation and schemes in later books or your course project.

### Study note

Section 8.2 on environmental impact assessment is much longer than the other five sections on specific legislation and schemes. This is for three reasons: (i) because EIA has a longer history than the other legislation, so there is more experience to comment on; (ii) because some stages of the EIA process have the potential to illustrate well what it means to start off systemically (or not); and (iii) I have explored the overall effectiveness of EIA and included an account of the broader evolution of environmental assessment at the end of that section.

## 8.1 The Aarhus Convention – more information, participation and justice?

In 1998 the UN Economic Commission for Europe prepared a Convention on Access to Information, Public Participation in Decision Making and Access to Justice in Environmental Matters (the Aarhus Convention). The European Commission subsequently developed two new directives (in 2003) and proposed one further one in order to implement the provisions of this convention. The Aarhus Convention is a relatively recent development in environmental legislation and although it has attracted a lot of attention from policymakers and other stakeholders, it has yet to become 'mainstream'. Hence, it might seem an odd place to start our inquiry into specific legislation and schemes. But I consider it first here because it is particularly relevant to this book and the potential for environmental decision making to start off systemically. Some of the issues of involving stakeholders, valuing multiple perspectives and starting off participatively have already been discussed in Part 1. They are all relevant to developing systemic awareness and to being able to formulate multistakeholder problems, opportunities and systems of interest.

## Reading 8

Read the article 'New EU directives to implement the Aarhus Convention' by AndrewRyan.

### SAQ 41   New EU directives to implement the Aarhus Convention

(i) What does Andrew Ryan mean by the 'three pillars' of the Aarhus Convention?

(ii) Briefly describe the main requirements for public authorities to provide information under the three EU directives derived from the Aarhus Convention.

### Activity 38   Implications of the Aarhus Convention

How do you think that implementation of the Aarhus Convention will affect

(i) how environmental decision-making situations are explored?

(ii) how problems, opportunities and systems of interest are formulated?

The Aarhus Convention and its derived EU directives on public participation and environmental information are relevant to other legislation. The directive for public participation brought in changes to the public participation procedure required in other legislation. For instance, it requires that the public is consulted in drawing up plans and programmes specified in several other environmental directives, including the Water Framework Directive. Another example comes from the Environmental Impact Assessment Directive where Article 6 in the Aarhus Convention covers 'Public participation in decisions on specific activities' and includes the wording:

> The public concerned shall be informed, either by public notice or individually as appropriate, early in an environmental decision-making procedure, and in an adequate, timely and effective manner, inter alia, of ... the fact that the activity is subject to a national or transboundary environmental impact assessment procedure.

(Source: UNECE, 1998, Article 6.2)

As Andrew Ryan commented, whether the implementation of the directives and the convention will have much effect remains to be seen, but it is likely to result in challenges. Some of these challenges may well be to those working with legislation that has been long-established as an integral part of practice. One such example is environmental impact assessment.

## 8.2 Environmental impact assessment and its broader evolution

Environmental impact assessment was first introduced in the USA as a result of the National Environmental Policy Act of 1969. It became part of European law in 1985 when an EIA Directive (85/337/EEC) was introduced in what was then the European Economic Community. The directive required that member states should have procedures in place for assessing the environmental effects of certain land-use projects such as power stations, waste disposal installations, road, rail and airport construction and extractive and other industries. In practice this requirement was interpreted differently in different countries and there was considerable variation in, for example, the degree of regulation, the number of EIAs carried out and the degree of public participation in the process.

The directive was amended in 1997 (Amending Directive 97/11/EC). Further legal obligations were introduced at that stage. Both the range of developments requiring an EIA and member states' responsibilities concerning screening of projects were extended to ensure that the need for an EIA is explicitly considered by a competent authority. An additional requirement was for the outcome of this process to be formally publicised in every case. Small as well as large projects are covered by Annex II, so in practice a system of thresholds was developed.

Use of environmental impact assessment extends well beyond Europe. Glasson et al. (2005) identified 120 countries where EIA takes place, as shown in Figure 39. Many of them have full regulations, some have partial or draft regulations and some have guidelines.

There is not space here to give a comprehensive account of EIA processes. Writers such as Wathern (1988), Canter (1996), Morris and Therivel (2001), Wood (2002) and Glasson et al. (2005) have done that elsewhere, and there is a vast literature on both EIA theory and practice. My purpose here is to introduce EIA as an example of a formal technique that supports environmental decision making that is required by law, with particular emphasis on the early stages of decision making. EIA is highly relevant to this book as the whole process could be seen as one of exploring and re-exploring situations and formulating problems and opportunities.

### 8.2.1 Public participation and consultation in EIA

The stages of the EIA process that are most relevant for exploring the situation, and formulating problems and opportunities and systems of interest, are usually the stages of screening, scoping and preparation of the environmental impact statement. We will go on to look at what some of these stages aim to achieve in detail later, after we have taken an overview of participation and consultation in the process by looking at some examples. Who explores and formulates what and how is particularly relevant to whether or not a systemic start is made to decision making, as discussed in Part 1.

8 HOW SPECIFIC ENVIRONMENTAL LEGISLATION AND SCHEMES FRAME A SITUATION AND OUR PRACTICES

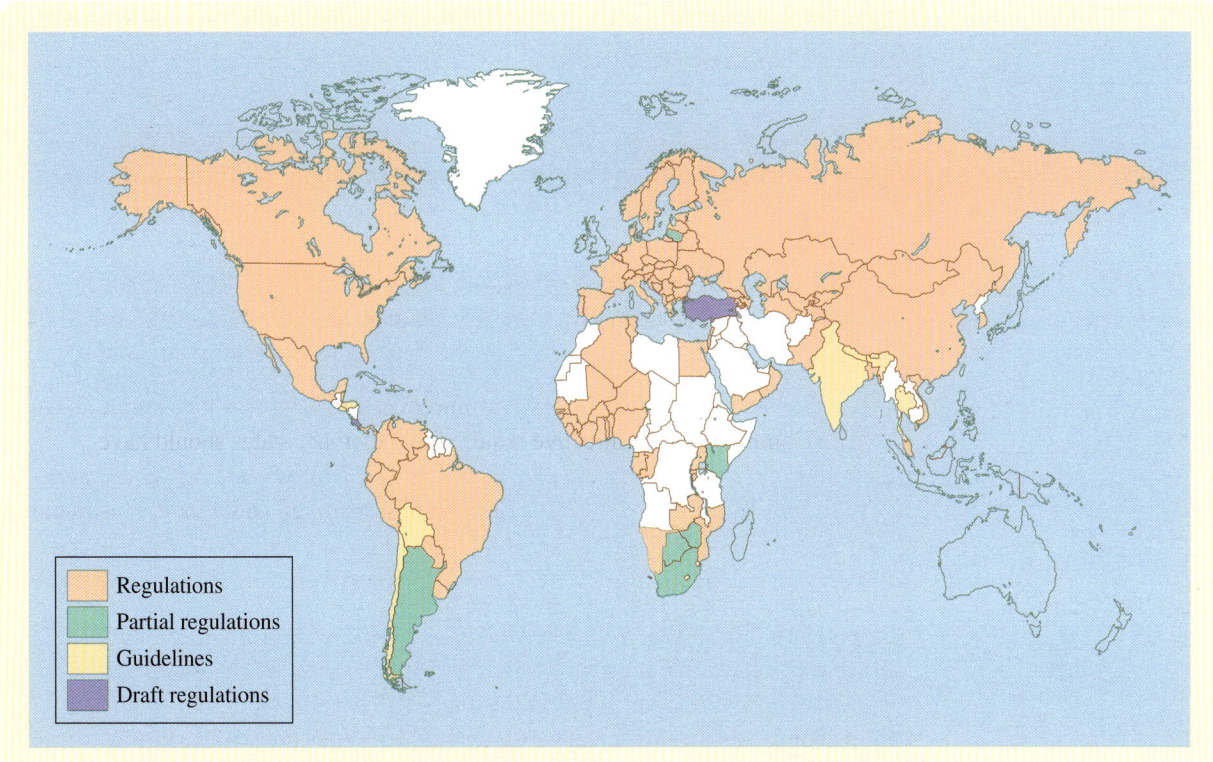

Figure 39    EIA systems worldwide (the authors apologise for any omissions or inaccuracies) (Source: Glasson et al., 2005, p. 37)

Hence public consultation and participation is a recurring theme in this section. Where there is iteration and review, there may also be re-exploration of the situation and further problems and opportunities may be formulated even in the post-decision phase.

How do access to information and public participation in decision making and access to justice in environmental matters, as proposed in the Aarhus Convention and discussed in the previous section, work in practice? And do they help stakeholders in starting off systemically? Some examples of consultation and participation in environmental decision making have already been considered in Part 1 of this book. I will now use some examples of EIA processes to further address these questions.

### 8.2.2 Examples from EIA practice

The three short case studies in Box 16 are all examples of consultation and participation in EIA processes at the early stages. They are taken from the UK IEMA's 2002 book *Perspectives: Guidelines on Participation in Environmental Decision Making.* As you read through the case studies and answer the associated SAQ and activity, keep in mind some of the issues of consultation and participation discussed in Part 1.

## Box 16  EIA case studies

### Case study 1:  Consultation throughout the EIA process for a new container terminal at Dibden Bay

#### Context

Associated British Ports (ABP) proposed the construction of a new container terminal on land at Dibden Bay, Port of Southampton. ABP published details of the scheme in 1998 following two years of consultation with local authorities, industry and the community.

#### Mechanism for participation

The following mechanisms for public participation were employed. Figure 40 illustrates how the programme was integrated into the EIA process.

#### Preliminary discussions

Preliminary discussions were held with local planning authorities, statutory consultees, Government departments and interest groups before a scoping document of the EIA was produced. A total of 18 organisations and councillors from county, district, town and parish councils were consulted. The concept behind the preliminary discussions was to provide an opportunity to ensure that the range of environmental issues examined was suitably comprehensive before the scope of the EIA was released for general comment.

#### Scoping document

A scoping document was then circulated which explained the main likely consequences which the EIA was expected to address. The scoping document was sent out to all those involved in the preliminary discussions, plus several additional organisations.

#### 'Dibden Update'

In a 17-month period, five issues of the 'Dibden Update' were published. 'Dibden Update' was a regular briefing note that outlined the Port of Southampton's proposals for its land at Dibden Bay. An average of 90,000 copies of each of the five issues were printed and distributed to the local community, informing the public of the proposals and providing an opportunity to write to the port company expressing their views.

#### Dibden Forum meetings

A forum was established to provide for the exchange of information between the developer and the local community concerning the proposed port development and local issues. The group was made up of key members from the community and included parish councillors, local businesses, Government officials, local authority officers and ABP officers. Six meetings were held, each concentrating on a specific issue.

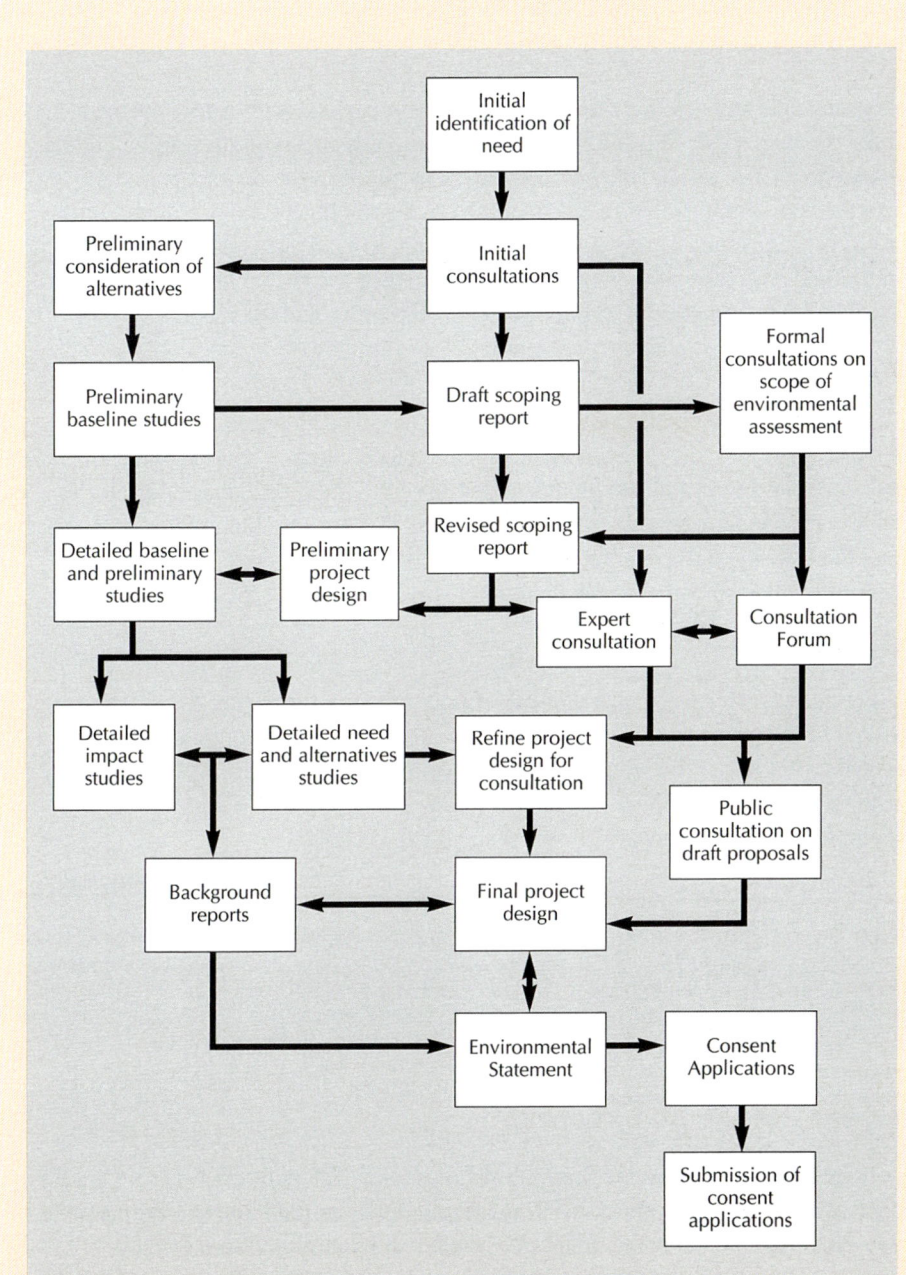

Figure 40  Dibden Terminal consultation process

## Presentations

Informal presentations of the initial draft proposals were made to officers and members of a number of relevant authorities and statutory bodies. Similar presentations were also made to the relevant nature conservation interest groups within the region and other interested parties including the CBI, Solent Forum, Royal Geographical Society, County Surveyors' Society and Chartered Institute of Transport.

### Public exhibitions

A public exhibition of the draft proposals was presented at five sites during a three month period. This allowed the public to view the exhibition and facilitate discussions. The public had an opportunity to question the developer and the EIA authors about specific aspects of the development and to make comments as to the acceptance or otherwise of the project, as well as highlighting their individual concerns. A total of 2456 people visited the five exhibitions. The exhibition was also previewed to the port community and the media.

### Meetings with local residents and landowners

A number of individuals raised particular issues about the proposed port development that were related to specific locations, such as residences. The developer and relevant consultants undertook individual consultation exercises with these concerned residents at their homes. The concept behind this approach was to allow the developer to become aware of individual concerns and hopefully allay some of the adjacent-landowner fears about the development.

### Outcome

Where it was realistic, practical and justified to alter the scheme, the design and layout of the proposals and mitigation measures were adjusted to accommodate issues raised during the consultation and participation exercise. One result of the extensive consultation was that measures designed to mitigate impacts were incorporated into the scheme rather than added as extras.

(Source: Smith, 1997)

### Case study 2: Scoping of the Strangford Lough Sea Defences environmental statement (ES)

A scoping document for the Strangford Lough Sea Defences ES was sent out for consultation to 29 organisations. A scoping report was then issued, summarising the issues and concerns identified in the initial consultation phase. A more detailed secondary consultation phase followed with a wide range of interest groups using a working group. The working group was asked to scope the key issues raised by the project and the options available. A round-table discussion agreed the options for further consideration at subsequent meetings.

(Source: Binnie, Black and Veatch, 1997; Smith, 1997)

## Case study 3: Preparation of an ES by interested parties

Local residents and surrounding communities organised an action group opposed to the extraction of sand and gravel at a site in Bedfordshire. A copy of the full planning application was delivered to the action group one week prior to its submission to the planning authority inviting comment. The action group negotiated an extension to the consultation period to enable them to prepare an independent ES as part of a formal objection to the planning authority. Having taken into account the ES prepared by the action group and other representations, the planning authority granted planning permission. However, a modified version of the application was approved, which included a reduced extraction period, improved screening and changes in phasing of extraction.

(Source: Commonwealth Environment Protection Agency, 1994)

## SAQ 42 Consultation and participation in EIA case studies

(i) What means of consultation or participation were used in each of the case studies?
(ii) Identify some examples of use of models in the means of consultation and participation you have identified in part (i).
(iii) Look at the diagram of the Dibden Bay consultation process and describe to what extent the consultation process was iterative.
(iv) Who was consulting with whom in the Dibden Bay and Strangford Lough Sea Defences cases?
(v) Briefly summarise the outcomes of the processes of consultation and participation in each case.

## Activity 39 Formulating questions to ask stakeholders

Draft a set of five questions that you might address to stakeholders in the consultation and participation processes described in the three cases, with the purpose of finding out whether or not these processes started off systemically.

Some further points about public participation will be made later in this section in relation to specific stages of EIA. I now want to look in more depth at what EIA tries to achieve and how the whole process starts off.

### 8.2.3 The stages of EIA

Internationally, while EIA definitions and processes vary, most involve at least three stages: (i) collecting data and preparing a written environmental statement; (ii) consultation based on the statement: (iii) a stage where the environmental statement and results of the consultation are taken into account in the development consent process. A key question raised when considering the role of EIA in decision making is which perspectives are represented.

Glasson et al. (2005) in their book *Introduction to Environmental Impact Assessment* described EIA as a process, shown in Figure 41.

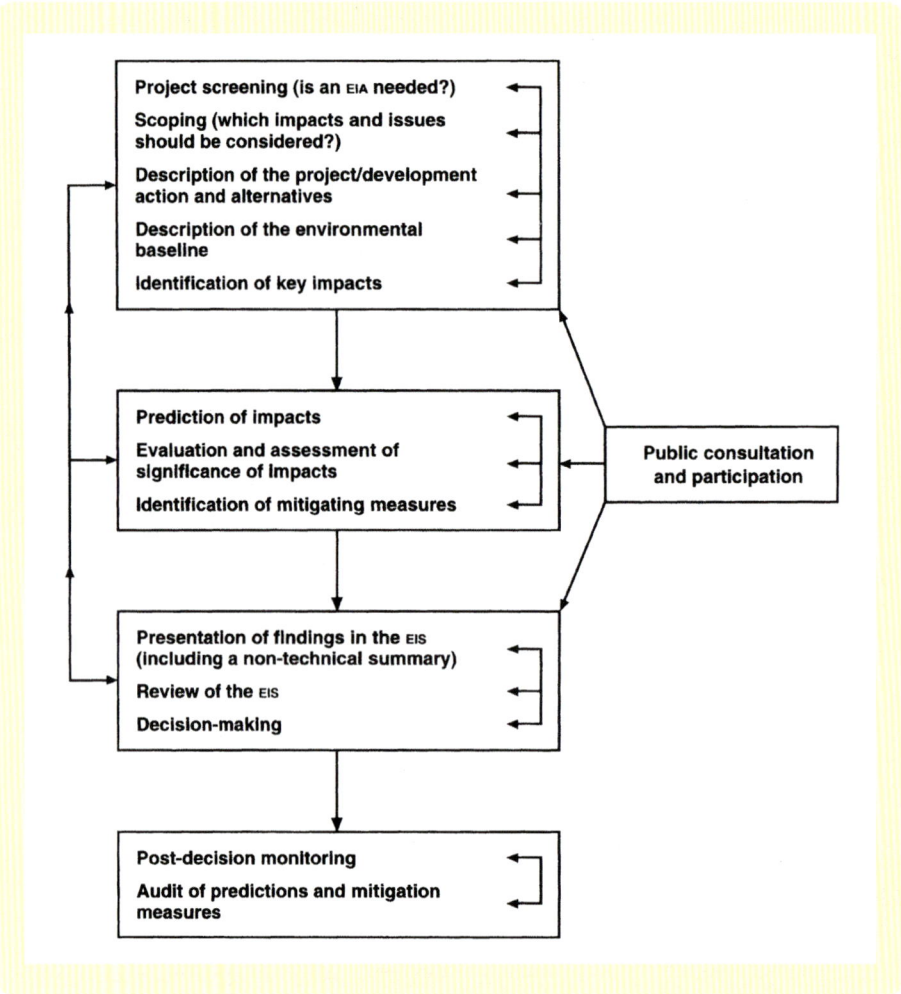

Figure 41   Important steps in the EIA process (Source: Glasson et al., 2005, p. 4)

Glasson et al. also briefly described each step in the list that follows (Box 17), noting that, although the steps are set out in a linear fashion, EIA should be a cyclical process. (We will discuss this process later on in this section.) Some of the steps shown are not required by some EIA legislation (e.g. monitoring is not mandatory in many EIA procedures).

### Box 17   Descriptions of steps in environmental impact assessment

*Project screening* narrows the application of EIA to those projects that may have significant environmental impacts. Screening may be partly determined by the EIA regulations operating in a country at the time of assessment.

*Scoping* seeks to identify at an early stage, from all of a project's possible impacts and from all the alternatives that could be addressed, those that are the crucial, significant issues.

*The consideration of alternatives* seeks to ensure that the proponent has considered other feasible approaches, including alternative project locations, scales, processes, layouts, operating conditions and the 'no action' option.

*The description of the project/development action* includes a clarification of the purpose and rationale of the project, and an understanding of its various characteristics – including stages of development, location and processes.

*The description of the environmental baseline* includes the establishment of both the present and future state of the environment, in the absence of the project, taking into account changes resulting from natural events and from other human activities.

*The identification of the main impacts* brings together the previous steps with the aim of ensuring that all potentially significant environmental impacts (adverse and beneficial) are identified and taken into account in the process.

*The prediction of impacts* aims to identify the magnitude and other dimensions of identified change in the environment with a project/action, by comparison with the situation without that project/action.

*The evaluation and assessment of significance* assesses the relative significance of the predicted impacts to allow a focus on the main adverse impacts.

*Mitigation* involves the introduction of measures to avoid, reduce, remedy or compensate for any significant adverse impacts.

*Public consultation and participation* aims to ensure the quality, comprehensiveness and effectiveness of the EIA, and that the public's views are adequately taken into consideration in the decision-making process.

*Environmental impact statement (EIS) presentation* is a vital step in the process. If done badly, much good work in the EIA may be negated.

*Review* involves a systematic appraisal of the quality of the EIS, as a contribution to the decision-making process.

*Decision making* on the project involves a consideration by the relevant authority of the EIS (including consultation responses) together with other material considerations.

> *Post-decision monitoring* involves the recording of outcomes associated with development impacts, after a decision to proceed. It can contribute to effective project management.
>
> *Auditing* follows from monitoring. It can involve comparing actual outcomes with predicted outcomes, and can be used to assess the quality of predictions and the effectiveness of mitigation. It provides a vital step in the EIA learning process.
>
> (Source: Glasson et al., 2005, pp. 5–6)

Glasson et al.'s representation of a cyclical process of EIA is one of many. Another diagram of the EIA process, from Wood (1995), can be found as Figure 25 in the *Techniques* book (see Environmental assessment: EIA) and a further diagram, linking EIA and the project cycle, is given below in Figure 42.

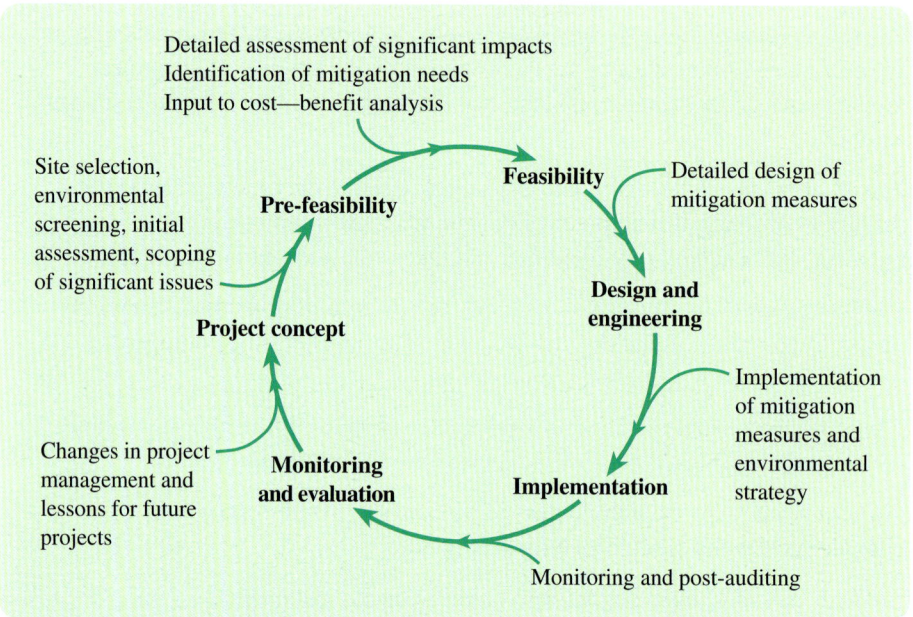

Figure 42   EIA and the project cycle (Source: based on UNEP, 1988)

When considering whether or not decision making in environmental impact assessment starts off systemically, it is necessary to take a closer look at how these processes are both represented and used.

The purpose of the following activity is primarily to encourage you to look at a range of representations of EIA and to begin to consider how they start off. In doing this, remember that the diagrams are models of processes and as such are simplifications (as discussed in Part 1). Although the diagrams are useful to give a rapid overview of a process and to prompt questions, care must be taken when using them in isolation as they indicate only a part of what is going on or a part of what the person drawing them is describing.

## Activity 40  Comparing EIA diagrams

Consider Figure 25(T) (from the *Techniques* book) with Figures 41 and 42 here.

(i) List the main words that appear in Figures 25(T) and 42.

(ii) Compare the two lists and diagrams with each other and with Glasson et al.'s list of steps in Box 17. What are the main similarities and differences in the three diagrams?

(iii) Identify and describe in a few sentences the starting points and initial stages in each of the three processes represented in Figures 25(T), 41 and 42. State any assumptions you make or difficulties you had in doing this.

(iv) Does any one of the diagrams indicate who is involved in the processes? What further questions does the answer to this question raise for you?

---

As you will see from my answer to this activity, I found it quite difficult in two of the diagrams to see where these cyclical processes started. In practice, individuals taking part in an EIA process, or in other environmental decision-making processes, may start off at different stages. I also found that I would need to consider examples of EIA in practice to be able to fully understand the processes represented.

EIA is meant to happen before a decision is made, but decisions about individual projects are often constrained by previous decisions regarding policy and programmes, as was shown in the aviation case study in Book 1. Peter Wathern recognised that decision making starts well in advance of formal project proposals:

> EIA is a process having the ultimate objective of providing decision makers with an indication of the likely consequences of their actions. Over the years, it has become increasingly evident that the authorization of proposals is not the sole decision point. There are many decision makers involved in the evolution of a set of development proposals and the influence of most of them is exerted long before the submission of an application for formal project authorization ... In the past, attention has tended to focus on the most spectacular decision point, authorization, and the importance of well-integrated appraisal in the refinement of development proposals has largely been undervalued. EIA is no longer seen as an add-on process. Indeed, the greatest contribution of EIA to environmental management may well be in reducing adverse impacts before proposals come through to the authorization phase.
>
> (Wathern, 1988, p. 6)

Out of context, Wathern's optimism that EIA was no longer seen as an add-on process might be questioned, given that interpretation of EIA in different parts of the world is very variable. However, the quote is from a book that refers to parts of the world where EIA was fairly long-established and Glasson et al. (2005) also suggest that there is general acceptance of the value of EIA. Other writers too have noted that there are many decisions, not just a final decision, to be made and that a range of decision makers is involved.

Before moving on to look at some of the separate stages of EIA, it is useful to consider who makes the decisions about EIA.

> Decision making takes place throughout the EIA process. Many decisions are made by the proponent (e.g. choices between various alternatives). Others may be made jointly by the proponent and the decision-making and environmental authorities (e.g. screening and scoping decisions). However, the main decision in the EIA process, whether or not to allow the proposal to proceed (or, less frequently, which alternative to implement) is always taken in the public domain. While the decision-making body may have given previous indications of the likely outcome of this decision, it is normally taken by a government agency, following consultation and public participation.
>
> (Wood, 1995, p. 181)

Issues about which perspectives are represented, who decides what is a significant issue and who makes the decisions frequently recur in EIA. There is evidence of stakeholder involvement in many decisions that involve EIA, for example in scoping. Examples of different approaches at the various stages are included in this section. Some of them are more systemic approaches than others, in that they describe situations where people work out their systems of interest together and there is iteration in decision making. There is a need for a systemic approach to ensure that multiple perspectives are taken into account. Some of the more general issues relating to who makes decisions and who decides what issues are significant are similar to those discussed on the DVD in (i) the video on participating in environmental decision making that you will have watched with Part 1 and (ii) the videos accompanying the aviation case study.

### Screening

> A screening mechanism seeks to focus on those projects with potentially significant adverse environmental impacts or whose impacts are not fully known. Those with few or no impacts are 'screened out' and allowed to proceed to the normal planning permission and administrative processes without any additional assessment or additional loss of time and expense.
>
> (Glasson et al., 2005, pp. 89–90)

So, who decides which projects require an EIA and how is it decided? EIA regulations that determine screening procedures exist in some countries. Criteria such as project type, location, size and the nature of likely impacts have been used in many countries to draw up lists of projects that should be subject to EIA. For the EU, categories of projects where an EIA is mandatory, or where an EIA is required if member states decide it is likely to cause significant effects, are listed in Annex I (mandatory) and Annex II (discretionary) of the European Council Environmental Impact Assessment Directive (97/11/EC). The lists were extensively modified and extended in 1997 when the directive was amended. Further guidelines were also included in these amendments to improve EIA practices regarding Annex II projects – for example, an extra annex was added which lists criteria to be used to screen Annex II projects.

The following list, in Box 18, summarises the types of project included in Annex I for which an EIA is mandatory in the EU. Thresholds and detailed criteria and specifications are not included here as the list is long and I only want to give an indication of the types of project covered by the legislation.

> ### Box 18  EC EIA Directive Annex I projects
>
> 1. Crude oil refineries, installations for coal/shale gasification and liquefaction
> 2. Thermal power stations and other combustion installations; nuclear power stations and other nuclear reactors
> 3. Irradiated nuclear fuel and radioactive waste processing and/or storage installations
> 4. Cast-iron and steel smelting works and installations for production of non-ferrous crude metals
> 5. Asbestos extraction, processing and transformation
> 6. Integrated chemical installations
> 7. Construction of railways, airports, motorways, express and four-lane roads
> 8. Inland waterways and ports; trading ports and piers for larger vessels
> 9. Hazardous waste disposal installations for incineration or chemical treatment
> 10. Large non-hazardous waste disposal installations for incineration or chemical treatment
> 11. Large-scale groundwater abstraction or recharge schemes
> 12. Large-scale works for transfer of water resources (excluding piped drinking water)
> 13. Large waste-water treatment plants
> 14. Large-scale extraction of petroleum and natural gas for commercial purposes
> 15. Large dams and reservoirs
> 16. Large and/or long gas, oil and chemical pipelines
> 17. Large installations for intensive rearing of poultry or pigs
> 18. Industrial plants for production of pulp, paper and board
> 19. Large quarries and open-cast mining
> 20. Construction of long and high-voltage overhead electrical power-lines
> 21. Large installations for storage of petroleum, petrochemical and chemical products
>
> (Source: summarised from Annex 1 to EC directive 97/11/EC, 3 March 1997)

Projects listed in Annex II of the directive (Box 19) are those where an EIA is required when they are likely to cause significant effects, which is decided by member states against guidelines and specifications made in the directive. Hence, they do not always require an EIA, as in the case of Annex I projects.

> **Box 19  EC EIA Directive Annex II projects**
>
> *All these categories have sub-categories that are not included here.*
> 1   Agriculture, silviculture and aquaculture
> 2   Extractive industry
> 3   Energy industry
> 4   Production and processing of metals
> 5   Mineral industry
> 6   Chemical industry (projects not included in Annex 1)
> 7   Food industry
> 8   Textile, leather, wood and paper industries
> 9   Rubber industry
> 10  Infrastructure projects
> 11  Other projects (as specified)
> 12  Tourism and leisure
> 13  Changes to Annex I and Annex II projects already authorised and temporary Annex 1 projects for development of new methods or products
>
> (Source: summarised from Annex II to EC directive 97/11/EC, 3 March 1997)

The lists in Annexes I and II of the directive indicate that people who have developed European legislation and national governments have gone through a process of considering certain categories of project in the light of past experience. Enough is known by those people about the potential impacts of those types of project to suggest that an EIA is needed.

Stephenson et al. (1995), in examining a range of informal opportunities for public participation in EIAs, found that there were opportunities at the screening stage. They found, for example, in the context of land drainage and improvement schemes that, if a decision is taken not to undertake an EIA, strong opposition from other parties can lead to the decision being reversed.

### SAQ 43  Screening

(i) What is screening?

(ii) What is the difference between the types of project listed in Annex I and Annex II of the EC directive for environmental impact assessment?

### Scoping

> The process of scoping is that of deciding, from all of a project's possible impacts and from all the alternatives that could be addressed, which are the significant ones.
>
> (Glasson et al., 2005, p. 91)

This definition immediately raises questions about what constitutes a significant issue and who decides which issues are significant. There is no single answer to this because different procedures are adopted in different countries. Scoping decisions often have to be made by people who are described by Wood (1995, p. 131) as 'individuals with the appropriate levels of knowledge and expertise who are able to say from past experience: what significant effects are likely to arise; how they are likely to impact on the environment; and what steps might be taken to deal with them'. These individuals might include consultants employed by developers, government employees, members of the public and representatives of organisations, or they may be 'expert panels' and formally constituted groups of representatives of different interest groups.

Considerations about the scale of a development, the sensitivity of its location and the nature of its adverse effects take place at the screening stage to determine whether or not a project needs an EIA. By the scoping stage, some possible impacts will have been identified and scoping usually focuses on a range of potentially significant impacts. It is at this stage that priority issues are identified.

The main scoping is at an early stage in the EIA process. However, to a limited extent it is iterative as it continues throughout the process as issues are examined and discarded, if it is determined that they are not significant, and as other issues come to the fore.

EIA legislation and practice vary. Scoping is usually done through discussions among the developer, relevant agencies, competent authorities and in some cases the public. For example, in a method used in Canada small community-based meetings were held before formal EIA hearings where local residents discussed their concerns in the presence of an assessment panel and representatives of the developer. Government agencies and research establishments also made representations to the panel. The purpose of these hearings was to increase understanding of potential environmental effects and perceptions of the issues identified by the community (Beanlands, 1988).

Opportunities for the public to be involved in scoping vary. Commenting before the EIA Directive was amended, Clark (1994) was one of many writers who pointed out the need for public participation at early stages of the EIA, such as scoping, to identify key issues. At that time, public participation often focused on when an EIA was complete rather than during the EIA process itself. In France, for example, unless a public inquiry was required as part of the consent procedure, an EIS only had to be published after a decision was taken. In the Netherlands, by contrast, traditions of public participation at an early stage in the process were already well established. The 1997 amendments to the directive require public review to take place before development consent is granted. Some changes have also resulted from the Aarhus Convention as discussed in Reading 8. There may however be both advantages and disadvantages of public participation in EIA, depending on your point of view. Glasson et al. (2005, pp. 158–9) pointed out that 'historically public participation had connotations of extremism, confrontation, delays and blocked development'. They also identified advantages: 'public participation can be used positively to convey information about a development, clear up misunderstandings, allow a better understanding of relevant issues and how they will be dealt with, and identify and deal with areas of controversy while a project is still in its early planning phases'.

While many countries do require scoping to take place, Wood (1995) observed that in the UK and New Zealand it was not obligatory. Even the amended European EIA

Directive only places the obligation on the competent authority to scope an EIA if requested to do so by the developer.

Where there is public involvement in scoping it is not always through discussion. Questionnaires and surveys may be used. Beanlands (1988) notes that there are issues about low return rates of surveys and inappropriate questionnaire design that make these methods less desirable than discussion where different perspectives can be heard in one place. However, it could be said that all techniques used to engage the public in participation have their limitations, including discussion.

Beanlands also acknowledged that detailed results of a scoping exercise will depend on a specific project, but noted several themes that seem to recur:

> The primary concern of the public with respect to environmental matters is human health and safety. All others will be subordinate when man's health is in jeopardy as a result of a proposed development. The public will have a great concern for potential losses of important commercial species or commercially available production. The converse would hold true regarding an increase in the numbers of undesirable species. Society can be expected to place a high priority on species of major recreational or aesthetic importance, whether or not they support commercial activities of any consequence. Special interest groups will usually gain broad support in their concern for rare or endangered species on the basis that mankind has special custodial responsibilities regarding their preservation. Finally, the public can normally be expected to be concerned over habitat losses which represent a foreclosure on future production. In all of these cases, public concern will be heightened in relation to perceived imbalances between supply and demand of species or habitats within a local, regional or national context.
>
> (Beanlands, 1988, p. 35)

A specific example of an issue that was seen as a priority in one location is provided by Cook and Donelly-Roark in a chapter on public participation in environmental assessment in Africa in a World Bank publication. The example also highlights that there may be differences in views over what constitute the priority issues:

> the Mozambique Agricultural Services EA reports that NGOs were extremely concerned that most of the fertile land in the project area would be used for cotton crops rather than food crops. The EA team did not agree with this assessment and responded with a five-page analysis of the relationship between food and cotton production. However, this type of response did nothing to allay the real and valid concerns raised by NGOs. Instead, it denied the validity of their locally based views in comparison to those of the expert who may or may not be able to predict the outcome more successfully.
>
> (Cook and Donelly-Roark, 1994, p. 95)

Finally, it is worth noting that the way in which scoping is done can also affect subsequent stages of the EIA process. Sadler and Fuller commented that:

> many countries report difficulties in 'closing the scoping diamond' ... narrowing the range of concerns to identify the impacts and issues that matter. When this closure is not achieved, the determination of significance is compromised, the ES becomes a voluminous and descriptive document and the process of decision making becomes protracted, inefficient and unfocused.
>
> (Sadler and Fuller, 1997, p. 14)

A series of techniques has been developed to support EIA. One example is the use of matrices for scoping (and in Canada for screening). These techniques will not be covered in this section but some of the techniques for environmental decision making discussed in the *Techniques* book and elsewhere in the course are relevant to EIA. For example, some of the participatory rural appraisal techniques seen in the video you watched in Part 1 may support activities such as scoping and consideration of alternatives.

> ### SAQ 44   Scoping
>
> (i)   What is scoping?
> (ii)  What perspectives are sought in scoping?
> (iii) How are different perspectives sought in scoping and by whom?

### Preparation of an environmental impact statement

Preparation of an environmental impact statement (EIS) is a central part of the EIA process. It is a statement that includes details of screening, scoping, the nature of the development, the findings of 'baseline studies' (which are sets of environmental data against which change caused by the development can be measured), impact prediction and evaluation, mitigation and monitoring measures.

In the UK, the importance of environmental statements in decision making increased when new EIA regulations were introduced in 1999 as a result of the 1997 amendment to the European EIA Directive. (Previous UK EIA regulations had been in place since 1988.) This happened because, from 1999, local planning authorities were required to ensure that environmental statements provided a minimum level of information.

In order to focus on examples of practices that relate to the topic of this book, I will now consider the purpose of EIA – and of the EIS – in relation to decision making in more depth. Relevant observations in this respect include the following:

> [The purpose of EIA is to] predict, analyse and evaluate the impacts of a proposed action on the environment and ensure that information regarding these impacts is taken into account in decision making.
>
> (Roberts, 1995, p. 120)

One function of EIA is to provide decision makers with an indication of the environmental consequences of the options open to them. Environmental issues, however, rarely form the sole basis for a decision related to the implementation of a particular set of proposals. Politicians may perceive a pressing need for economic development, jobs and revenue generation or for remedying some social ill as an overriding consideration despite consequent environmental degradation. Thus, the case for development often seems overwhelming. Nor must it be assumed that development and protection of environmental quality are necessarily conflicting. Indeed the converse may be true, as experience from some LDCs [less developed countries] clearly points to the serious environmental impact of poverty. Even when sanctioning a development appears the only decision which can be countenanced, applying EIA may still yield benefits. An EIA may reveal other ways of achieving the same objectives, but with less environmental disruption. In addition, there may be economic benefits from using EIA. Mitigating measures identified during EIA may be incorporated more economically at the design stage than subsequently.

(Wathern, 1988, pp. 28–9)

The purposes of EIA therefore include:

- predicting and understanding the environmental effects of an action before decisions are made
- evaluating alternative courses of action
- bringing forward environmental considerations so that they can be considered alongside economic and social considerations
- seeking courses of action that minimise environmental disruption.

EIA can be thought of as a tool for environmental decision making.

Two areas referred to in the above quotes warrant closer attention. The first is the reference to 'information' in Roberts' quote. I have selected the area of information because it is the primary focus of public consultation and participation in EIA and, as discussed in Part 1, the nature of consultation and participation is highly relevant to whether or not a decision-making process starts off systemically. The way in which requirements for information are interpreted in EIA raises issues about whose situations are explored and whose problems and opportunities are formulated.

The second area for closer attention is how environmental issues can be considered in the process of economic and social development – I will not consider this aspect here but in the next section, on strategic environmental assessment, in the context of how EIA and related techniques have evolved and might evolve in future so that the wider context of a project or programme can be explored and informed.

### 8.2.4 Information for EIA

Figure 43

There is a range of theories about information and knowledge and how individuals respond to data. Some of them have already been explored in Part 1 in relation to the aviation case study. One aspect that is relevant in using EIA and in preparing an EIS is that, while there are many people who accept the principle that it is within an individual that a particular meaning is attributed to data, it is still difficult (some would say impossible) for one person to imagine how another will receive or respond to the data. In site-based interpretation – an activity that focuses on the visitor's experience in national parks, museums, historic and other sites – there is some acknowledgement of this difficulty and attempts have been made to find out about a visitor's experience from their point of view, asking them to explain using words or pictures what their visit and the data that were presented meant to them. This follows the example of Freeman Tilden (1977), a pioneer of interpretation in North American national parks, who included as one of six principles of interpretation (initially in 1957):

> Any interpretation that does not somehow relate what is being displayed or described to something within the personality or experience of the visitor will be sterile.
>
> (Tilden, 1977, p. 9)

To develop 'good' or 'meaningful' interpretation, some interpreters take into account the feedback obtained from visitors in preparing future interpretive materials:

> Information is data that has been processed into a form that is meaningful to the recipient and is of real or perceived value in current or prospective decisions.
>
> (Davis, 1974)

Davis' definition suggests that the form that data takes is important in terms of data's potential to become information. The degree to which information is meaningful to a recipient depends on whether the recipient's perspective has been taken into account in collecting, processing and presenting the data. Even though there is uncertainty about how data is received, interpreters have shown that efforts can certainly be made to get feedback from those who receive data and to find out what the data meant to them. In the case of EIA, this could include whether people found the data useful in decision making. One sign that this is starting to be done is in work reviewing the quality of EISs.

The quality of environmental statements has come under increasing legal scrutiny in the UK since the 1999 regulations were introduced. The magazine of the IEMA reported in August 2001 that recent court cases concerning EIA had signalled a far more rigorous attitude about the requirement to comply with the EIA Directive. One commonly cited example that led to some clarification of what information was required concerned a business park in Rochdale in the UK.

Glasson et al. (2005) raised the issue of 'quality for whom?' in considering EIS quality, pointing out that in a UK Department of the Environment (1996) study researchers found little agreement about EIS quality among planners, consultees and the researchers. Interestingly, from the viewpoint of considering whether some of these EIA processes started off systemically, they also noted that planning officers, consultees in the EIA process and developers/consultants often had very different perceptions of purpose of the EIS (perhaps different systems of interest?) and hence evaluated it differently.

There is some recognition that data presented must be meaningful to different people in that a non-technical summary of the EIS is usually required. However, a term such as 'non-technical' is open to interpretation. In most cases the responsibility for preparing the statement lies with the developer and it might not be in the developer's interests for details to be accessible to all who might object to a development.

Other perspectives are represented in the EIS. Consultants are often brought in to undertake EIAs including to help in conducting baseline studies and in some cases to prepare EISs. Various consultees who have relevant data and perspectives are involved. There is often an opportunity, or in some cases a requirement, for public review of the statement and an opportunity for the public to submit comments. Stephenson et al. noted that:

> Although there are no data available to describe the extent to which public participation occurs in the preparation of EISs, it is believed that practice is variable and does not occur in the majority of cases as most developers will meet only the minimum (i.e. formal) requirements, unless it is in their interests to do more.
>
> (Stephenson et al., 1995, p. 24)

Given that the process of EIA is intended to ensure that public and not just private interests are taken into account in decision making, the issue of public participation in EIA is an important one in bringing forward information for decision making, as in the case of screening. Practices vary around the world as to who else besides the developer is involved in the preparation of environmental impact statements. In the Netherlands an 'expert panel' is appointed by an EIA commission that is independent of Government and was established by royal decree. This expert panel draws up guidelines on what should be included in the EIS. There is opportunity for public and advisers' comments before an EIS is prepared. In the UK, there is a legal requirement for 'statutory consultees' to be consulted before a decision is made and they are required to provide the developer with information in their possession which is likely to be relevant to the EIS; but there is no requirement for public views to be taken into account until after the EIS has been submitted. Iceland and Japan have a history of two-stage EISs, with opportunity for the public and others to comment before the final EIS is submitted, so members of the public might be involved in bringing forward information. It is not just a case of what is legally required and how or whether those legal requirements are implemented. Stephenson et al. (1995), in a study of public participation in EIA in Europe and the UK, identified a wide range of informal opportunities for public participation in EIA in the UK before the stage when the public had a legal right to express their views.

There are clearly many issues in EIA around consultation and participation and quite a lot of them in the early stages are associated with the generation, collection, processing and presentation of data. This applies in the case of statutory consultees who have to judge what additional data to submit, to the public who want to know whether their interests are represented, and to those officials who have to interpret and judge whether a project should go ahead on the basis of details presented to them. Whether the type of data made available and the form in which it is presented really support decision making as much as is possible is questionable, and an issue that continues to be a challenge for those seeking to improve the process of environmental impact assessment.

### 8.2.5 Exploring the effectiveness of EIA and the evolution of environmental assessment techniques

Before leaving EIA, I want you to consider how it frames a situation and our practices by taking an overview of practice from some different perspectives.

## Reading 9

Read 'Everything you already know about EIA (but don't often admit)' by Robert Beattie (1995).

> ### SAQ 45  Everything you already know about EIA
>
> (i) What is Beattie's perspective on EIA?
> (ii) What are the three main points Beattie seems to be making against EIAs?
> (iii) Why does Beattie think that, in spite of all their shortcomings, EIAs are valuable and necessary?
> (iv) What suggestions does Beattie make for improving EIAs?

Driving forces for environmental decision making are of two main types – the 'pull' force and the 'push' force (also known as 'carrots' and 'sticks'). An example of a pull force might be the business opportunity of developing new 'clean' technologies. Complying with legislation tends to be a push force in that it is driven by fear of prosecution and the resultant loss of public confidence in an organisation's activities. Pull forces are usually perceived as opportunities and push forces as problems, although there may be different perceptions of whether, say, a single item of legislation or the development of a new product constitutes a problem or an opportunity.

In terms of exploring situations before formulating problems and opportunities and systems of interest, the legal context is certainly one that influences environmental decision making and action. The EC directive for environmental impact assessment means that certain projects require an exploration of a situation, through an EIA, to be carried out in advance of a decision about whether a development goes ahead. But whether this exploration occurs before formulating problems, opportunities and systems of interest – i.e. whether EIA processes encourage a systemic start to environmental decision making – is debatable. And does legislation such as EIA encourage re-exploration of a situation to meet the needs of different stakeholders in practice?

Just how flexible is EIA legislation? Who ensures that there is compliance? If objectives set down by law are not met by a developer or a government agency are they open to negotiation, or does prosecution automatically result? Consider the press release from the European Commission, discussed in Box 20.

> ### Box 20  Environmental impact assessment – how effective?
>
> In June 2003, the European Commission published its five-year report on how member states implement the directive on environmental impact assessment (EIA). The report criticised the member states for failing to fully implement the legislation. It also gave some indications of attitudes to EIAs and how the Commission viewed them. A quote in the Commission's press release
>
>

(EUROPA, 2003) from Environment Commissioner Margot Wallström said 'Environmental Impact Assessments have been a very useful tool for promoting environmental protection, but some project developers still see them, wrongly, as a bureaucratic obstacle. In fact, thorough EIA can simplify their lives by making decisions easier, while ensuring that the Environment is protected. The Directive also enables citizens to voice their concerns and take part in the decision making process'.

Many infringement cases were reported. Spain was identified as the member state with most infringement procedures open at that time, though only Denmark had no current open cases.

According to the press release the report outlined nine shortcomings in the following areas:

- The unsystematic 'screening' of Annex II projects. Annex II of the directive lists the categories of projects that have to undergo an EIA if they are likely to have a significant impact on the environment.

- Wide variation between member states in the criteria for 'screening'. This means that a certain project would be subject to an EIA in one member state but not in another.

- Poor 'scoping'. Scoping is the process of identifying the content of environmental impact studies.

- Insufficient consideration of the cumulative effects of projects.

- Processing of transboundary EIAs requires more formal and informal consultation.

- Poor quality control systems for the EIA process. Setting quality control systems is not an obligation deriving from the directive itself but it is left to the member states.

- Variable levels of EIA activity between member states, i.e. different numbers of EIAs carried out in the member states.

- The inadequate incorporation of EIA results in development decisions.

- Incomplete transposition of directive 97/11.

Interestingly, the Commission was not responding to these shortcomings by amending the directive, at least for the time being. This is partly because an amendment had already been adopted recently for additional obligations regarding public participation and access to justice (in line with the Aarhus Convention – directive 2003/35/EC). Also, the Strategic Environmental Assessment Directive was currently being adopted (see next section). Instead, they planned to tackle the implementation gaps through continuous monitoring and by preparing guidance in consultation with member states, the new member states and stakeholders like NGOs, local and regional authorities and industry. They also planned to carry out targeted research and encourage capacity building programmes.

(Source: EUROPA, 2003)

> ### Activity 41  A European Commission perspective on EIA
>
> (i) Summarise in a few sentences the European Environment Commissioner, Margot Wallström's perspective on EIA according to the press release.
>
> (ii) Which of the shortcomings identified are most relevant to starting off systemically in EIA?

John Alder suggested that the general framework of English law was inadequate to secure the aims of the EIA directive and noted that

> the handful of cases brought by environmentalists against what they considered to be inadequate implementation of the Directive have all been unsuccessful. In particular the courts appear to apply traditional English judicial review principles without taking account of the broader obligation to interpret legislation implementing European policies in the light of those policies.
>
> (Alder, 1993, p. 61)

Alder concluded that 'the framework of English law gives local authorities and central government considerable discretion as to whether to implement the EIA Directive broadly or narrowly'. However, he also admitted that the directive was 'often vague and evasive' so perhaps it is not surprising that there is a range of interpretations. Alder was referring to the 1985 EIA directive. There were hopes then that the 1997 amendments would improve this situation, but the 2003 EC report suggests there are still weaknesses to be addressed. However, both strengths and weaknesses have been identified in the operation of the amended directive (Glasson et al., 2005, pp. 49–50).

Alder suggested that an independent environmental impact assessment panel should be set up to monitor and advise on practice and procedures. He noted that 'The watchwords of the environmental impact assessment panel might be "scoping, screening and participation". As the law stands the UK's environmental impact procedures fail to ensure compliance with these basic techniques'. While the 1997 amendments to the EIA directive, the Aarhus Convention and the growth of strategic environmental assessment may have improved some aspects of EIA since the time when Alder was writing, Glasson et al. (2005) still include scoping and the roles of participants in the EIA process as current issues.

The legal context of EIA therefore has several dimensions that are relevant to this book. There are different degrees of flexibility in the legal frameworks of different countries and in the interpretation of the acts and regulations. Even with laws in place, factors such as the costs of challenging a planning decision and the way in which public interests are represented and monitored mean that legislation in practice can be more supportive of some perspectives being heard and taken into account in decision making than others.

> **SAQ 46   Exploring effects of environmental legislation**
>
>
>
> Write down three ways in which environmental legislation can affect how environmental decision-making situations are explored and problems and opportunities are formulated.

Since EIA was introduced in the 1970s, the technique has evolved and a whole range of other impact assessment techniques have emerged. Sadler (1994) charted its evolution up to 1990.

Table 9   The evolution of environmental assessment (EA)

| Phase and date | Trends and innovations |
| --- | --- |
| 1 Prior to 1970<br>Pre-EIA | Project review based on engineering and economic studies, e.g. cost–benefit analysis; limited consideration of environmental consequences. |
| 2 1970–75<br>Methodological development | EA introduced in some developed countries; initially focused on identifying, predicting and mitigating biophysical effects; opportunity for public involvement in major reviews. |
| 3 1975–80<br>Social dimensions included | Multidimensional EA, incorporating social impact assessment (SIA) and risk analysis; public consultation integral part of development planning and assessment; increased emphasis on issues of justification and alternatives in project review. |
| 4 1980–85<br>Process and procedural redirection | Efforts to integrate project EA with policy planning and follow-up phases; research and development focusing on effects of monitoring, on EA audit and process evaluation and on mediation and dispute resolution approaches; adoption of EA by international aid and lending agencies and by some developing countries. |
| 5 1985–90<br>Sustainability paradigm | Scientific and institutional frameworks for EA begin to be re-thought in response to sustainability ideas and imperatives; search begins for ways to address regional and global environmental changes and cumulative impacts; growing international cooperation on EA research and training. |

(Source: Roe, D. et al. (1995) after Sadler, B. (1994))

Since 1990 many of the trends that Sadler identified have continued. The need to consider assessment of environmental impacts together with economic, social and other dimensions of sustainable development has led to a focus on a more strategic level of operation and increased emphasis on strategic environmental assessment. Integration of EA with other kinds of assessment could perhaps be the title given to the phase from 1990 onwards, but I did not extend Sadler's table in this direction as efforts to integrate were in evidence long ago, and I felt it to be a bit too optimistic given some of the shortcomings of EIA discussed in the last section. Part of the need for integration has come about from proliferation of assessment techniques along with legislation and regulation, leading to, for instance, regulatory impact assessment, which will be discussed in the next section. This proliferation and the response to it is another feature of the past decade that could be seen as part of the evolution of environmental assessment, but again it was already in evidence before that.

The two 'emerging directions' for impact assessment identified by Roe et al. (1995) were strategic environmental assessment and cumulative effects assessment. Both these techniques draw wider boundaries around impact assessment processes than traditional EIA by acknowledging that considering a project or just some of its effects in isolation from its context will give only a partial view of a system. Strategic environmental assessment (SEA) has been introduced into European legislation (SEA Directive 2001/42/EC). Member states started implementing the directive from 2004. It requires a formal environmental assessment of a range of public plans and proposals. It has the potential to take into account cumulative impacts between projects, policies and programmes. Cumulative effects assessment is intended to consider the combined effects of projects and programmes. Examples of cumulative effects given by Roe et al. (1995) include groundwater depletion and linkages between fisheries decline and wetland losses.

### SAQ 47  Evolution of environmental assessment

How has the technique of environmental assessment evolved since the 1970s?

The evolution in EIA techniques reflects attempts to bring environmental, social and economic considerations together. In some ways, it is indicative of the boundaries of the techniques being changed to cope with priority issues that emerge in the course of EIAs. While there is evidence of some learning and adaptation of techniques to cope with increasing recognition of the links between environmental, social and economic issues with the increased international focus on 'sustainable development' (discussed in Book 1), there is still criticism of the way in which this learning is limited.

McCulloch (1996) was critical of the way in which the EA process was often represented:

> In the way it is almost always presented ... the EA process can be characterised as being an important part of project management and as being highly self-contained. Its representation in this way implies three things:
>
> 1 EA is an activity which takes place in relative isolation from its wider social environment
>
> 2 The feedback from the EA process is directed largely toward the project from which it came rather than feeding into the larger environment within which the project is situated and
>
> 3 the inputs to the EA process are threefold (EA-related skills, data and consultation) and the outputs singular (project-related environmental impacts mediated through the appropriate decision makers).
>
> This characterisation of the EA process is problematic in that it unnecessarily focuses our thinking on the internal dynamics of the process rather than upon the wider environment within which the process takes place. This encourages us to neglect the wider possibilities which stem from the fact that the world's societies

[are] having large numbers of EAs undertaken each year and also from having ongoing programmes of monitoring together with the associated data. Put bluntly, we are not encouraged to think of EA as something which can play a role as a societal resource, rather we tend to think of it in very narrow terms.

(McCulloch, 1996, pp. 3–4)

> ### SAQ 48 Considering McCulloch's objection
>
>
>
> Summarise, in fewer than 100 words, McCulloch's main objection to the way in which environmental assessment is characterised.

Many of McCulloch's criticisms are of environmental assessment at the project level and while still valid in some EA practice, some practitioners around the world have moved on to take account of some of these criticisms. Developments in strategic environmental assessment are a case in point.

## 8.3 Strategic environmental assessment

Strategic environmental assessment was defined by Sadler and Verheem (1996) as:

> a systematic process for evaluating the environmental consequences of proposed policy, plan or programme initiatives in order to ensure they are fully included and appropriately addressed at the earliest appropriate stage of decision-making on par with economic and social considerations.

(Sadler and Verheem, 1996)

Mercier and Ahmed (2004) also drew attention to the purpose more recently assigned to SEA by the World Bank:

> A participatory approach for upstreaming environmental and social issues to influence development planning, decision making and implementation processes at strategic level.

(Mercier and Ahmed, 2004)

Bina (2003) observed three key trends in the development of SEA:

1 the shift away from the traditional 'object' of assessment (draft PPPs) towards a more encompassing view of the policy process and its political dimension, with special attention to decision making;

2 the growing focus on the promotion of sustainable development, with the implicit need to combine hard and soft sciences, and to develop dialogical processes; and

3 the reduced emphasis on the positivist dimension of assessment of impacts within the overall SEA process, accompanied by an increased attention to SEA's contribution to, and integration in, the 'formulation' of strategic initiatives.

I am not able to substantiate or dispute Bina's claims here and note Dalal-Clayton and Sadler (2004) comments that 'policy-makers have reservations about the value added by SEA' and that 'impact assessment practitioners, development planners and policy analysts appear to occupy different universes ... and could benefit from sharing experience and lessons'. But I am drawn to Bina's trends because of the special attention to decision making, the focus on dialogical processes and the potential contribution of SEA in the formulation of initiatives. All these focuses are highly relevant to this book. I will therefore go on to explore the links between decision making and SEA a bit later in this section.

Another trend affecting SEA that is relevant to starting off systemically in environmental decision making is the way that some are aligning it with sustainability appraisal, i.e. not just focusing on 'environment'. There is a table that shows this in detail in the *Techniques* book (see Environmental assessment: SEA).

Sean Nicholson in *The Environmentalist* (IEMA's magazine) also explored some of the links between sustainability appraisal and the SEA Directive (2001/42/EC) and explained why he felt the two should be linked:

> Sustainability appraisal (SA) of Regional Planning Guidance is now mandatory and the Government is proposing to make SA mandatory for new Local Development Frameworks. Many recent development plans have been subjected to SA. The draft guide encourages SEA to be undertaken within the context of a broader SA but I think this should be mandatory rather than discretionary. There are four reasons for this:
> 
> - The concept of sustainable development is about achieving 'win–win–win' solutions and to separate out the assessment of environmental impacts from social and economic ones seems a backward step;
> - The SEA Directive requires consideration of impacts on population, health and material assets so there are clear linkages to social and economic considerations that should be dealt with in an integrated way;
> - Paragraph 3.3.9 of the draft guide suggests that inclusion of economic and social considerations could dilute environmental considerations. My experience of SAs that have incorporated a range of objectives is that this is not the case. This comment could encourage authorities to only consider environmental considerations, which would be contrary to sustainable development; and
> - The draft guide recommends an objectives-led approach to SEA which fits well with the existing approach to SA.
>
> (Nicholson, 2003, pp. 16–18)

## Activity 42 Starting off in SEA and sustainability appraisal

Look at Table 4 (entitled 'Stages, decisions and outputs of SEA and sustainability appraisal') in the Environmental assessment: SEA section of the *Techniques* book. How do the processes of SEA and sustainability appraisal appear to start off? What potential does there appear to be for starting off systemically?

Having considered how SEA legislation has come about and how it is used in parallel to other legislation and techniques, I now want to return to its role in decision making.

## Reading 10

Read 'Decision making and strategic environmental assessment' by Mins Nilsson and Holger Dalkmann and answer the following SAQ.

### Study note

This is quite a long reading and to some extent repeats material that you have already come across but it focuses it in a different way, raising questions about SEA, and in my view this reading has the potential to help you consolidate some of your learning in the course so far. There are, for instance, links that can be made between this reading and some of the ideas about limited rationality in decision making discussed in Book 1. Use your learning journal to build on your previous notes about decision making rather than repeating them. You will probably not have time to go into all the material included in the paper in depth, so use the SAQ to focus on what is required here and make notes of any concepts you do not understand or any other points that you find insightful so you can more easily return to this reading later in the course if you wish.

> ### SAQ 49 Decision making and strategic environmental assessment
>
>
>
> (i) What, in the authors' view, does environmental assessment provide for decision makers?
>
> (ii) Summarise the critiques of rationalism referred to by the authors.
>
> (iii) What are incremental models and why were they developed?
>
> (iv) What is the difference between impact-driven and decision-driven approaches to SEA, according to the authors?
>
> (v) Why, in the authors' view, does SEA often seem to fail in influencing real decisions?
>
> (vi) What steps do the authors identify in their description of a strategic decision-making process based on 20 case studies in a published EU-funded project?
>
> (vii) Do the authors indicate which steps are to be used in starting off in decision making? If so make a note of which these are.
>
> (viii) Summarise the authors' conclusions.

## 8.4 Regulatory impact assessment

Regulatory impact assessment (RIA) is intended to assess the effects of any proposed new regulation and evaluation of existing regulation, mainly as a systematic appraisal of costs and benefits. Regulation means rules and is a form of secondary legislation that deals with how primary legislation is implemented. The detail of implementation of RIA are not entirely relevant to the first two stages of the T863 framework but the assumptions and thinking behind the approach, and the way in which those affected by the proposal are given opportunity to comment, certainly are.

The UK Government introduced RIAs in 1998 based on previous experience with cost compliance assessments and the Organization for Economic Co-operation and Development (OECD)'s work on impact analysis. These RIAs have not just applied to environmental regulations but RIAs have been used, for instance, with the Department of Environment, Food and Rural Affairs' (DEFRA) Waste Strategy 2000 and the UK's Sustainable Development Strategy 2005.

The overall intent behind RIA is for 'better regulation' but what does that mean? Better from whose perspective and in what terms? Colin Kirkpatrick and David Parker considered this in an editorial they wrote for an issue of *Public Money and Management* in October 2004. (See Box 21.)

### Box 21 Regulatory impact assessment – an overview

*by Colin Kirkpatrick and David Parker*

While the role of an effective regulatory regime has always been of concern to public sector researchers and policy-makers, the particular meaning attached to 'better regulation' and its translation into public policy have shifted over time. The importance of good regulation has come to forefront today because of the rise of the 'regulatory state' (Majone, 1994, 1997), in which governments are said to 'steer' rather than 'row' (Osborne and Gaebler, 1992).

State regulation that promotes economic and social welfare needs to be both *effective* and *efficient*. Effective in the sense of achieving its planned goals, and efficient in the sense of achieving these goals at least cost, in terms of government administration costs and the costs imposed on the economy in terms of complying with regulations. There is, therefore, a compelling case for the systematic appraisal of the positive and negative impacts of any proposed or actual regulatory change. The purpose of *regulatory impact assessment* (alternatively referred to as *regulatory impact analysis*) is to 'explain the objectives of the [regulatory] proposal, the risks to be addressed and the options for delivering the objectives. In doing so it should make transparent the expected costs and benefits of the options for the different bodies involved, such as other parts of Government and small businesses, and how compliance with regulatory options would be secured and enforced' (NAO, 2002, p. 51). The appraisal should encompass the likely economic, environmental, social and distributional consequences of a regulatory measure, thereby providing a comprehensive analysis of its impact.

The underlying rationale for regulatory impact assessment (RIA) is that regulations need to be assessed on a case-by-case basis, to see whether they contribute to strategic policy goals. It has the potential to strengthen regulation efficiency and effectiveness by examining the possible impacts arising from

> planned government actions and communicating this information to decision-makers in a way that allows them to consider (ideally) the full range of positive and negative effects (benefits and costs) that are associated with a proposed regulatory change. This is known as *ex ante* RIA. Equally, RIA has the potential to improve the monitoring of *existing* regulatory policies—called *ex post* RIA (SIGMA, 2001). This might lead to revisions to an existing regulation to improve its performance or even the outright cancellation of a regulation.
>
> (Source: Kirkpatrick and Parker, 2004, p. 267)

### SAQ 50  The purpose of RIA

In Kirkpatrick and Parker's view, what is the purpose of regulatory impact assessment?

Some insights into what constitutes an effective RIA come from a paper by Ed Humpherson concerning the UK National Audit Office's evaluation of RIAs in 2003.

> The NAO found that it is the process of preparing the RIA and consulting those likely to be affected that adds value. ... RIAs that added value tended to be characterised by:
>
> - *Starting at a sufficiently early stage*. RIAs are more likely to add value if they are prepared while policy-makers are still considering options for achieving their policy objectives, so that the analysis in the RIA informs the design and choice of the options. Those being consulted are more likely to respond constructively if they feel that their comments will have an impact on the development of policy. For this to happen, consultation needs to start very early in the process.
>
> - *Consulting effectively with those affected by the proposal*. Although knowledgeable in their field, policy-makers do not always have practical experience of applying regulation. To ensure that proposals are workable, and have minimal side-effects, policy-makers need to draw on the experience of others during policy design. Persuading businesses and other interested parties to comment on the likely impact of something that could happen in the future is a challenge. The judicious use of face-to-face and group methods may add value to paper-based approaches to consultation. ...
>
> - *Analysing appropriately the likely costs and benefits of the proposal*. A key purpose of the RIA process is to help examine whether the benefits justify the costs. Comparing costs with benefits of policy options can add value.
>
> (Humpherson, 2004, p. 278)

> **Activity 43 Effective RIA – a systemic and systematic approach?**
>
> What aspects of the features identified by the National Audit Office would you interpret as part of a systemic or systematic approach, and why?

Given the considerable growth in regulations and legislation over the past two decades, their evaluation has become important. Which and whose data is used for that evaluation, and how it is used, are questions to keep in mind if considering whether environmental decision making has started or could start systemically. In the UK case of aviation expansion, discussed in Book 1, the Department for Transport undertook an RIA basing most of the analysis on data produced by the various national and regional studies.

### Study note

If you would find it useful to look at an example of an RIA, at time of writing there were many examples linked to aviation issues, including the Aviation White Paper mentioned in the Book 1 case study, available online on the UK Department for Transport's web pages concerning aviation: http://www.dft.gov.uk/stellent/groups/dft_aviation/documents/sectionhomepage/dft_aviation_page.hcsp.

## 8.5 Environmental management systems standards: ISO 14001 and EMAS

### 8.5.1 Background

'Standards' for environmental management systems (EMSs) began to emerge in the late 1980s and early 1990s in the context of the Uruguay round of the international GATT (General Agreement on Tariffs and Trade) negotiations, which concentrated on the need to reduce non-tariff barriers to trade, and the Rio Earth Summit on Environment and Development (UNCED) held in 1992 (discussed in Book 1). EMSs have evolved in parallel to environmental legislation following and/or linking with traditions such as standards for quality systems and health and safety. EMS standards may be used formally, in which case an organisation seeks a certificate for a standard and must demonstrate to an accredited external auditor that it meets requirements which are set down in a written standard. Alternatively, as Martin Baxter pointed out in his abstract in Section 7.3, they can be developed informally and certification is not sought.

Some examples of the principles behind environmental management systems (EMSs) are shown in Table 10, mostly suggested by Nigel Riglar, when he was with the UK's Local Government Management Board.

Table 10  Examples of the principles behind environmental management systems

Voluntary

Self-regulating

Polluter pays principle

Market instrument

Business- or site-based (industry)/administrative unit-based (local government)

Focuses on direct process effects (industry)/indirect service delivery or product effects (local government)

Promotes continual improvements in environmental performance

Source: Riglar, Personal communication

The principle of continual improvement in environmental performance is particularly important as it is at the core of EMSs. In 2004, when ISO 14001 was revised, there was an additional emphasis that the process of continual improvement must be a recurring one.

The 'polluter pays' principle is exemplified in EMS standards by the way in which organisations that pollute (or could pollute) their environment pay for external independent validation of their EMS. The market instrument principle is clearly defined as such in the EU's fifth Programme of Policy and Action – Towards Sustainability.

In systems terms, an EMS describes a set of components and processes that are interconnected for the purpose of managing natural resources and human activities to minimise negative and maximise positive environmental effects. There is often a range of different perspectives on what is inside and outside an EMS boundary and what its purpose is (there might also be different views on what constitute 'negative' and 'positive' environmental effects). In addition, there are various interpretations of how an EMS works in practice. Several standards and schemes have been devised to guide those involved in environmental management on what should be included within an EMS and how its objectives can be achieved.

Two initiatives will be considered in some detail in this section, namely EMAS and ISO 14001. The two schemes evolved at different international levels (European and worldwide) but have been brought together.

EMAS is the European Commission's Eco-Management and Audit Scheme and is a voluntary regulation that came into operation in April 1995 in all member states of the EU. It was initially for industry, but was adapted at that time for use in local government. EMAS has since been revised and relaunched as EMAS2 in 2001 when its scope was broadened.

ISO 14001 'Environmental management systems – specifications with guidance for use' is the international standard for EMSs. (It is part of a series of voluntary environmental standards and guidelines, known as the ISO 14000 series.) Its European code became EN ISO 14001 when it was adopted by the European standards body (CEN) as a European standard and its British code became BS EN ISO 14001 when the standard was published in the UK in 1996. General guidelines on the principles, systems and supporting techniques have also been provided in a separate standard, ISO 14004. Revised editions of ISO 14001 and ISO 14004 were published in 2004 (BSI, 2004).

I will look at what is involved in meeting the requirements of EMAS and ISO 14001 and how these initiatives can be used for environmental decision making later in this section.

Firstly, let's consider what EMAS and ISO 14001 aim to achieve, how they came about – in particular their links with quality systems – and the extent to which they have been taken up.

While ISO 14001 is described as a 'standard', which implies a level to be attained, and EMAS as a 'regulation', which implies rules that must be obeyed, they fulfil very similar functions. These are to improve the quality of environmental management and to help organisations to gain public recognition and/or competitive advantage from these improvements. They are both 'voluntary', in that organisations can choose whether or not to try to reach the standard or to comply with the regulation. The procedures that must be followed if an organisation wants to achieve either EMAS or ISO 14001 are required rather than voluntary but ISO 14001 allows self-certification as well as certification by a third party. Since 2001, ISO 14001 and EMAS have become more integrated. The new EMAS2 scheme adopted ISO 14001 as its environmental management system core. EMAS has additional requirements over ISO 14001, including mandatory public reporting of environmental performance. With the revisions to EMAS, there is increased compatibility between the two schemes and there is potential for straightforward progression from ISO 14001 to EMAS2.

In the UK, EMAS and ISO 14001 replaced BS 7750, the UK standard for environmental management systems which was developed by the British Standards Institution initially in 1992 and revised in 1994. BS 7750 is important in a historical context as it preceded and contributed a great deal to the other standards. Another initiative from BSI in 2003 was the development of a new British standard from the ACORN project – BS8555 – which leads to more gradual implementation of ISO 14001 and ISO 14031 and which they describe as 'A phased approach to environmental management'. This standard has been designed to meet the needs of small and medium-sized businesses, particularly those where external certification is necessary to demonstrate effective environmental management to stakeholders, especially suppliers.

The development of standards for environmental management has grown considerably in recent years. According to the International Organization for Standardization there were 90,569 ISO 14001 certificates at the end of 2004, an increase of 37% over the previous year (ISO, 2005). Numbers for EMAS are lower as more is required and now that ISO 14001 has become integrated within EMAS there is overlap between the numbers of certificates for EMAS and ISO 14001. The ISO 14000 family of standards and guidelines for environmental management extends beyond ISO 14001 to include, for example, standards for auditing, labelling, environmental performance evaluation, life-cycle assessment, life-cycle impact assessment and integrating environmental aspects into product design and development. Further standards include those for environmental communication and greenhouse gas quantification, monitoring and reporting on emissions and removals. To comply with the standards, organisations must demonstrate that they have followed certain stages in developing their environmental policy and practice and attained a certain level of achievement.

Recognition of the need for high standards in management practices goes much further than environmental management practices. For example, there are management system principles that are common to both the international quality systems standards (the ISO 9000 series) and the international environmental management standards (the ISO 14000 series) and the two standards have been brought into closer alignment as they have developed. Parallels between the 'quality' and 'environmental' standards extend to areas such as auditing which are also relevant to other stages of the T863 decision-making framework considered in subsequent books. A joint ISO 9000 and ISO 14000 audit standard – ISO 19011 – replaced existing auditing standards in the ISO 9000 and ISO 14000 series in 2002. To some extent the environmental management standards have been modelled on quality standards, and the correspondence between ISO 9001 quality management systems and ISO 14001 is explained in some detail in Annex B of the published standard ISO 14001 (2004).

However, whereas the claimed aim of quality management systems such as ISO 9001 is to maintain the quality of a product to deliver a customer specification, an environmental management system has a very different primary objective, that of continual improvement in environmental performance. In systems terms, this implies that they are different systems of interest, with different combinations of components and processes, different purposes and different boundaries. The example of the ISO standards (ISO 9001 and ISO 14001) helps to draw out the differences as well as the similarities between them. While a course of action might sometimes meet the primary objectives of both systems, there will be times when they are in conflict.

Many activities that, say, save energy, reduce waste and prevent pollution have both economic and environmental benefits. However, if an organisation's primary outputs are products that have largely negative environmental effects, such as planes or powerful cars that use large amounts of fossil fuels, it remains to be seen how those organisations will make trade-offs in the long run between environmental and economic considerations as discussed in Part 1 in relation to the aviation case study. The objectives of quality and environmental management systems will not necessarily be fully complementary.

### SAQ 51 Comparing EMSs and quality systems

What is the major difference between the primary objectives of environmental management systems and quality systems such as ISO 9001?

EMS standards continue to evolve. It is important to be aware of this evolution of these initiatives in your environmental decision making. If you want to use the standards in your work, detailed operational guidelines, guides and training materials can be obtained for the standards from the national and international standards bodies. Further details are available on websites such as:

- the European Commission's EMAS helpdesk at http://www.europa.eu.int/comm/environment/emas/
- the UK EMAS website at http://www.emas.org.uk/

- ISO's management systems website at http://www.iso.org/iso/en/iso9000-14000/index.html – which gives details of both the ISO 14000 and the ISO 9000 series.

There is a range of perspectives on how the standards work in practice and it is worth keeping in mind that an organisation wanting to improve environmental performance but less concerned about obtaining a certificate can develop an EMS without going for one of the standards. While ISO 14001 and EMAS have both become very popular, there is a range of issues that has arisen in their use. The following is a selection of 'news' headlines from the *ENDS Report* regarding some of their issues:

> **March 2005 Maintaining momentum on EMSs.** The number of firms boasting ISO 14001 certificates to testify that they have a sound environmental management system (EMS) continues to spiral. Once on the conveyor belt, however – for whatever reason – companies have to maintain their certificates or lose face. (*ENDS Report* 362, 2005, pp. 34–5)
>
> **December 2003 UKAS 'We let EMS standards slide'** The UK's governing body for the certification of environmental management systems has fired a shot across practitioners' bows for letting standards slip. The UK Accreditation Service accepts some of the blame for the loss of credibility in certification and is pledging to do what it takes to meet stakeholders' expectations. (*ENDS Report*, 2003, pp. 3–4)
>
> **December 2003 EMS survey reveals widespread concerns over certification.** An opinion survey conducted by ENDS and the Institute of Environmental Management and Assessment has revealed significant concerns about the effectiveness of environmental management systems and the quality of their certification. (*ENDS Report*, 2003, pp. 19–21)
>
> **May 2005 ISO 14001 certification bodies complain of unfair competition...** being undercut by competitors who are not recognised by the official UK Accreditation Service (UKAS) or any affiliated body. (*ENDS Report* 364, 2005, pp. 3–5)
>
> **April 2005 Certified EMSs boost export potential.** Having a certified environmental management system boosts a company's chance of winning export contracts, a study by researchers in Israel suggests. Firms in EU countries were more likely to favour suppliers with ISO 14001 certificates. Japanese and US firms tended to balance these with economic considerations. (*ENDS Report* 363, 2005, pp. 34–5)

## 8.5.2 EMS standards and environmental decision making

EMSs support environmental decision making by providing a structured approach for organisations to consider, develop and review environmental policies, programmes and management systems.

I will now consider the requirements and principles of ISO 14001 and EMAS with a view to finding out what they contribute to the first two stages of our environmental decision-making framework that are the subject of this book, i.e. how much they can encourage or discourage exploration of the environmental decision-making situation, before problems and opportunities and systems of interest are formulated.

### ISO 14001

Take a few minutes to look closely at (i) the notes on ISO 14001 in Box 22, (ii) Figure 44, the diagram for ISO 14001 (which also appears as Figure 27 in the *Techniques* book), and (iii) Box 23 which describes the kind of methodology ISO 14001 is based on.

Note that EMAS2 renumbered its clauses to mirror ISO 14001.

> **Box 22   ISO 14001 – environmental management system requirements** *(clause numbers and headings extracted from BS EN ISO 14001: 2004)*
>
> 4   Environmental management system requirements
>   4.1  General requirements
>   4.2  Environmental policy
>   4.3  Planning
>     4.3.1  Environmental aspects
>     4.3.2  Legal and other requirements
>     4.3.3  Objectives, targets and programme(s)
>   4.4  Implementation and operation
>     4.4.1  Resources, roles, responsibility and authority
>     4.4.2  Competence, training and awareness
>     4.4.3  Communication
>     4.4.4  Documentation
>     4.4.5  Control of documents
>     4.4.6  Operational control
>     4.4.7  Emergency preparedness and response
>   4.5  Checking
>     4.5.1  Monitoring and measurement
>     4.5.2  Evaluation of compliance
>     4.5.3  Nonconformity, corrective action and preventive action
>     4.5.4  Control of records
>     4.5.5  Internal audit
>   4.6  Management review
>
> The ISO 14001 EMS model and the ongoing process of continual improvement are shown in Figure 44.
>
> (Source: BSI, 2004, pp. 4–9)

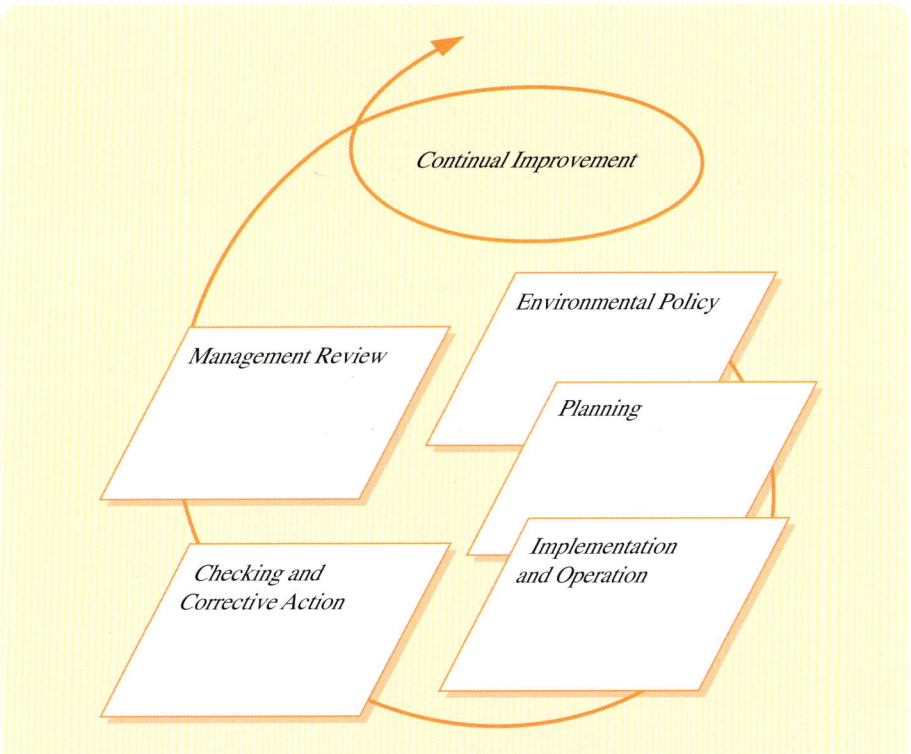

Figure 44  EMS model for ISO 14001 (Source: BSI BSEN ISO 14001, 2004, p. vi)

### Box 23  Plan–do–check–act methodology

This international standard is based on the methodology known as plan–do–check–act (PDCA). PDCA can be briefly described as follows:

**Plan:** establish the objectives and processes necessary to deliver results in accordance with the organisation's environmental policy

**Do:** implement the process

**Check:** monitor and measure processes against environmental policy, objectives, targets, legal and other requirements, and report the results.

**Act:** take actions to continually improve performance of the environmental management system.

Many organisations manage their operations via the application of a system of processes and their interactions, which can be referred to as a process approach. ISO 9001: 2000 promotes the use of the process approach. Since PDCA can be applied to all processes, the two methodologies are considered to be compatible.

(Source: BSI, 2004, p. vi)

### EMAS

Now consider a representation of EMAS in Figure 45. Note the way that ISO 14001 is identified as the integral environmental management system linked to market and stakeholder needs by performance and environmental reporting for credibility.

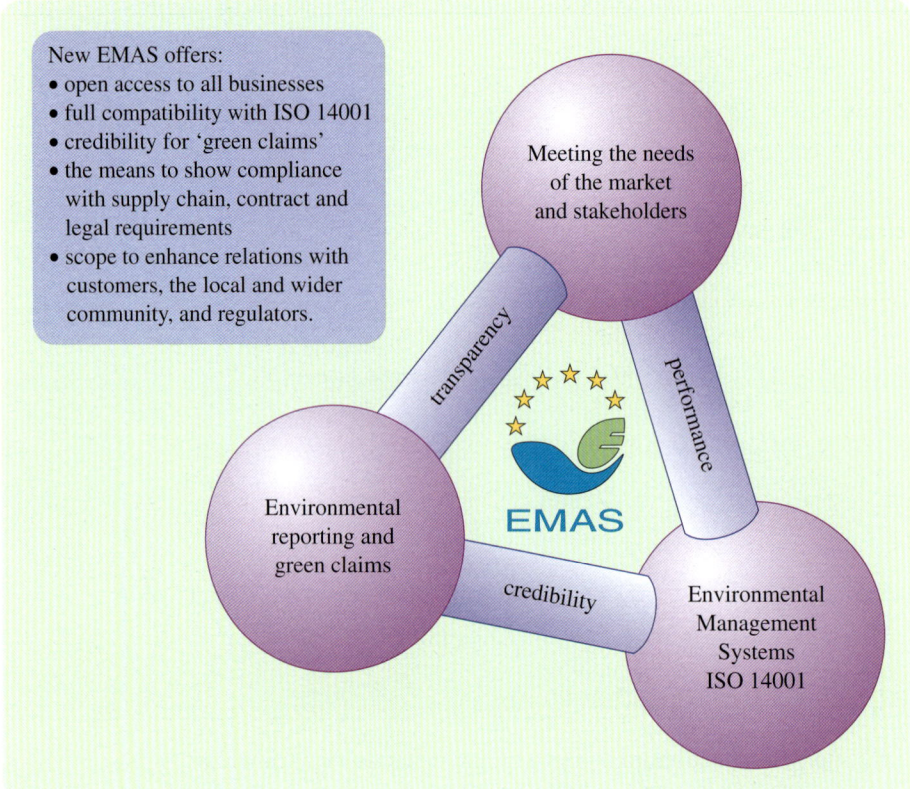

Figure 45  A representation of 'new' EMAS (Source: EMAS website and *Environment Business Magazine*, 68, September 2001, p. 23)

### Activity 44  Starting off in ISO 14001 and EMAS

(i) Using your experience of studying Book 2 so far, how do you think the ISO 14001 process could start off to enhance systemic awareness among stakeholders?

(ii) What may EMAS add to ISO 14001 in terms of encouraging the environmental management systems process to start off systemically?

### Activity 45  Different interpretations of phrases in ISO 14001 and EMAS

Consider Figures 44 and 45, and the notes in Boxes 22 and 23. Identify up to six phrases, words or symbols used that might be open to different interpretations.

Most of the terms for both EMAS and ISO 14001 are explained in more detail in the standards' guidelines, but there is still scope for different interpretations. This is important in considering whether there is scope for a systemic approach to environmental decision making with the emergence of problems and opportunities and the involvement of stakeholders. A term such as 'review' or 'audit', for instance, could imply a systemic or purely systematic approach, or both. The way in which the initiatives are assessed will probably have considerable influence on how they are interpreted. However, the motivations and thinking of those applying for the standards do vary and will also affect interpretation. To see how the standards are used in environmental decision making, it is necessary to look not just at what is written but at what happens in practice.

Often an initial environmental review or developing an environmental policy is the starting point of an EMS for an organisation. It is the stage at which the organisation considers its overall environmental aims and commitments to continuous improvement. Individuals involved in the process may join in at several different stages. The diagrams alone do not explain whether or not an environmental policy that meets EMAS's two main requirements (compliance with environmental regulations and commitment to continual improvement) is devised systemically. For it to be a systemic approach it would need a range of stakeholders, probably mainly from within the organisation, to work out which environmental issues are relevant to them and what they want or need to do about them. In other words, they would work out their shared system of interest together. A systemic approach also needs the people involved to consider the whole system of interest rather than the parts and to concentrate on basic principles of organisation rather than on the building blocks. In terms of an EMS this might, for instance, mean considering the links between services provided by the unit considered rather than individual services in isolation.

### Activity 46    Identifying more scope for exploring and formulating

Identify other stages in ISO 14001 and EMAS besides the environmental policy and review stages where there is scope for exploring or re-exploring situations before formulating problems, opportunities and systems of interest.

There is certainly evidence of the involvement of a range of stakeholders in some EMS projects. As you work through the following reading look for indications of achieving EMAS process and the way stakeholders worked together as well as the outcomes and achievements.

### Reading 11

Read the case study of achieving EMAS from Kirklees Metropolitan Council.

## Activity 47 EMAS and Kirklees Metropolitan Council

(i) What technique was used by Kirklees Metropolitan Council to reflect on what they had learnt? Where else in T863 have you come across this technique?

(ii) Seek out in the reading all comments made on how the project started out. Do these comments give any indications of whether or how situations were explored or re-explored or how problems, opportunities and systems of interest were formulated? If so, describe some of them.

(iii) What evidence is there in the case study of systems thinking, evaluating, negotiating and modelling? Identify an example of each if you can, and in each instance consider whether this applied in the early stages of decision making or later on.

(iv) In doing this activity, what questions occurred to you that are not explained in the report? Which stakeholders would you like to address these questions to if given a chance?

### 8.5.3 Environmental reporting

Here is an example of environmental reporting under EMAS. It comes from the London Borough of Sutton in the UK. (This foreword gives an overview. Further or different extracts may be taken from the full document to show how it works in practice. The full document could be found (at the time of writing, January 2006) under 'articles' on IEMA's reading room website: http://www.iema.net/readingroom/show/614/c190).

### Box 24 London Borough of Sutton Annual Environmental Statement, 2003/04

**Foreword**

**Councillor Colin Hall, Lead Councillor for Environment**

Welcome to Sutton's Annual Environmental Statement.

We live in a world where environmental issues are swiftly becoming one of our foremost concerns. As over-consumption of the earth's resources continues at an alarming rate, local environmental problems are contributing to regional and global issues. Unlike just a few years ago, environmental concerns have become mainstream news. Newspapers and television frequently feature articles on climate change, the amount of consumer waste produced and the loss of bio-diversity. These issues inevitably affect every society and every individual; our legacy will also affect future generations. So we need to act and act now.

Sutton is committed to protecting and improving the local environment and helping our community play its part in seeking solutions to local, regional and global environmental issues.

- On a local level Sutton Council is addressing its direct and indirect impacts on the environment. This Environmental Statement details the actions we are taking to reduce our impact. Examples include reducing use of fuel by making council homes and buildings more energy efficient, reducing our use of natural resources and creating planning policies to ensure development has less environmental impact.
- Regionally Sutton is involved in European projects to protect plant and animal species, by preserving and improving local habitats and by developing tools to help businesses and other authorities purchase goods in an environmentally responsible manner.
- Our community is also playing its part in tackling global warming by making their homes more energy efficient and recycling waste.

EMAS (Eco-Management and Audit Scheme) is an externally accredited management system that Sutton uses to manage its environmental impacts. It is a European standard and we are audited every 6 months to ensure our operations comply with these standards. EMAS ensures environmental considerations are represented in policymaking and service provision and that we set targets for continuous environmental improvement.

This statement is produced so the residents and other stakeholders can be informed of the environmental performance of their council. It is an update to the 2001 Environmental Statement and reports on the period April 2003 – March 2004. We welcome your comments and feedback on our environmental performance and this Statement.

This is an exciting time. We are currently consulting the public on our Community Strategy (see the Council Website) which seeks to improve quality of life for now and for the future. Environmental targets sit alongside those for economic and social well-being. I am pleased to launch this update of our Environmental Statement at a time when all our partners are looking at environmental issues as an essential element of our quality of life.

Colin Hall

(Source: London Borough of Sutton Environmental Statement, 2003/04, p. 1, IEMA reading room website)

### SAQ 52 London Borough of Sutton – environmental reporting

What do you understand to be the purpose of the London Borough of Sutton's environmental statement?

> ### Activity 48 Framing a situation and practices through an environmental statement
>
> Write down three points you have noticed in reading this statement in answer to the following questions.
>
> How do you think this environmental statement frames:
> (i) the situation in the London Borough of Sutton?
> (ii) the practices of stakeholders in this situation?

So, what are some of the issues of environmental reporting as part of environmental management systems? How useful is environmental reporting in exploring situations and formulating systems of interest? Don't try to answer these questions yet. We will return to them at the end of the next section.

## 8.6 Corporate social (and environmental) responsibility

Other kinds of reporting have surfaced in recent years besides environmental reporting. Corporate social, and sometimes environmental, responsibility reporting is another example.

Wikipedia defines corporate social responsibility (CSR) as:

> an expression used to describe what some see as a company's obligation to be sensitive to the needs of **all** of its stakeholders in its business operations. The principle is closely linked with the imperative of ensuring that these operations are 'sustainable' i.e. that it is recognised that it is necessary to take account not only of the financial/economic dimension in decision making [but] also the social and environmental consequences.
>
> (http://en.wikipedia.org/wiki/Corporate_social_responsibility)

### Study note

*Wikipedia is a useful source of information on many subjects. However, you should bear in mind that the information there is not refereed and is subject to change. There are many other sources of information. For more information, go to http://en.wikipedia.org/wiki/Wikipedia:Researching_with_Wikipedia.*

CSR will be considered in Book 4 in relation to the whole T863 framework. At this stage of the course, I am concerned mainly with its role in exploring or re-exploring situations or in formulating problems, opportunities and systems of interest so, as you read through the following two examples and a reading which is a dialogue about CSR, keep this in mind.

The following is an extract from the Corporate Social Responsibility Report for Taylor Woodrow, a housing and development company working across the UK and in selected markets in North America, Spain and Gibraltar.

## Box 25   Corporate Social Responsibility Report – Taylor Woodrow

### Introduction

*The development and construction industry has a direct impact on society, the natural and built environment and upon the many stakeholders with whom it interacts.*

Taylor Woodrow recognises the increasingly important role that social and environmental issues play in the continued success of our business and we have responded by continuing to develop our Corporate Social Responsibility (CSR) Strategy.

CSR matters to Taylor Woodrow because:
- many of our stakeholders have an interest in the broader performance of the company, not just in our financial performance;
- there are legislative, fiscal, customer, investment community and societal drivers encouraging adoption of a positive CSR agenda; and
- good performance on CSR will benefit the company, wider society and the environment.

Enhancing shareholder value is our primary objective as a commercial organisation and hence the investment community is a key stakeholder group for Taylor Woodrow. Parts of the investment community are increasingly seeking engagement with us on CSR issues. We welcome this engagement and seek to respond positively in our communications with investors. One particular example of this was the interaction with Insight Investment, the investment arm of HBOS. Their survey of sustainability in the UK housebuilding sector, carried out in conjunction with WWF, was published in January 2004. Taylor Woodrow performed well, scoring nearly 70%, and we were ranked third of 13 publicly listed UK development companies.

Taylor Woodrow also recognises that by demonstrating good and continually improving CSR performance, we will enhance our credentials with ethical investors and with indices such as the Dow Jones Sustainability Index.

Sustainability is a key feature of Government policy in the UK and also within the European Union. Whilst the development industry in both Europe and North America is already heavily regulated through the planning system and through building regulations, we recognise that regulatory pressures will continue to grow.

Taxation is also an important vehicle for Government to influence corporate behaviours, for example through the Climate Change Levy, Aggregates Tax and Landfill Tax, and enhanced tax allowance schemes for use of specified environmentally friendly products. Taylor Woodrow participates in two-way communication with Government to further the understanding and implementation of sustainable development.

> A number of NGOs (non-governmental organisations) are very active in promoting CSR issues in our sector. WWF is one notable example through its One Million Sustainable Homes initiative.
>
> Employees and supply chain partners are important stakeholder groups. We engage our employees in CSR in a number of ways, one of which is the CSR Improvement Group process and this is detailed later in the report. We have been progressing our communication with supply chain partners by various means including the development of partnering agreements.
>
> CSR issues material to Taylor Woodrow's activities are summarised as:
>
> - sustainable development – long-term impacts arising from the communities that we help to develop, including energy efficiency of dwellings, transport, social inclusion, redevelopment of brownfield land and local economic benefits; and
> - direct impacts arising from how we do things – health and safety, environmental and community issues during construction, employee and supply chain aspects.
>
> This report summarises our approach to CSR and the progress we have made in the past year. It is organised into three main sections:
>
> **What we do;**
>
> **How we do it;** and
>
> **How we are performing.**
>
> In developing our CSR programmes we also take advice from consultants who provide us with an external perspective.
>
> We trust that the report will be of value to:
>
> - stakeholders with whom we already have significant dialogue on CSR issues: the investment community, Government, NGOs, business-to-business customers, planning authorities, supply chain partners and our employees; and
> - other stakeholders, such as customers, who may have an interest in the wider activities of Taylor Woodrow.
>
> (Source: Taylor Woodrow Corporate Social Responsibility Report, 2003)

The next example is related to the T863 aviation case study, as it is presented by BAA, one of the stakeholders in aviation expansion. It is a summary report and there is also a full report available online through the BAA website (http://www.baa.com accessed 9 March 2006). The full report includes statements on many more aspects of the company's policy and practice.

## Box 26 Corporate Responsibility – Doing the Right Thing

### What Corporate Responsibility Means to BAA

BAA's approach to corporate responsibility is guided by our well-established policies on sustainable development and ethics. In 2003, we published a sustainable development policy, based on input from a range of stakeholders, including investors and community groups. On 7 March 2005, the Government published *Securing the Future*, its new strategy for sustainable development. We will be reviewing our sustainable development policy in light of this new strategy, and will publish our revised policy on our website www.baa.com/corporateresponsibility

...

BAA has a clear process of accountability to ensure its policies and strategies are delivered throughout the organisation. Strategies, goals and measures of corporate responsibility are embedded at every level of the Company's core management processes. Both the Board and Executive Committee are actively involved in how we manage corporate responsibility. ... [Below is] an overview of the key issues affecting our business and related performance indicators. These are not dealt with in any particular order of priority. For a more in-depth look at our progress please refer to our website.

### Our People

Our goal is to be the employer of choice wherever we operate. To achieve this we are committed to offering opportunities to all our staff based on merit. We aim to provide learning and development opportunities, varied career paths, equality in a workplace free from bullying and harassment, fair reward and recognition for work, and a range of benefits designed to recruit and retain the best people for our business.

...

Our pension scheme has 8,858 active members and 6,330 pensioners. Under Financial Reporting Standard 17 a pension scheme deficit, net of deferred tax, of £138 million is included in BAA's net assets at 31 March 2005 (2004: £111 million). BAA contributed 14% of pensionable pay per annum to the pension scheme from 1 April 2004. This was equivalent to £34 million in 2004/05. From 1 April 2005, the level of contribution has increased to 17%, equivalent to £43 million for 2005/06.

...

### Health, Safety and Security

We place paramount importance on achieving the highest standards of health, safety and security in the workplace. BAA continued to ensure that our airports remain safe working environments for travellers, staff and business partners. Health and safety remains the responsibility of our Board and Executive Committee members.

...

### Our Environment Climate Change

Aviation is a relatively small but growing contributor to climate change. We believe aviation's greenhouse gas emissions will respond most effectively to market mechanisms, and that emissions trading represents a smarter way to address the industry's climate impacts than crude taxes, which will raise Government revenues without making any direct impact on emissions. And we recognise that a global solution will take time, and fully support the UK Government's commitment to regional action on aviation's emissions at a European level as an interim step.

...

BAA has established an absolute $CO_2$ emissions reductions target of 15% below 1990 levels by 2010, despite a projected growth in passenger numbers of around 70% during this period, and have put a comprehensive strategy in place to help us achieve it. In fact, over the past three years, BAA's $CO_2$ growth has been virtually zero, despite passenger growth of 8.3 million and the introduction of new facilities

...

### Noise

Aircraft noise is one of the most sensitive local community issues. BAA continued to work with airlines, government agencies and local groups to seek reductions in aircraft noise at source, by bringing quieter engines and aircraft into operation, and by improving compliance with quieter operating practices. We are also working to improve our communication about noise impacts and, through research, to understand better the effects of noise on people and communities.

...

### Waste

All airports exceeded their 20% recycling target in 2004/05 – a further step towards our long-term goal to recycle 40% of waste by 2010. In the previous year recycling initiatives focused on our tenanted areas only, but during this year, they were extended to include third parties such as retailers, airlines and property tenants.

...

### Our Communities

BAA is committed to gaining and maintaining the trust of the communities around our airports. This year we launched a new community relations strategy which targets our resources on issues of greatest concern to them. As a result, over the past 12 months, BAA's airports have supported a wide-range of community activities

...

### BAA Communities Trust

BAA's own charity, the BAA Communities Trust, supports projects which are brought forward by staff. Although these projects are local to our airports they have an international element. They reflect our commitment to the local community and also to our links across the world. BAA is the main source of income for the charity, donating 0.15% of pre-tax profits, excluding exceptional items, to the charity, amounting to £955,500 for 2004/05.

...

### Best Practice and Benchmarking

BAA enters the key corporate responsibility indices to benchmark its performance and to ensure best practice.

In 2004/05, we were highly-ranked within a number of corporate responsibility league tables, in many cases improving our scores compared to the previous year. BAA was in the top quartile in *The Guardian*'s Giving List, and sixth in the Global Reporters Survey. In BiTC's Corporate Responsibility Index, BAA topped the transport sector and moved 21 places up the overall rankings to joint fifth. In BiTC's Business in the Environment Index, we scored 95%, once again placing us in the 'Premier League' of corporate performers.

BAA again featured in the PerCent Standard, a voluntary benchmark that measures contributions by companies through cash donations, staff time, gifts in kind and management time, as a percentage of pre-tax profits. In 2003/04, BAA contributed £5.7 million or 1.1% of pre-tax profits to community investment.

(Source: BAA Annual Review, 2004/05, p. 11)

### SAQ 53  Why does CSR matter?

(i) Why do Taylor Woodrow and BAA think corporate social responsibility matters to them?

(ii) Who do Taylor Woodrow and BAA think their report will be of value to, and how may this relate to the early stages of environmental decision making?

## Reading 12

Read the 'corporate social responsibility' debate between Tom Burke and Joel Bakan.

### Study note

Be sure to read this debate critically – e.g. do you think these two debaters answer each other's questions or do they appear to you to sidestep some of the issues?

### SAQ 54  Corporate social responsibility – a debate

(i) Briefly describe Tom Burke and Joel Bakan's roles and experience that inform their perspectives.
(ii) Why does Joel Bakan describe CSR as an oxymoron?
(iii) What is Tom Burke's view of where corporate responsibilities lie?
(iv) Summarise both Burke and Bakan's views of the relationship between CSR and legal regulation.

I will now return to the questions on environmental reporting framed at the end of the previous section and, in Activity 49, I want you to review them in the context of CSR.

### Activity 49  Issues and uses of CSR reporting

(i) What are some of the issues of CSR reporting?
(ii) How useful is CSR reporting in exploring situations and formulating systems of interest?
(iii) Do you think the issues raised regarding environmental and CSR reporting will be the same?

## 8.7 The future for environmental legislation and schemes and systemic decision making

What does the future hold for environmental legislation and schemes? Some of the readings in this book have already highlighted some aspects that are not working well where improvements need to be made.

### Activity 50  Reviewing trends and calls for improvement

(i) Go back through Part 2 of this book and make some notes of improvements that have been called for and potential future trends that have been noted regarding environmental legislation and schemes. Be sure to indicate the perspective the call for improvement has come from.
(ii) Try to cluster the calls for improvements and the trends you have identified and give each cluster a name, therefore identifying future themes for improvement.
(iii) How are the clusters you have identified linked to systemic and systematic factors in decision making?

I have not this time supplied my response to this activity because I want to include some discussion of the improvements called for and potential future trends here rather

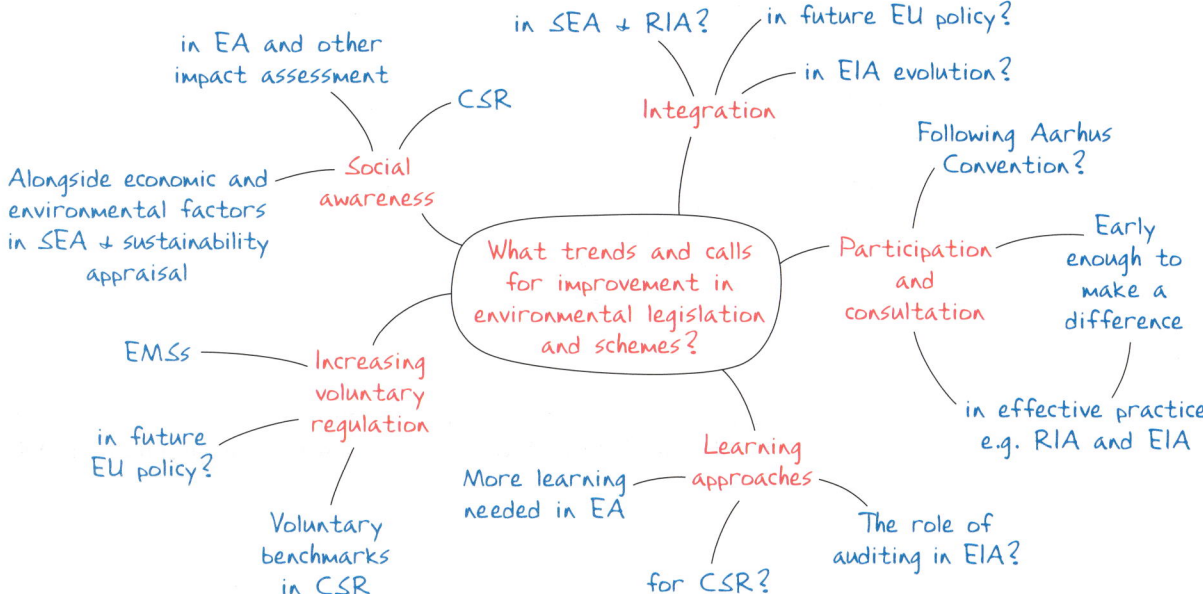

Figure 46    Spray diagram of some of the trends and calls for improvements in Book 2 Part 2

than at the back of the book. There are five areas that I have drawn out for closer scrutiny. I have represented them in a spray diagram in Figure 46.

How do these areas compare with those you identified? Some of the themes identified here will be considered further in Books 3 and 4, but in bringing this part to an end I want to now return to some of the discussion of what it means to start off systemically introduced in Part 1.

I think that all five of these trends or calls for improvement I have drawn out in Figure 46 suggest that more systemic approaches are called for in use of environmental legislation and schemes in decision making. Recognition of interconnections is evident in calls for integration of one set of legislation or schemes with another, and in the rise of awareness of social as well as economic factors in environmental decision making. Calls for more participation and early consultation seem to recognise the need for valuing multiple perspectives to be able to formulate problems, opportunities and systems of interest. Recognition of a need for learning approaches suggests to me an iterative process where learning from one situation can be built on in another. The rise and success of some voluntary regulations suggest to me some recognition that legislation alone cannot control decision makers, and that conditions have been created in which people can respond voluntarily to some of the challenges of environmental decision making and management. There are undoubtedly systematic elements that could also be identified in most of these trends, for example in auditing, assessment and appraisal.

Am I, perhaps, from my perspective of writing part of a course on systems approaches, not taking enough account of my own biases in identifying and interpreting these trends?

I could have instead approached this part of the book as a critique and found plenty of evidence that legislation and schemes are not set to become more systemic. On the evidence of the specific legislation and schemes considered in Section 8, I find it difficult not to conclude that the traditions of environmental legislation and schemes as exemplified by EIA, SEA, RIA, environmental management systems standards and corporate social and environmental responsibility have in the past been largely systematic, as Nilsson and Dalkmann suggested for environmental assessment. This has clearly served some stakeholders' needs in environmental decision making and it is important that systematic traditions continue in some aspects of environmental decision making (for rigour, consistency, etc.). But on the evidence of cases considered in Part 2, there are also signs of change and there appears to be potential for environmental legislation and schemes to start out more systemically in some cases than they do at present. This would involve multiple stakeholders working together to explore their situations before formulating problems, opportunities and systems of interest and in the process increasing their awareness of cycles, counterintuitive effects and possible unintended consequences.

Indeed among people who have been working 'to the spirit' of some of the legislation and schemes rather than in their literal translation, there are examples to be found of practitioners who have approached environmental decision making *both* systemically and systematically. In some of the critiques of environmental legislation and schemes included in this part it is also possible to see increased recognition of the need for them to start off more systemically. The Aarhus Convention, with its requirements for public participation, might encourage more systemic decision making, particularly if it starts early on in environmental decision-making processes. Some of the legislation not considered in this book, such as the Water Framework Directive, has also taken a different approach to preceding legislation and may, in the longer term, develop into a more systemic tradition of environmental legislation.

# Part Three  Monitoring and evaluating your own learning

## 9  Managing a learning system

Part 3 is designed to take one week to study, alongside doing your TMA. My aim in this part is to begin to enable you to deepen your understanding of evaluation, and associated monitoring, and to link this to changes in your own understanding and practice – i.e. learning (or lack of it). In this process I want you to explore:

1. whether your stakeholding in environmental issues and the course has changed as a result of your study so far
2. your own developing use and critique of the environmental decision-making framework and your capacity to use it as part of your own practice
3. the extent to which your systemic awareness in relation to complex, uncertain situations has changed
4. how the course framework and your skills in exploring situations and formulating systems of interest could be used to think about your project.

Pleased do not be alarmed by the heading of this part – whilst I am shifting the focus from environmental decision-making situations to you and your engagement with them, the material is still highly relevant to systemic environmental decision-making practices.

I regard monitoring as a sub-system of evaluation; monitoring usually involves the collection of data over time for the purpose of evaluation. Data for evaluation may be both quantitative and qualitative. If it is to inform evaluation and new cycles of decision making, then data must be interpreted – someone must attribute meaning to it. A critical question that I pose for you here is 'who might participate in this process of attributing meaning?' Consider:

1. If all relevant stakeholders are involved in the decision-making process, and this is kept as open and transparent as possible, then interpretation of results is largely a public process, or open to negotiation and the social construction of meaning.
2. The same applies for monitoring and evaluation – an open, participatory process has to accommodate the learning of all those involved and must be, by its very nature, self-correcting (or evaluating) or else it will fail.
3. Coordination, communication and conflict-resolving mechanisms are key factors in the practice of integrated environmental management (which in turn arises from systemic environmental decision making).

Action is an emergent outcome which arises from the process when the conditions described above have been met – this does not mean that it just happens, as clearly a lot of work has to be done to achieve these outcomes. In case studies where this has been achieved, critical success factors include (i) the alteration of the institutional environment (culture, politics, tradition, history) and (ii) changes in the attitudes of managers and patterns of organisation and structure in the public and private sectors. However, they do not always make it clear how these can be achieved!

The action I am interested in here is your active participation in monitoring and evaluating your own learning. This section represents another change in level of abstraction – it is a move up a level from just being concerned with the course material to encompass both you and the course material and what is emerging! I said earlier that evaluation is something that should start at the beginning of any project or activity, and that for evaluation to be successful some form of monitoring would be required. But what do I mean by evaluation?

## 9.1 Evaluation

A common definition of evaluation used in environment and development contexts, particularly in relation to projects, is:

> An examination, as systematic and objective as possible, of an ongoing or completed project or program, its design, implementation, and results, with the aim of determining its efficiency, effectiveness, impact, sustainability, and the relevance of its objectives. The purpose of an evaluation is to guide decision makers.
>
> (OECD, 1986)

This definition also refers to programmes. For the moment I will leave it to you to consider whether this definition is adequate for an environmental decision – which is not mentioned specifically.

Wadsworth argues that:

> We evaluate all the time. From the minute we meet someone new, or sift through the day's mail, or walk into a shop or office, or decide on the week's activities, we are evaluating. We decide whether things are valuable or unimportant, worthwhile, or not 'worth it', whether things are good or bad, right or wrong, are going OK or 'off the rails', are attractive, difficult, exciting, offputting, useful, undesirable, functional, effective, boring, expensive, too much, too little, just right, interesting, too simple, much too complex, or a disaster! Every time we choose, decide, accept, or reject – we have made an evaluation.
>
> (Wadsworth, 1997b, p. 1)

She goes on to say that evaluation begins when we notice a discrepancy between what we expected (or did not expect) or wanted (or did not want) and what actually has occurred:

> A difference between an 'is' and an 'ought' (or an 'ought not'). Or more accurately, the difference between a valued (or it might be an unvalued) 'is' and a valued (or unvalued) 'ought' or expectation.
>
> (Wadsworth, 1997b, p. 1)

From this perspective evaluation is the process of valuing – something mentioned in Book 1. In environmental decision making, the attribution of economic value has predominated, especially through the process of cost–benefit analysis (which will be discussed in Book 3). Wadsworth's perspective challenges this narrow focus on evaluation.

My own perspective is that evaluation needs to be practised as an ordinary, everyday part of what we do, but not to the extent of digging up the tree to see if its roots are growing. I mean 'light-touch' evaluation. If it is thought of otherwise it always looms as that thing which has to be done at the end and which in practice there never seems time to do. Of course, if evaluation is left to the end, how do we know that we are still on track? Evaluation from this perspective is not something that necessarily needs to be left to an outside expert to do. Obviously, there are cases where this might be desirable or the only practical way to evaluate. So, following Wadsworth (1997a, b), I am suggesting the need to break out of a trap in our thinking which sees evaluation as difficult, uncomfortable, time-consuming and done by someone else, preferably an 'expert'.

By now, you may have gathered that I am going to use the term evaluation rather broadly. Patton observes that:

> Human beings are engaged in all kinds of efforts to make the world a better place. These efforts include assessing needs, formulating policies, passing laws, delivering programs, managing people and resources, providing therapy, developing communities, changing organisational culture, educating students, intervening in conflicts and solving problems. In these and other efforts to make the world a better place, the question of whether the people involved are accomplishing what they want to accomplish arises. When one examines and judges accomplishments and effectiveness, one is engaged in evaluation. When this examination of effectiveness is conducted systematically and empirically through careful data collection and thoughtful analysis, one is engaged in evaluation research.
>
> (Patton, 1990, p. 11)

When Patton and Wadsworth use the term 'research' they do not mean something done by an expert in a white coat or a university – they mean research as part of everyday life. In this sense research is the same as learning, but being aware of what and how we learn. Doing an evaluation is actually doing a bit of research on your own or other people's evaluation of things.

Wadsworth claims that the questions driving evaluation are:

> meant to be self-consciously value-driven (although some evaluation pretends to proceed as if it isn't). This makes it both easier and also more difficult to sort out whose values are predominating [Figure 47]. On the one hand it is easier because it is clear – even just from the term 'evaluation' – that values are being used to judge practices. On the other hand, it can be more difficult because evaluation can try to appear 'objective' (for purposes of legitimacy, certainty, agreement, etc.) but without real agreement around values. This may make it more difficult to realise that value is not inherent in what is being evaluated, but is ascribed by those observing it.
>
> (Wadsworth, 1997, p. 8)

McCallister (1980) in his book *Evaluation in Environmental Planning* goes further, arguing (p. 280) that 'evaluation can rightly be considered a branch of ethics'. It is because evaluation is concerned with values, ethics and our judgements that I consider it to encompass monitoring and auditing (as discussed in Part 2).

Figure 47  Who is the evaluation for? (Source: Wadsworth, 1997b, p. 7)

### SAQ 55  Evaluating what?

In Box 11 in Part 1 Section 6.3.2 you were introduced to 'three Es' as examples of measures of performance of a system of interest. Which one of these does Patton seem to claim is the main basis for evaluation?

## 9.2  Monitoring

The word 'monitor' comes from the Latin *monitum* which means 'to show or warn'. The most common reason for monitoring is to aid decision making or planning. Another might be to take control action by introducing feedback and learning into a system of interest. Several definitions of monitoring can be found:

- the systematic measurement of variables and processes over time (Spellerberg, 1991)

- monitoring is a process not a result, a means to an end rather than an end in itself (Hellawell, 1991)

- a periodic, rather than one-off, reassessment of indicators chosen to determine the effects of certain interventions or policies, or change in general (cited in Abbot and Guijt, 1998)

- an objective process for obtaining unambiguous data to detect clear-cut change (cited in Abbot and Guijt, 1998)

- assessment of whether or not a program is (a) operating in conformity to its design and (b) reaching its specified target population (Rossi et al., 1979)

- an activity undertaken to provide specific information on the characteristics and functioning of environmental and social variables in space and time in order to see whether an impact occurred as a consequence of the project and to estimate its magnitude to see if it is of significance (Litchfield, 1996).

Burnside (1993) suggests that there are at least four common roles associated with monitoring in a managed system:

1. a mechanism for education and awareness about the working of a system that operates within a personal problem-solving model (for example, cholesterol checking)
2. a normative decision aid operating within a formal decision support model (for example, monitoring pest and predator activity as part of integrated pest management)
3. a means of evaluating the level of achievement of objectives for management (for example, factory output)
4. a means of regulating behaviour within a system (for example, urban water usage on which charges are based).

For me, these definitions of monitoring have in common (i) the collection of data over time and (ii) that data collection is a means to some other end.

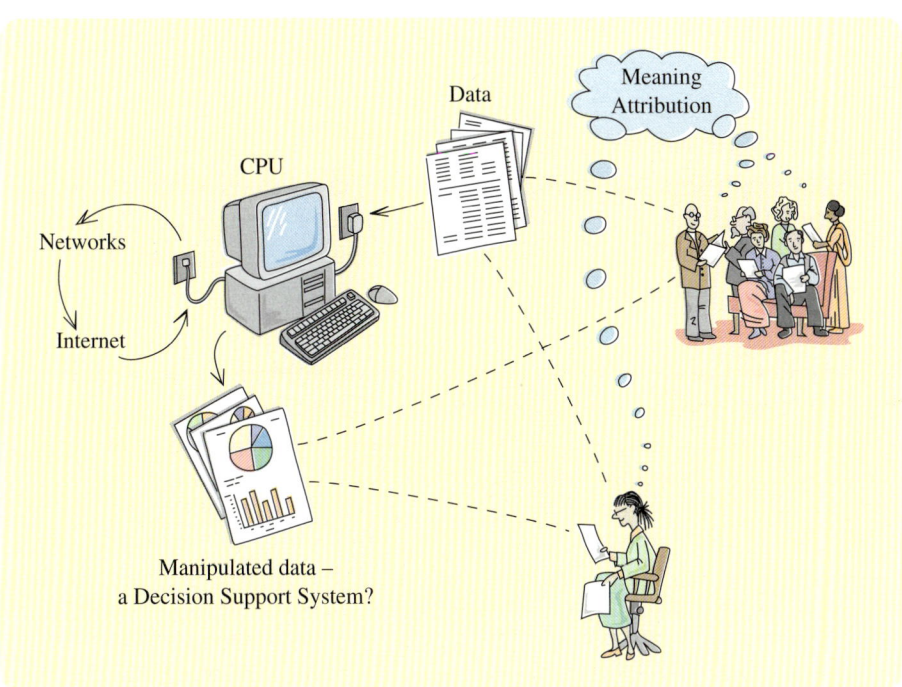

Figure 48   Who attributes meaning to data? Computers, computer networks and the internet do not produce information (Source: adapted from Checkland and Scholes, 1990, in Stuth and Lyons, 1993)

I also recognise epistemological differences amongst those proposing the definitions which can be related to the ideas in Box 27. Implicit in all of the definitions is the notion that the data must be analysed and interpreted by someone and that, through the process of analysis and interpretation, either (i) new data becomes available to inform policy makers, participants, evaluators, etc. or (ii), following the logic of Figure 48, those involved in analysing and interpreting the data, if they are the decision makers, construct new meanings which inform their ongoing actions. Monitoring is concerned with revealing particular patterns (I would regard a trend as part of a pattern but not synonymous with it) and discontinuities in environmental and social variables that someone has considered worth measuring. Of course, monitoring cannot be separated from measuring, which may be quantitative or qualitative.

> ### Box 27  The truth, the whole truth and the limitations of data
>
> Why is data so often of minimal value? Monitoring everything is impossible. It is impossible in theory because we do not know enough about the biophysical world to know all the aspects we could record – and new techniques and approaches are being developed all the time. It is impossible in practice because there will never be enough resources – time, money, equipment, expertise – to record everything. Therefore, data collection is necessarily selective. This means that an assemblage of data is not objective fact: rather it is a particular view of objective fact; and viewpoints change with time as knowledge and theory progress – which is why past data is of dubious value in answering future questions.
>
> Monitoring happens from different standpoints, with each standpoint affecting the results:
>
> - Monitoring data as reality
>
>   Some people argue that monitoring data provides a direct representation of reality. This perspective holds that the monitoring data reflects objective science and can therefore be used as evidence that supports or dismisses a cause.
>
> - Monitoring as politically expedient
>
>   In contrast, other people may see reality as a matter of perspective, objectivity as impossible, and therefore monitoring data as a manifestation of political ideology and propaganda. Based on this view, monitoring data can be moulded to support the cause being pursued (or data selected on the basis that it supports the cause).
>
> (Source: Abbot and Guijt, 1998, after Roberts, 1991)

From my perspective there is considerable confusion about the way in which these terms are being used. An aspect of this confusion is also the question of just what is being evaluated and monitored? This is not always made clear – is it 'the environment', a range of development options (with potentially different environmental effects), the decision-making process, etc.?

Brady (2005) differentiates between a 'monitoring approach', 'monitoring technique' (the scientific principles behind measurement including sampling and analysis) and 'monitoring method' – the documented procedure for use of techniques so as to ensure standardisation. He recognises three approaches to monitoring: (i) continuous monitoring – measurements carried out continuously with few, if any, gaps in the data produced; (ii) periodic monitoring – measurements carried out at intervals, e.g. weeks, month, years; and (iii) surrogate monitoring – the factor of interest (e.g. pollutant) is not itself measured but is estimated from some other parameter where a known relationship exists. The approaches described in Part 2 draw heavily on these distinctions about monitoring and measurement.

Greater clarity to what is meant by monitoring might be achieved when a 'system of interest' has been formulated by relevant stakeholders. It then becomes possible to talk about evaluation and monitoring because the purpose of the system is made explicit. The use, and therefore meanings, of terms such as evaluation, monitoring and auditing is in a state of flux with different communities of interest (e.g. environmentalists, scientists, development professionals, businesses, planners) using them in different ways. This may not be a bad thing – it certainly suggests that a lot of thought is being given to these matters. However, I would like you to decide for yourself.

Earlier I said that it is not possible to ascribe purpose to a system of interest without, at the same time, considering the measure of performance of a system against which purpose is judged. The potential need for different measures of performance by different stakeholder groups has led Wadsworth (1997b) and others to identify two dominant approaches to evaluation: 'audit review evaluation' and 'open inquiry evaluation' (Table 11). Both of these are discussed in the *Techniques* book (see Evaluation), and you will have considered some aspects of audit review already in Part 2.

I can think of other terms which are used synonymously for these two approaches (Table 11). They are not mutually exclusive categories. My reason for making the distinctions is that I think it is important to be aware, when engaged with others in decision making, of when we are operating predominantly in one or other mode. At this stage I am not going to say more about these two distinctions – they will be discussed in more detail in Book 3.

Table 11  Some possible synonyms for open inquiry and audit review evaluation

| Open inquiry evaluation | Audit review evaluation |
| --- | --- |
| Systemic | Systematic |
| Process-based | Objective |
| Illuminative | Standards-based |
| Learning-based | Performance-based |

My view that monitoring and auditing are subsidiary processes of evaluation can be linked to the experiential learning cycle – Figure 11 in Book 1 – and also to the process of formulating systems of interest in situations of complexity that I first discussed in Part 1 (Sections 5 and 6).

## 9.3 Evaluation of a system of interest

In Section 6, I introduced you to the process of formulating systems of interest as a device for developing your understanding of complex environmental decision-making situations with a view to improving them. In this section I want to review how the logic of evaluation works within an SSM-style approach to formulating systems of interest in order to help you to apply the approach to your own situation as much as to particular environmental decision-making situations. I am assuming the situation you are in – having to complete your study and prepare a project – could be one you are experiencing as complex.

### Activity 51  Monitoring and evaluating a system of interest

Return to Box 11 in Part 1 and look at the system of interest that is modelled in that example – this is the example of 'a system to communicate with Mum by writing and posting a letter to her in order to maintain good relations with her'. Write an explanation in your own words of how monitoring and evaluation have been treated in this example. Include in your explanation a description of how measures of performance of the system of interest have been dealt with.

When you have finished writing this description suggest some measures of performance for your study of Book 2 conceptualised as a system to do P by Q because of R.

---

My own response to this activity is in the text below.

In the example given in Box 11, a conceptual model has been developed based on eight activities which give rise to the transformation:

>  need to communicate with Mum → need met by letter writing

These activities were each described by a verb. However, these eight activities on their own do not guarantee that the system will meet its purpose (the why) – of maintaining good relations with Mum. To ensure that the purpose is met it is required to monitor all the activities (i.e. monitor the operations of the system). It is necessary to specify criteria which would constitute appropriate measures of performance for the system of interest. In this case, three have been defined:

> $E_1$ = efficacy (i.e. did the system work by Mum receiving letters?)
>
> $E_2$ = efficiency (i.e. did this system make the best use of resources such as time?)
>
> $E_3$ = effectiveness (i.e. did the system achieve its espoused purpose – maintaining relations with Mum?)

On the basis of defined measures of performance and monitoring of the eight activities then control action can be taken. Notice that in Box 11 there are three activities outside the boundary of the system – 'define Es', 'monitor 1–8' and 'take control action'. These three activities together in SSM equate to evaluation – i.e. they can be seen as three key activities in any evaluation system. Peter Checkland describes how he understands this process (Checkland, 2000):

> For many years the concept of measures of performance was felt to be sufficient for use in models, but was then enriched by an analysis which flows from the consideration that SSM's models are simply logical machines for carrying out a purposeful transformation process expressed in a root definition. Measuring the performance of a logical machine can be expressed through an instrumental logic which focuses on three issues: checking that the output is produced; checking whether minimum resources are used to obtain it; and checking at a high level, that this transformation is worth doing because it makes a contribution to some higher level or longer term aim. This gives definitions of the '3Es' which will be relevant for every model: the criteria of efficacy ($E_1$), efficiency ($E_2$), and effectiveness ($E_3$), first developed in 1987. This core set of criteria can be extended in particular cases – for example by adding $E_4$ for ethicality (is this

transformation morally correct?) and $E_5$ for elegance (is this an aesthetically pleasing transformation?). Since it will not be possible to name the criteria for effectiveness without thinking about the aspirations of the notional system owner (O in CATWOE), this analysis is another contribution which prevents the modeller's thinking being restricted only to one level, that of the system itself.

(Checkland, 2000)

> ### SAQ 56  Measures of performance
>
> What other measures of performance for a system of interest does Checkland suggest, i.e. $E_4$ and $E_5$?

Please remember at this point that Checkland's approach does not set out to model real systems, or to imply that social situations can be reduced to simple machine-like behaviour. His approach involves a rigorous logic for learning about situations which are experienced as complex and all of the models that are built in this process are done so for heuristic purposes, i.e. to learn about the situation and to enable debate or dialogue about desirable and feasible change (which will be discussed in Book 3).

In real world situations, it may not be possible or desirable to monitor everything – think for an example of a system to monitor water dynamics and quality in a river catchment. Nevertheless the logic of an SSM approach can be used to gauge whether the monitoring you are doing will allow you to understand, and thus take control action in the system of interest.

As I said above, within SSM logic evaluation arises from three interconnected activities: (i) monitoring against; (ii) articulated measures of performance, including purpose; as well as (iii) taking control action (which might include revising the formulation of the system of interest). As Checkland (2000, p. S29) observes: 'the core systems image is that of a whole entity which can adapt and survive in a changing environment. So our models, to use systems insights, need to be cast in a form which in principle allows the system to adapt in the light of changing circumstances ... The core structure of the monitoring and control sub-system is always the same: a "monitor" activity contingent upon definition of the criteria by which system performance will be judged and an activity rendered as "take control action" which is contingent upon the monitoring'.

In conceptual terms, systemic understandings of communication and control are at the core of the SSM approach to evaluation (Box 28). I have introduced Box 28 because in my experience many people have what I call a first-order understanding of communication and control which is not always helpful. Think of how control is expressed metaphorically in our language – e.g. 'pulling the levers', 'identifying the drivers', 'exerting pressure', 'measuring up', 'meeting the targets', etc. This language is fine for control of mechanistic processes and for some simple biophysical processes, but one can never escape the fact that people are usually part of the system of interest (as for example in Figure 48). Each of these metaphors reveals a particular view of control that is basically mechanistic and inappropriate in complex, uncertain, contested situations such as those associated with environmental decision making.

From a systemic perspective, control action emerges from the local operation of a system and in relation to purpose and boundary judgements. If one is not aware of these distinctions then it is likely that monitoring, evaluation and definition of measures of performance will be inadequate, i.e. that the evaluation system will not work or will bear no resemblance to the system of interest. From my perspective, traps – associated with how communication and control are understood – have the potential to affect your evaluation practices. The main ones are:

1. Situations where what is communicated as part of attempting to take control action is merely a summary of activity (i.e. some statement about whether the activity was undertaken and how often). In the field of agricultural extension, where there are specialist advisers called 'extension officers', I have frequently encountered situations where what is monitored is the type and amount of activity (e.g. number of visits to farms or farmers; number of attendees at events; number of press releases, etc.). There is often an accompanying, mistaken, belief that reporting on this activity constitutes reporting on effectiveness (which it does not) and that the actual reporting itself will constitute an effective control action because 'a message has been sent' (see Box 28).

2. When adherents to a strictly rationalist approach to decision making (as discussed in Book 1) believe that what is written down (e.g. guidelines, rules, procedures) constitutes messages that will be perfectly understood by readers and that such a procedure can, by itself, be central to an evaluation system.

3. When externally imposed targets distort the functioning of a local 'adaptive whole' because behaviour changes to enacting a 'system to meet the targets' (with accompanying communication to sell success or deflect approbation) rather than the phenomenon for which the targets were developed.

4. Where the use of different understandings of human communication, as embodied in the metaphors in Table 12, either distort or make ineffective an evaluation system. This can be linked to what is acceptable or unacceptable evidence in an evaluation system. For example, in evaluating your own learning you may be reliant on those measures put in place by the course team (TMAs, Project report, SAQs and Activities) and you could report on your activity in relation to these, e.g. number attempted, number attempted successfully, mark for TMA, mark for Project report. Whilst these are all important and necessary, do they constitute, in aggregate, an evaluation system for your own learning? Consider this question when you read through the material in Box 28 and Table 12 where the distinction is made between a first-order and a second-order learning or evaluation system.

As further preparation for reading the material in Box 28 please complete the following activity.

### Activity 52  Control models

If you have not already done so go to the *Techniques* book and read the material on Diagramming: control model diagrams. After you have read through this material, fully label the basic model reproduced below and write some notes in your learning journal about how different aspects of your engagement with T863 could be understood through the operation of a control model.

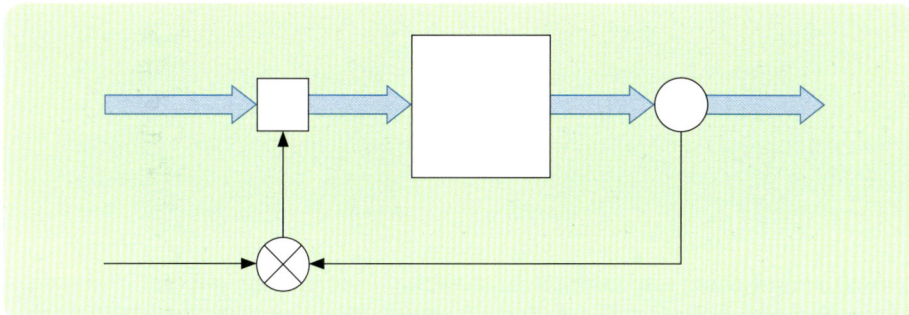

Figure 49    A control model

I have provided my own response to this activity at the back.

### Box 28    Communication and control

Cybernetics, although often applied to the control of machines, has long been one of the foundations of thought about human communication, its central notion being circularity. Cybernetics 'arises when effectors, say a motor, an engine, our muscles, etc., are connected to a sensory organ which, in turn, acts with its signals upon the effectors. It is this circular organisation which sets cybernetic systems apart from others that are not so organised' (von Foerster, 1992). In first-order cybernetics, it was the idea of feedback control which mainly occupied the practitioners (the classic example is that of a thermostat controlling the temperature of a room). Too often human communication is understood in terms of a simple, first-order feedback loop but human communication is not mechanistic – it has a biological basis.

As originally conceived, control models (see Figure 49) indicate the application of control to a process to ensure the objectives or standards of that process are achieved. They can be developed from input–output diagrams by sensing/monitoring the outputs and feeding this information back to a comparator that can then control the inputs through an actuator. They are often used to analyse control problems. A control model can also be seen as a simple model of a 'learning system' in that feedback can lead to learning and thus a change of goals (purpose) for the system of interest based on some form of evaluation. When used in this way the question 'what controls the controller' comes into view (Glanville, 1995a, b) and the property of circularity becomes the focus of attention once again.

Second-order cybernetics is a theory of the observer rather than what is being observed. Heinz von Foerster's phrase 'the cybernetics of cybernetics' was apparently first used by him in the early 1960s as the title of Margaret Mead's opening speech at the first meeting of the American Cybernetics Society when she had not provided written notes for the Proceedings. '[The understandings which have arisen from second-order cybernetics…] requires a loosening of our grip on the supposedly certain knowledge that is acquired objectively, about a reality existing independently of us, and a willingness to consider the constructivist idea (see Mahoney, 1988) that we each construct our own version of reality in the course of our living together. The virtue of objectivity was that the properties of the observer should be separate from the description of what is being observed. This led to what von Foerster (1992) called the Pontius Pilate attitude of abrogating responsibility because the observer is an innocent bystander who can claim he or she had no choice. The alternative attitude, which seems to be less popular today, is to own a personal preference for one among various alternatives' (Fell and Russell, 2000, p. 34).

A second-order perspective gives rise to different understandings of human communication which are revealed and concealed by different metaphors (Table 12). Understanding human communication as a biological phenomenon is best exemplified through the dance–ritual metaphor. A second-order evaluation system might consider questions like:

- What would I have to do to enable X to provide me with feedback about the quality of my work?
- How will I know when and if my purpose in studying this course has changed?
- How could I create the circumstances where the stakeholders in this environmental decision-making situation could articulate a purpose and design an evaluation system?
- How do the things I am doing enable me to recognise when control action might be required and what would such action look like?

Table 12   Metaphors of communication

| Metaphor | Example | Some implications |
|---|---|---|
| Language as a container | 'Her thoughts were locked in cryptic verse' <br> 'What did you get out of the lecture?' | The idea that communication consists of sending discrete messages that contain something is pervasive <br> Non-content or relational aspects of communication are rarely addressed <br> Communication contents become entities with objective properties <br> Communication is associated with transportation – messages, etc. are carried from here to there; 'sharing' is seen as the logical consequence of 'good' communication |
| The conduit metaphor | 'That message got to her' <br> 'A national information highway' <br> 'Let's not upset communication flows' | The wire became a tube through which something could flow from a source to a sink as in a plumbing system <br> The notion of channels of communication becomes pervasive <br> Communication is affected by 'noise' <br> What comes out of the channel cannot be qualitatively different nor quantitatively exceed what entered it. |

| Metaphor | Example | Some implications |
|---|---|---|
| The control metaphor | 'The weather report caused the University to cancel the field trip' <br> 'She advanced compelling arguments' | Communication is a causal phenomenon used as a means to achieve particular ends or as an instrument – it calls for the invention of forces <br> It entails fundamental social asymmetries – the controller and the controlled as in e.g. targeted messages <br> Authors, etc. as producers of communications assume the privileged position of knowledgeable agents <br> Communication becomes limited to successful communication – all assertions about success and failure derive from this metaphor <br> It brings in one perspective and suppresses other perspectives (i.e. difference) |
| The transmission metaphor | 'Have you received the message?' <br> 'Getting the message across' <br> 'Sending the right message' | Comes from cryptography and is linked to the work of Shannon and Weaver (1949) <br> Sees information as the measure or extent that coding processes are reversible and thus preserve a pattern <br> It is a radical departure from the container and conduit metaphors in that meanings reside in human understanding and not in the signals transmitted <br> It reveals the cognitive burden placed on communicators both as senders and receivers, e.g. interpretation <br> It can be used as the basis of campaigns to change behaviours – 'getting the message across' |
| The war metaphor | 'He attacked every weak point in the argument' (i.e. arguments can be won or lost) | More associated with talk than writing or mass communication (but what about storming in groups; and flaming online)? <br> This too is pervasive in Western societies (and conceals cultural differences where argument or debate – literally 'to put down' – is central rather than say dialogue – meaning 'running through') |
| The dance–ritual metaphor | The habitual reading of the paper or course units on the train <br> Ceremoniously asking 'how are you?' or saying goodbye <br> Conversation – having a yarn, gossip? | Entails continuity and repetitiveness – in a ritual authors are unimportant, in a dance it is the overall pattern of movement <br> It is always possible to re-create the conversation with different people as long as participants recognise the same process <br> It is a cooperative and communal activity in which the autonomy of the others is respected <br> Entering into a conversation is experienced as an invitation. <br> It leaves something recognisable behind which is every participants' construction |

(Source: following Krippendorf, 1993)

## Activity 53 Communication ideas influence understandings of control

Look back over your learning journal and see if you can spot instances where the metaphors for human communication outlined in Table 12 dominated your thinking. Make some notes on how you now understand the idea of control.

## 9.4 Evaluating the course framework and your use of it so far

In Section 4.2, I introduced two metaphors relating to practice – those of hammering and a concert performance. In this section I want to provide an opportunity to review your performance, your practice, with the T863 course framework. I do so to enable you to monitor and evaluate the progress you have made as well as to prepare you for the rest of the course.

In Book 1, one of the final activities you were asked to do involved exploring the T863 course framework on the DVD (Activity 23 in Book 1). I would like you to return to look at the framework now in the light of your engagement with, and learning from, Book 2 (Activity 54). My concern at this stage is to review what you have done in this book in the light of the framework and how your use of it has, or has not, enabled you to better understand the airport expansion decision-making case study.

## Activity 54 Re-exploring the T863 environmental decision-making framework

Go once again to the Resources section of the DVD and work through Part 2 of the animation on the T863 framework if you haven't already done so. (It explains how each book focuses on different aspects of the framework.) Notice from the animation the focus of Book 2 in relation to both the framework and the other books. Look at the notes you made when you attempted Activity 23 in Book 1 and answer the following two questions:

(i) Have you now addressed any of the questions you had about the framework as you were finishing Book 1? (e.g. has the meaning of parts of the framework or how it may be used become any clearer?) If so briefly write down how.

(ii) What further questions occur to you regarding the framework and your use of the framework, now that you have nearly finished Book 2? Write them in your journal to return to later on.

To answer this activity I would expect that you would say something about how your understandings of environmental decision-making situations had changed and, possibly, your practices. I acknowledge that, at this stage, the main practices to have changed are likely to have been those associated with studying the course – using new techniques, completing activities, etc. – but of course you may have already begun to incorporate some of the course ideas into your understandings and practices in situations outside of the course. I certainly hope so.

One way of monitoring how things have changed would be to review how, if at all, your understanding of the aviation expansion situation has changed and the decision-making processes associated with it. For example, how do you now evaluate the decision-making process? How, if at all, has your own stakeholding in the situation changed? For my own part I have become more aware of just how much the aviation industry is being subsidised and how inadequate the decision-making process has been in dealing with what I, and many others, regard as systemically desirable to do. At the beginning of this book I claimed that systemic awareness comes from understanding:

1. cycles
2. counterintuitive effects
3. unintended consequences.

From my perspective, the aviation expansion case study falls down on all three of these points. Judged in the longer term it may well lead to systemic failure. On the other hand, seen as a system to deliver a decision to support economic expansion and a stable planning and investment climate for the main investors – stakeholders in aviation expansion – it was undoubtedly very successful. It also looks as if the decision will stick – hence it was culturally acceptable or feasible even if not systemically desirable. The challenge as I see it is to be able to move more towards transforming situations through decision making which is both systemically desirable and culturally feasible, ideas which are taken up in Book 3.

So my understanding of the situation has changed significantly but what about my practices? I could claim that my practices as an academic by working on this case study and making it accessible to a wider audience is an example of changing my behaviour and being more responsible. On the other hand this could be a cop out – after all when writing this I did take two flights with 'cheap' airlines despite my concern about the sustainability of aviation! My own behaviour highlights what I see as a major issue for sustainable development – how can individuals be more responsible, and at the same time, how can the circumstances be created to enable individuals to be more response-able (Figure 50). At the moment what is enabled, or facilitated, in relation to air travel is more and more consumption without any clear evidence that new social technologies (e.g. carbon trading schemes) will change things for the better.

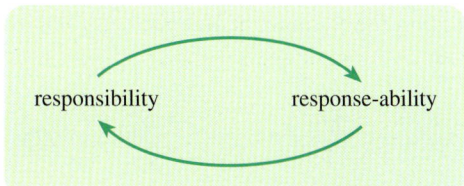

Figure 50    The recursive relationship between responsibility and response-ability

## 9.5 Monitoring and evaluating your systemic awareness

In this book we have been using both the adjectives systemic and systematic. I now want to introduce a table of the characteristics that distinguish between systemic thinking and action and systematic thinking and action (Table 13). I have constructed the table in such a way so that you can add your own examples of each characteristic if you wish to – but this is not an expectation. Used in this way, it could be an opportunity for you to monitor and evaluate your own understandings of the differences between systemic thinking and practice and systematic thinking and practice.

I also provide an opportunity for you to review your understandings of the systems concepts that have been introduced in this book (Activity 55).

You will have further opportunities to refine and deepen these understandings in Books 3 and 4 where the distinctions between systemic and systematic and audit review and open inquiry methods will be taken up again.

Table 13  A summary of the characteristics that distinguish systemic thinking and action and systematic thinking and action

| Systemic thinking | Example | Systematic thinking | Example |
| --- | --- | --- | --- |
| Properties of the whole differ, they are said to emerge from their parts. | The wetness of water cannot be understood in terms of hydrogen and oxygen. | The whole can be understood by considering just the parts through linear cause–effect mechanisms. | |
| Boundaries of systems are determined by the perspectives of those who participate in formulating them. The result is a system of interest. | | Systems exist as concrete entities; there is a correspondence between the description and the described phenomenon. | |
| Individuals hold partial perspectives of the whole; when combined, these provide multiple partial perspectives. | | Perspective is not important. | |
| Analysis is systemic; situations are characterised by feedback; may be negative, i.e. compensatory or balancing; or positive, i.e. exaggerating or reinforcing. | | Analysis is often reductionist, linear or deterministic. | |

| Systemic thinking | Example | Systematic thinking | Example |
|---|---|---|---|
| Systems cannot be understood by analysis of the component parts. The relevant properties of the parts are not intrinsic properties, but can be understood only within the context of the larger whole through studying the interconnections. | | A situation can be understood by step-by-step analysis followed by evaluation and repetition of the original analysis. | |
| Concentrates on basic principles of organisation. | | Concentrates on basic building blocks. | |
| Systems are seen as nested within other systems – they are multilayered and interconnect to form networks. | | There is a foundation on which the parts can be understood. | |
| Contextual or synthetic. | | Analytical. | |
| Concerned more with process and relationships. | | Concerned more with entities and properties. | |
| The properties of the whole system are destroyed when the system is dissected, either physically or theoretically, into isolated elements. | | The system can be reconstructed after studying the components. | |

| Systemic action | Example | Systematic action | Example |
|---|---|---|---|
| The espoused role and the action of the decision maker are very much part of the situation. How the researcher perceives the situation is critical to the 'system' being studied. The role is that of participant conceptualiser. | | The espoused role of the decision maker is that of participant observer. In practice, however, the decision maker claims to be objective and thus remains 'outside' the 'system' being studied. | |
| Different ethics are perceived as applying at different levels. What might be good at one level might be bad at another. Responsibility replaces objectivity in whole-systems ethics. | | Ethics and values are not addressed as a central theme. They are not integrated into the change process; the researcher/decision maker takes an objective stance. | |

| Systemic action | Example | Systematic action | Example |
|---|---|---|---|
| It is the interaction of the practitioner, a system of interest and the context (the environment) that is the main focus of exploration and change. | | The 'system' being studied is seen as distinct from its environment. It may be spoken of in open-system terms but intervention is performed as though it were a closed system. | |
| Perception and action are based on experience, especially the experience of patterns that connect entities and the meaning generated by viewing events in their contexts. | | Perception and action are based on a belief in a 'real world'; a world of discrete entities (including systems) that have meaning in and of themselves. | |
| There is an attempt to stand back and explore the traditions of understanding in which the practitioner is immersed. | | Traditions of understanding may not be questioned although the method of analysis may be evaluated. | |

### SAQ 57 Systemic and systematic

Select one set of distinctions between systematic and systemic from Table 13 that have the most significance for you. Briefly explain why.

### Activity 55 A systematic review of concepts associated with a 'systems' approach

Carry out a systematic review of the concepts associated with a 'systems' approach that you have come across in Book 2. Use the following table as a basis for conducting your review. To complete the review, answer the following questions:

(i) Does your understanding of the concept accord with the definition given?

(ii) Try to locate where the concept was introduced or discussed and give one example which demonstrates the concept in relation to environmental decision making.

(iii) If you cannot find the concept, do a web search and find an example of the concept which can be related to environmental decision-making situations.

## 9 MANAGING A LEARNING SYSTEM

Table 14  Definitions of some generalised systems concepts used in this course

| Concept | Definition |
| --- | --- |
| Boundary | The borders of the system, determined by the observer(s), which define where control action can be taken: a particular area of responsibility to achieve system purposes |
| Communication | (i) First-order communication is based on simple feedback (as in a thermostat) but should not be confused with human communication, which has a biological basis<br>(ii) Second-order communication is understood from a theory of cognition which encompasses language, emotion, perception and behaviour. Amongst human beings, this gives rise to new properties in the communicating partners who each have different experiential histories |
| Connectivity | Logical dependence between components or elements (including sub-systems) within a system |
| Difficulty | A situation considered as a bounded and well defined problem where it is assumed that it is clear who is involved and what would constitute a solution within a given time frame |
| Emergent properties | Properties which are revealed at a particular level of organisation and which are not possessed by constituent sub-systems. Thus these properties emerge from an assembly of sub-systems |
| Environment | That which is outside the system boundary and which affects and is affected by the behaviour of the system; alternatively the 'context' for a system of interest |
| Feedback | A form of interconnection, present in a wide range of systems. Feedback may be negative (compensatory or balancing) or positive (exaggerating or reinforcing) |
| Hierarchy | Layered structure; the location of a particular system within a continuum of levels of organisation. This means that any system is at the same time a sub-system of some wider system and is itself a wider system to its sub-systems |
| Measure of performance | The criteria against which the system is judged to have achieved its purpose. Data collected according to measures of performance is used to modify the interactions within the system |
| Mess | A mess is a set of conditions that produces dissatisfaction. It can be conceptualised as a system of problems or opportunities; a problem or an opportunity is an ultimate element abstracted from a mess |
| Monitoring and control | Data collected and decisions taken in relation to measures of performance are monitored and controlled action is taken through some avenue of management |
| Networks | An elaboration of the concept of hierarchy which avoids the human projection of 'above' and 'below' and recognises an assemblage of entities in relationship, e.g. organisms in an ecosystem |
| Perspective | A way of experiencing which is shaped by our unique personal and social histories, where experiencing is a cognitive act |
| Purpose | What the system does or exists for; the raison d'être which in terms of a model developed by people is to achieve the particular transformation that has been defined |
| Resources | Elements which are available within the system boundary and which enable the transformation to occur |
| System | An integrated whole whose essential properties arise from the relationships between its parts; from the Greek *synhistanai*, meaning 'to place together' |
| System of interest | The product of distinguishing a system in a situation, in relation to an articulated purpose, in which an individual or a group has an interest (a stake); a constructed or formulated system, of interest to one or more people, used in a process of inquiry; a term suggested to avoid confusion with the everyday use of the word 'system' |

| Concept | Definition |
|---|---|
| Systemic thinking | The understanding of a phenomenon within the context of a larger whole; to understand things systemically literally means to put them into a context, to establish the nature of their relationships |
| Systematic thinking | Thinking which is connected with parts of a whole but in a linear, step-by-step manner |
| Tradition | Literally, a network of pre-understandings or prejudices from which we think and act; how we make sense of our world |
| Transformation | Changes, modelled as an interconnected set of activities which convert an input to an output which may leave the system (a 'product') or become an input to another transformation |
| Trap | A way of thinking which is inappropriate for the situation or issue being explored |
| Worldview | That view of the world which enables each observer to attribute meaning to what is observed (sometimes the German word *Weltanschauung* is used synonymously) |

(Source: adapted from Wilson, 1984; Capra, 1996; Pearson and Ison, 1997)

## 9.6 Taking control action with respect to your own learning

Spend some time taking stock of your answers to the activities in Part 3. You could do this by constructing a spray diagram which on one side explored the main things you feel you have learnt from the course so far and on the other the concepts, ideas or techniques which still cause you concern. At the end of such an activity, I would expect you to act responsibly by taking control action with respect to your own learning and as preparation for the study of Book 3. The following activity is designed to help you do this.

### Activity 56  Monitoring your own situation

Develop a rich picture of your own situation at this point in the course. Make sure you include yourself in your rich picture and that you make reference to your project.

Identify the five main themes that your rich picture reveals. Rank these in terms of importance to your ongoing learning at the moment. Think about how you could decide what was systemically desirable and culturally feasible to do about this theme.

# Learning outcomes

After working through Book 2, you should be able to:

- explore and re-explore environmental decision-making situations systemically
- start off an environmental decision-making process systemically by:

    being aware of the biophysical dynamics in a situation

    recognising different types of models and modelling

    using systems concepts as tools for thought, creativity, communication, representation and process design in environmental decision making

    appreciating how interconnected 'cycles', counterintuitive effects and unintended consequences operate or arise

- use some diagrammatic modelling techniques to represent aspects of situations, as part of a decision-making process
- use creative techniques and tools for thinking and action to start and sustain processes of environmental decision making
- recognise why different environmental decisions are likely to be reached if more attention is paid to how the process is started and who participates
- conduct a stakeholder analysis
- recognise and accommodate multiple perspectives
- appreciate how problems and opportunities come into being through social processes
- distinguish between consultation and different forms of participation
- recognise the implications of starting off, or not starting off, an environmental decision-making process in a participatory manner
- formulate systems of interest in complex environmental decision-making situations.
- appreciate a range of legislation and schemes used for environmental decision making and their declared purposes
- understand why these legislation and schemes are used, by whom and how and in what contexts, including some aspects of variation in use within and between different countries
- understand some of the advantages and disadvantages of different kinds of legislation and schemes
- understand how environmental legislation and schemes can be used in systemic (incorporating systematic) environmental decision making, particularly when starting off
- take stock of your experience of environmental legislation and schemes
- understand how environmental legislation and schemes can be used in improving environmental performance
- structure and interpret descriptive examples of environmental legislation and schemes
- interpret and compare diagrammatic representations of environmental legislation and schemes

- understand some of the issues of participation, consultation, information and motivation in using, implementing or reporting on environmental legislation and schemes
- understand the evolution and overall trajectory (past, present, future) of some environmental legislation and schemes and their use
- understand the difference between 'the spirit' and the literal translation of legislation and schemes for environmental decision making
- recognise that evaluation of any planned action starts at the beginning, not the end, and that to evaluate some form of monitoring is required throughout to check how you are going
- improve your own learning and performance and adopt a critical perspective.

# References

Abbot, J. and Guijt, I. (1998) 'Changing views on change', Working Paper on Participatory Monitoring of the Environment, London, IIED.

ACI Europe (2004) *Airports and Environmental Legislation: A Summary of EU Environmental Legislation and Additional Standards and Recommendations Directly and Indirectly Related to Aviation, Version 1.3,* Airports Council International.

Ackoff, R.L. (1974a) 'The systems revolution', *Long Range Planning*, vol. 7, pp. 2–5.

Ackoff, R.L. (1974b) *Redesigning the Future*, New York, Wiley.

Ackoff, R.L. (1980) 'The systems revolution' in Lockett, M. and Spear, R. (eds) *Organizations as Systems*, Milton Keynes, Open University Press.

Adnan, S., Barrett, A., Nurul Alam, S.M. and Brustinow, A. (1992) *People's Participation: NGOs and the Flood Action Plan*, Dhaka, Research and Advisory Services.

Alder, J. (1993) 'Environmental assessment: the inadequacies of law' in Holder, J., Lane, P., Eden, S., Reeve, R., Collier, U. and Anderson, K. (eds) *Perspectives on the Environment. Interdisciplinary Research Network in Environment and Society,* pp. 61–82, Aldershot, Avebury.

BAA Annual Report 2004/05 *Success through Innovation* BAA Corporate and Public Affairs: England.

Baden, J. and Stroup, J. (1977) 'Property rights, environment quality and the management of national forests' in Hardin, G. and Baden, J. (eds) *Managing the Commons*, San Francisco, W. H. Freeman.

Bawden, R.J. (1998) 'The community challenge: the learning response' *New Horizons*, vol. 99, pp. 40–59.

Beanlands, G. (1988) 'Scoping methods and baseline studies in EIA' in Wathern, P. (ed.) *Environmental Impact Assessment: Theory and Practice*, New York, Routledge.

Beattie, R.B. (1995) 'Everything you already know about EIA (but don't often admit)', *Environmental Impact Assessment Review*, vol. 15, pp. 109–14.

Beck, U. (1992) *Risk Society – Towards a New Modernity*, London, Sage Publications.

Bina, O. (2003) 'Re-conceptualising strategic environmental assessment: theoretical overview and case study from Chile', PhD thesis, University of Cambridge.

Binnie, Black and Veatch (1997) *Strangford Lough Sea Defences at Newtownards, Environmental Assessment Report,* appendices A–K.

Brady, J. (ed.) (2005) *Environmental Management in Organizations: The IEMA Handbook*, London, IEMA/Earthscan.

British Standards Institution (2004) *BS EN ISO 14001:2004 Environmental Management Systems – Requirements with Guidance for Use,* BSI.

Brown, L. (2004) *Earth Policy Institute* [online], http://www.chelseagreen.com/2004/items/limits (Accessed November 2005).

Brown, V., Smith, D.I., Wiseman, R. and Handmer, J. (1995) *Risks and Opportunities: Managing Environmental Conflict and Change*, London, Earthscan.

Bunch, M. (2003) 'Soft systems methodology and the ecosystem approach: a system study of the Cooum River and environs in Chennai, India', *Environmental Management*, vol. 31, pp. 182–97.

Burke, T. and Bakan, J. (2005) 'Corporate social responsibility – a debate between Tom Burke and Joel Bakan', *The Ecologist*, March, pp. 28–32.

Burnside, D. (1993) 'On ground monitoring and monitoring as a management tool', *Proceedings North West Pastoral Conference*, Katherine, Australia, Australian Rangeland Society.

Canter, L.W. (1996) *Environmental Impact Assessment*, New York, McGraw-Hill.

Capra, F. (1996) *The Web of Life: A New Synthesis of Mind and Matter*, London, HarperCollins.

Casti, J.L. (1994) *Complexification: Explaining a Paradoxical World through the Science of Surprise*, London, Abacus.

Chambers, R. (2005) *Ideas for Development*, London, Earthscan.

Checkland, P.B. (1993 [1981]) *Systems Thinking, Systems Practice*, Chichester, John Wiley.

Checkland, P. (1999) 'Soft systems methodology: a thirty year retrospective' in Checkland, P. and Scholes, J. (1999) *Soft Systems Methodology in Action*, Chichester, John Wiley.

Checkland, P.B. (2000) 'Soft systems methodology: a thirty year retrospective', *Systems Research and Behavioural Science*, vol. 17, pp. S11–58.

Checkland, P. (2002) 'The role of the practitioner in a soft systems study', notes of a talk given to OuSyS and UKSS, 8 December 2001, in *Open University Systems Society (OUSyS) Newsletter*, The Open University, Milton Keynes, no. 27, March pp. S5–11.

Checkland, P.B. and Scholes, J. (1999 [1990]) *Soft Systems Methodology in Action* (2nd edn), Chichester, John Wiley.

Churchman, C.W. (1971) *The Design of Inquiring Systems*, New York, Basic Books.

Clark, B. (1994) 'Improving public participation in environmental impact assessment', *Built Environment*, vol. 20, no. 4, pp. 294–308.

Collins, K.B., Ison, R.L. and Blackmore, C.P. (2005) *River Basin Planning Project: Social Learning (Phase 1)*, Bristol, Environment Agency.

Commission of the European Communities (2000) *White Paper on Environmental Liability*, 9.2.2000 COM (2000) 66 Final, Brussels, CEC.

Commonwealth Environment Protection Agency (1994) *Public Participation in the EM Process*, Barton, Australia, Commonwealth Environment Protection Agency.

Confederation of British Industry (1990) *Narrowing the Gap: Environmental Auditing Guidelines for Business*, London, CBI.

Cook, C.C. and Donelly-Roark, P. (1994) 'Public participation on environmental assessments in Africa' in Goodland, R. and Edmundson, V. (eds) *Environmental Assessment and Development 1994: An IAIA World Bank Symposium,* Washington, DC, World Bank.

Dalal-Clayton, B. and Sadler, B. (2004) *Strategic Environmental Assessment – A Sourcebook and Reference Guide to International Experience*, London, Earthscan.

Davis, G.B. (1974) *Management Information Systems: Conceptual Foundations, Structure and Development*, London, McGraw-Hill.

Delcourt, H.R., Delcourt, P.A. and Webb, T. (1983) 'Dynamic plant ecology: the spectrum of vegetation change in space and time', *Quarterly Science Review*, vol. 1, pp. 153–75.

Department for Transport (2003) *Aviation White Paper*, Department for Transport.

Department for Transport (2006) *Aviation* [online], http://www.dft.gov.uk/stellent/groups/dft_aviation/documents/sectionhomepage/dft_aviation_page.hcsp (Accessed 13 March 2006).

Department of Environment (1996) *Changes in the Quality of Environmental Statements for Planning Projects*, London, HMSO.

Dickinson, R.E. (1988) 'Atmospheric systems and global change' in Rosswall, T., Woodmansee, R.G. and Risser, P.G. (eds) *Scales and Global Change: SCOPE 35*, pp. 57–80, Chichester, John Wiley.

Dryzek, J.S. (1997) *The Politics of the Earth: Environmental Discourses*, Oxford, Oxford University Press.

EMAS – Eco-Management and Audit Scheme (2006) [online] http://www.emas.org.uk/ (Accessed 27 March 2006).

ENDS (2003a) 'UKAS EMS survey reveals widespread concerns over certification', *ENDS Report*, December, pp. 19–21.

ENDS (2003b) 'UKAS "We let EMS standards slide"', *ENDS Report,* December, pp. 3–4.

ENDS (2005) 'Certified EMSs boost export potential', *ENDS Report*, April, pp. 34–5.

ENDS (2005) 'Where next for EU environment policy?', *ENDS Report*, June, pp. 22–5.

ENDS (2005) 'Maintaining momentum on EMSs', *ENDS Report*, March, p. 2.

ENDS (2005) 'ISO 14001 certification bodies complain of unfair competition', *ENDS Report*, May, pp. 3–5.

Environment Agency (2003) 'Trends in air quality' [online], http://www.environment-agency.gov.uk/subjects/airquality/ (Accessed 26 August 2003).

*Environment Business Magazine* (2001), no. 68, September, London, GEE Publishing Ltd.

EUROPA (2003) 'Commission report shows inadequate implementation of environment directive reference: IP/03/876' [online], http://europa.eu.int/rapid/pressReleasesAction.do?reference=IP/03/876&format=HTML&aged=0&language=EN&guiLanguage=en (Accessed 13 March 2006).

European Commission's EMAS Helpdesk (2006) http://www.europa.eu.int/comm/environment/emas/ (Accessed 13 March 2006).

European Council (1997) 'Directive 97/11/EC amending directive 85/337/EEC on the assessment of the effects of certain public and private projects on the environment', *Official Journal*, no. L 073, 14 March 1997, p. 5.

Fell, L. and Russell, D. (2000) 'The human quest for understanding and agreement' in Ison, R.L. and Russell, D.B. (eds) *Agricultural Extension and Rural Development: Breaking Out of Traditions*, Cambridge, Cambridge University Press.

Fortmann, L. (1989) 'Peasant and official views of rangeland use in Botswana', *Land Use Policy*, July, pp. 197–202.

Fuller, K. (2004) 'What is strategic environmental assessment?' [online], http://www.iema.net/library/RR_SEA_ebriefing/RR_SEA_ebriefing.html (Accessed 27 March 2006).

Gilles, J.L. (1985) 'Slippery grazing rights: using indigenous knowledge for pastoral development', *Arid Lands: Today and Tomorrow*, Proceedings of an International Research and Development Conference, Tucson, AZ, 20–25 October, pp. 1159–66.

Glanville, R. (1995a) 'A (cybernetic) musing: Control 1', *Cybernetics and Human Knowing*, vol. 3, no. 1, pp. 47–50.

Glanville, R. (1995b) 'A (cybernetic) musing: Control 2', *Cybernetics and Human Knowing*, vol. 3, no. 2, pp. 43–6.

Glasbergen, P. and Cörvers, R. (1995) 'Environmental problems in an international context' in Glasbergen, P. and Blowers, A. (eds) *Environmental Policy in an International Context: 1 Perspectives*, pp. 1–29, London, The Open University/Arnold.

Glasson, J., Therivel, R., and Chadwick, A. (2005) *Introduction to Environmental Impact Assessment*, London, Taylor and Francis.

Gray, R.H. with Bebbington, J. and Walters, D. (1993) *Accounting for the Environment*, London, Paul Chapman Publishing.

Guijt, I. and Redd Barna Uganda (1996) 'The approach of Redd Barna Uganda to participatory planning: reflections and guidelines', unpublished report.

Hellawell, J.M. (1991) 'Development of a rationale for monitoring' in Goldsmith, F.B. (ed.) *Monitoring for Conservation and Ecology*, London, Chapman and Hall.

Heron, J. (1989) *Facilitators' Handbook*, London, Kogan Page.

Hopcraft, P.N. (1981) 'Economic institutions and pastoral resource management: considerations for a development strategy' in Galaty, J.G., Aronson, D.R. and Salzman, P.C. (eds) *The Future of Pastoral Peoples*, pp. 224–43, Ottawa, International Development Research Centre.

Humpherson, E. (2004) 'The National Audit Office's evaluation of RIAs: reflections on the pilot year', *Public Money and Management*, vol. 24, no. 5, pp. 277–82.

Institute of Environmental Management and Assessment (2002) *Perspectives: Guidelines on Participation in Environmental Decision Making*, IEMA.

Institute of Environmental Management and Assessment (2006) 'E briefings' [online], http://www.iema.net/readingroom/c146 (Accessed 13 March 2006).

Institute of Environmental Management and Assessment Reading Room (2006) 'London Borough of Sutton's EMA statement' [online], http://www.iema.net/readingroom/show/614/c190 (Accessed 13 March 2006).

International Chamber of Commerce (1989) *Environmental Auditing*, Paris, ICC.

International Organization for Standardization (2005) *The ISO Survey of Certifications 2004*, ISO.

International Organization for Standardization (2006) 'Management systems website' [online], http://www.iso.org/iso/en/iso9000-14000/index.html (Accessed 13 March 2006).

Kirklees Environment Unit (2004) 'Kirklees Metropolitan Council: a case study of achieving EMAS' [online], http://www.kirkleesmc.gov.uk/publications/environment/Achieving%20EMASCase%20StudyOct2004%20.pdf (Accessed October 2005).

Kirkpatrick, C. and Parker, D. (2004) 'Editorial: regulatory impact assessment – an overview', *Public Money and Management*, vol. 24, no. 5, pp. 267–70.

Klijn, F. and De Haes, H.A.U. (1994) 'A hierarchical approach to ecosystems and its implications for ecological land classifications', *Landscape Ecology*, vol. 9, pp. 89–104.

Knudtson, P. and Suzuki, D. (1992) *Wisdom of the Elders*, Sydney, Allen and Unwin.

Krippendorff, K. (1993) 'Major metaphors of communication and some constructivist reflections on their use', *Cybernetics and Human Knowing*, vol. 2(1), pp. 3–25.

Lakoff, G. and Johnson, M. (1980) *Metaphors We Live By*, Chicago, IL, University of Chicago Press.

Leunig, M. (1985) *Ramming the Shears: A Collection of Drawings by Michael Leunig*, Ringwood, Penguin Books.

Litchfield, N. (1996) *Community Impact Evaluation*, London, UCL Press.

Mahoney, M. (1988) 'Constructive meta-theory 1: basic features and historical foundations', *International Journal of Personal Construct Psychology*, vol. 1, pp. 1–35.

McCallister, D.M. (1980) *Evaluation in Environmental Planning: Assessing Environmental, Social, Economic and Political Trade-Offs*, Cambridge, MIT Press.

McClintock, D., Ison, R.L. and Armson, R. (2003) 'Metaphors of research and researching with people', *Journal of Environmental Planning and Management*, vol. 46, no. 5, pp. 715–31.

McClintock, D., Ison, R.L. and Armson, R. (2004) 'Conceptual metaphors: a review with implications for human understandings and systems practice', *Cybernetics and Human Knowing*, vol. 11, no. 1, pp. 25–47.

McCulloch, A. (1996) 'Environmental assessment, the learning society and the search for sustainable development', paper presented at Conference on Integrating Environmental Assessment and Socio-Economic Appraisal in the Development Process, University of Bradford, 24–25 May.

McKie, R. (2005) 'Planet in peril', *The Observer*, 26 June, pp. 1–2 (supplement).

Meadows, D.H., Meadows, D.L. and Randers, J. (1992) *Beyond the Limits*, London, Earthscan.

Meadows, D.H., Meadows, D.L., Randers, J. and Behrens, W.W. (1972) *The Limits to Growth*, London, Earth Island.

Mercier, J. and Ahmed, K. (2004) 'EIA and SEA at the World Bank', paper presented to Proceedings of the 8th Intergovernmental Policy Forum on Environmental Assessment, in association with the Annual Meeting of the International Association for Impact Assessment (IAIA), Vancouver, Canada.

Miller, A. (1983) 'The influence of personal biases on environmental problem-solving', *Journal of Environmental Management*, vol. 17, pp. 133–42.

Miller, A. (1985) 'Technological thinking: its impact on environmental management', *Journal of Environmental Management*, vol. 9, no. 3, pp. 179–90.

Morris, R.M. (2005) 'Thinking about systems for sustainable lifestyles', *Open University Systems Society (OUSyS) Newsletter*, no. 39 (Autumn), pp. 15–19.

Morris, P. and Therivel, R. (2001) *Methods of Environmental Impact Assessment* London, Spon.

Moscovici, S. and Doise, W. (1994) *Conflict and Consensus: A General Theory of Collective Decisions*, London, Sage.

NAO (2002), *Better Regulation: Making Good Use of Regulatory Impact Assessments*, HC 329, London, NAO.

NERC (2005) *Climate Change: Scientific Certainties and Uncertainties*, NERC.

Nicholson, S. (2003) 'Implementing the SEA Directive', *The Environmentalist*, no. 13, February.

Nilsson, M.A. and Dalkmann, H. (2001) 'Decision making and strategic environmental assessment', *Journal of Environmental Assessment Policy and Management*, vol. 3, no. 3, pp. 305–27.

North, D. (1990) *Institutions, Institutional Change and Economic Performance*, Cambridge, Cambridge University Press.

O'Brien, B. (1990) *CONsequences*, Kent Town, South Australia, Wakefield Press.

The Open University (2003) U216 *Environment*.

Organization for Economic Co-operation and Development (1986) *Methods and Procedures in AID Evaluation*, Paris, OECD.

Osborne, D. and Gaebler, T. (1992) *Reinventing Government: How the Entrepreneurial Spirit is Transforming the Public Sector*, Reading, MA, Addison-Wesley.

Patton, M.Q. (1990) *Qualitative Evaluation and Research Methods* (2nd edn), Newbury Park, CA, Sage Publications.

Pearson, C.J. and Ison, R.L. (1997) *Agronomy of Grassland Systems* (2nd edn), Cambridge, Cambridge University Press.

Plsek, P. (2001) 'Why won't the NHS do as it is told?', plenary address, NHS Confederation Conference, 6 July.

Porritt, J. (2003) 'Odd couple', *The Guardian*.

Pretty, J.N. (1994) 'Alternative systems of inquiry for sustainable agriculture', *IDS Bulletin*, vol. 25, no. 2, pp. 37–48.

Pretty, J.N. (1995) *Regenerating Agriculture: Policies and Practice for Sustainability and Self-Reliance*, London, Earthscan.

Reyes, A. (1995) 'A theoretical framework for the design of a social accounting system', PhD thesis, University of Humberside.

Reynolds, M. (2006) 'Evaluation based on critical systems heuristics' in Iman, I. and Williams, B. (eds) *Evaluation and Systems*, Fairhaven, MA, American Evaluation Association.

Roberts, K.A. (1991) 'Field monitoring: confessions of an addict' in Goldsmith, F.B. (ed.) *Monitoring for Conservation and Ecology*, London, Chapman and Hall.

Roberts, P. (1995) *Environmentally Sustainable Business: A Local and Regional Perspective,* London, Paul Chapman Publishing.

Roberts, P. (2005) *The End of Oil*, London, Bloomsbury.

Roe, D., Dalal-Clayton, B. and Hughes, R. (1995) *A Directory of Impact Assessment Guidelines*, London, IIED.

Rossi, P.H., Freeman, H.E. and Wright, S.R. (1979) *Evaluation: A Systematic Approach*, Beverly Hills, CA, Sage Publications.

Rowe, J. (2005) Posting to http://onthecommons.org [online] on 9 August 2005 (Accessed November 2005).

Russell, D.B. and Ison, R.L. (2000) 'The research–development relationship in rural communities: an opportunity for contextual science' in Ison, R.L. and Russell, D.B. (eds) *Agricultural Extension and Rural Development: Breaking Out of Traditions*, Cambridge, Cambridge University Press.

Ryan, Andrew (2004) 'New EU directives to implement Aarhus Convention', *Environmental Law Bulletin*, January, pp. 7–9.

Rylands v. Fletcher (1868) *Law Reports 3 House of Lords 330* (accessed through Westlaw UK, 2004).

Sadler, B. (1994) *Proposed Framework for the International Study of the Effectiveness of Environmental Assessment*, Federal Environmental Assessment Review Office (FEARO), Canada, and the International Association of Impact Assessment.

Sadler, B. and Fuller, K. (1997) 'Quality assurance in environmental assessment', *Environmental Assessment Magazine*, vol. 5, no. 1, pp. 13–16.

Sadler, B. and Verheem, R. (1996) *Strategic Environmental Assessment: Status, Challenges and Future Directions*, Report 53, The Hague, Ministry of Housing, Spatial Planning and the Environment.

Sagoff, M. (1989) *The Economy of the Earth*, Cambridge, Cambridge University Press.

Schön, D.A. (1979) 'Generative metaphor: a perspective on problem-setting in social policy' in Ortony, A. (ed.) *Metaphor and Thought*, pp. 254–83, Cambridge, Cambridge University Press.

Senge, P. (1990) *The Fifth Discipline: The Art and Practice of the Learning Organization*, New York, Doubleday.

Senge, P. (1999) *The Fifth Discipline: The Art and Practice of the Learning Organization*, New York, Random House.

Senge, P., Roberts, C., Ross, R.B., Smith, B.J. and Kleiner, A. (1994) *The Fifth Discipline Fieldbook: Strategies and Tools for Building a Learning Organization*, London, Nicholas Brealey Publishing.

SLIM (2004a) 'Developing conducive and enabling institutions for concerted action', *SLIM PB3* (available at http://slim.open.ac.uk).

SLIM (2004b) 'SLIM framework: social learning as a policy approach for sustainable use of water' [online], http://slim.open.ac.uk (Accessed 27 March 2006).

SLIM (2004c) 'Stakeholders and stakeholding in integrated catchment management and sustainable use of water', *SLIM PB2* (available at http://slim.open.ac.uk).

SLIM (2004d) 'Guidelines for capacity building for social learning in integrated catchment management and the sustainable use of water', *SLIM PB7* (available at http://slim.open.ac.uk).

SLIM (2004e) 'Ecological constraints in sustainable management of natural resources', *SLIM PB1* (available at http://slim.open.ac.uk).

Smith A. (1997) 'Scoping, public participation and the consultation process', *Environmental Assessment*, vol. 5, no. 4.

Spellerberg, I.F. (1991) *Monitoring Ecological Change*, Cambridge, Cambridge University Press.

Stephenson, D., Brooke, C.E. and Nixon, J.A. (1995) *Public Participation in EIA: A Review of Experience in Europe and the UK*, Aberdeen, Centre for Environmental Management and Planning.

Stop Stansted Expansion (2005) [online] http://www.stopstanstedexpansion.com/maps.html (Accessed August 2005).

Stuth, J.W. and Lyons, B.G. (1993) *Decision Support Systems for the Management of Grazing Lands: Emerging Issues*, UNESCO.

Sustainable Development Commission (2006) 'Commissioners' [online], http://www.sd-commission.org.uk/pages/commissioners.html (Accessed 13 March 2006).

Svensson, M. (2005) 'Archetypes in system analysis' [online], Lund University Centre for Sustainability Studies, URL (Accessed November 2005).

Tansley, A.G. (1935) 'The use and abuse of vegetational concepts and terms', *Ecology*, vol. 16, pp. 284–307.

Taylor Woodrow Corporate Social Responsibility Report (2003) [online] http://www.iema.net/library/Article_TaylorWoodrow/Taylor%20Woodrow.pdf (Accessed 13 March 2006).

Tilden, F. (1977) *Interpreting Our Heritage* (3rd edn), Chapel Hill, NC, University of North Carolina Press.

Ulrich, W. (1996) *A Primer to Critical Systems Heuristics for Action Researchers*, Hull, Centre for Systems Studies, University of Hull.

Ulrich, W. (2000) 'Reflective practice in the civil society: the contribution of critically systemic thinking', *Reflective Practice*, vol. 1, no. 2, pp. 247–68.

UNECE – United Nations Economic Commission for Europe (1998) 'Convention on Access to Information, Public Participation in Decision-Making and Access to Justice in Environmental Matters (the Aarhus Convention)' [online], http://europa.eu.int/comm/environment/aarhus/index.htm (Accessed 13 March 2006).

UNEP (1988) *Environmental Impact Assessment: Basic Procedures for Developing Countries*, Nairobi, United Nations Environment Programme.

Upham, P., Maughan, J., Raper, D. and Thomas, C. (2003) *Towards Sustainable Aviation*, London, Earthscan.

Vickers, G. (1972) *Freedom in a Rocking Boat*, London, Penguin.

von Foerster, H. (1992) 'Ethics and second-order cybernetics', *Cybernetics and Human Knowing*, vol. 1, pp. 9–19.

Wadsworth, Y. (1997a) *Do it Yourself Social Research* (2nd edn), Sydney, Allen and Unwin.

Wadsworth, Y. (1997b) *Everyday Evaluation on the Run* (2nd edn), Sydney, Allen and Unwin.

Waltner-Toews, D. (2005) *Ecosystem Sustainability and Health: A Practical Approach*, Cambridge, Cambridge University Press.

Wathern, P. (ed.) (1988) *Environmental Impact Assessment: Theory and Practice*, New York, Routledge.

Wikipedia (2006) [online] http://en.wikipedia.org/wiki/ (Accessed 13 March 2006).

Wilson, B. (1984) *Systems: Concepts, Methodologies and Applications*, Chichester, Wiley.

Wood, C. (1995 [2002]) *Environmental Impact Assessment: A Comparative Review*, Harlow, Longman.

Woodward, F.I. (1987) *Climate and Plant Distribution*, Cambridge, Cambridge University Press.

World Health Organization (1999) *Guidelines for Community Noise*, Geneva, WHO.

WWF/Birdlife International (2000) 'Comments on the European Commission White Paper on environmental liability', WWF European Policy Office, Brussels BirdLife ECO.

# Responses to Activities

## Activity 1   The food on your table – an environmental web

I have not provided an extensive answer to this activity as each situation will be unique. You may have realised that Figure 2b could be used to help you think about this activity. Some foods, e.g. prawns produced commercially in coastal and estuarine areas cleared of mangroves, often carry with them a greater environmental 'wake' and/or take more food miles to get to your table. Others are produced and transported in ways that are hardly sustainable or that produce huge amounts of environmentally damaging effluent (e.g. pig production in the Netherlands).

## Activity 3   Use of models in the *Terminal 5* example

I noted a number of different models, although several were possibly all different uses of the same underlying engineering design model of the proposed terminal structure. The first model presentation on the track was a highly stylised general illustration of the external appearance of the entire terminal, and a few seconds later, a more detailed picture of the terminal building, with its 'glazed façade and beautiful waveform roof'. Both of these illustrations may have just been architect's drawings, albeit using computer graphics technology, or they could be an output from the much more detailed model that was used to produce the 'walk through' and static internal views of different parts of the terminal. In the second half of the track, there were similar virtual reality model outputs of other aspects of the passengers' journey through the terminal, using animated figures to increase the sense of reality. The same combinations of static and animated outputs were used to show off the satellite buildings relative to the main terminal and some features of these satellites.

But what about the sequence between the initial general view and the close-up of the terminal? It began with an illustration, something between a map and a satellite photograph of Europe, centred on Heathrow. From this point, there grew an expanding series of what we were expected to recognise as aircraft contrails, flowing freely from Heathrow to a range of destinations, ending with a recognisable aircraft shape passing across the screen. This sequence is also a model, very highly stylised, that was designed to represent in an abstract way what BAA, as promoters of Terminal 5, saw as its very positive features for its intended customers.

## Activity 4   Developing a systems map

I started this activity by re-working my way through the case study as written up in Book 1. I extracted from it what I considered to be some of the main elements (things) in the situation. I then began to group together what I considered to be related elements. I first focused on airports and the number of runways – I was thinking of the physical aspects of airports, including terminals, and recognised that other forms of transport also had a physical/spatial dimension, so included the other main forms of transport here and called it 'UK transport system'. As depicted here this can be seen as a sub-system of my overall aviation expansion decision-making system, but when I reflect on it, I realise that in my next iteration I would want to separate the UK airports

<u>Elements in the situation</u>
- stakeholders
- aircraft
- cars
- airports
- air travellers (holiday makers etc.)
- flights (number of)
- greenhouse gas emissions
- global warming
- noise
- air quality
- airport workers
- regulations - health & safety pollutants
- waste - liquid, solid
- drains
- air freight (eg fruit, flowers)
- runways
- White paper
- $CO_2$ emissions
- public transport
- trains
- buses
- traffic congestion
- house prices
- airport operators
- airline companies
- travel agencies
- industrial suppliers
- NGOs
- consultants
- government departments (DfT) etc.
- European Union
- public inquiry
- Terminal 5
- GDP
- FAA
- London airports (Gatwick, Heathrow, Stansted, Luton)
- Freedom to fly coalition
- BAA
- Legislation (Bills)
- Legislative stages (consultation stage)
- religious organisations
- international treaties
- MPs
- political parties
- Green papers
- Act of Parliament
- Minister for Transport
- studies
- White paper documents
  - New Deal (1998)
  - Regional studies
  - Future of aviation
  - UK freight
  - Potential Impact
- Air traffic
- forecourts
- summary of responses
- Regional consultation summary of 7 studies
- Aviation and the Environment
- White paper
- Questions
- Forecasting models (SPAM SPASM)
- oil price (assumptions)
- contrails
- Land-take
- economic instruments
- voluntary agreements
- levy
- carbon trading scheme
- index value
- principles (eg polluter pays)
- subsidy ICAO
- Open Skies Agreement
- Airport watch
- FoE
- Energy White Paper
- SERAS framework
- Cliffe site
- cost-benefit analysis
- businesses (airline, catering, maintenance, hotels)
- SEEDA
- Stop Stansted expansion
- District Chamber of Commerce
- Recommendations (Decision)
- RSPB
- BA
- Keys to protocol
- EMAS ISO14001

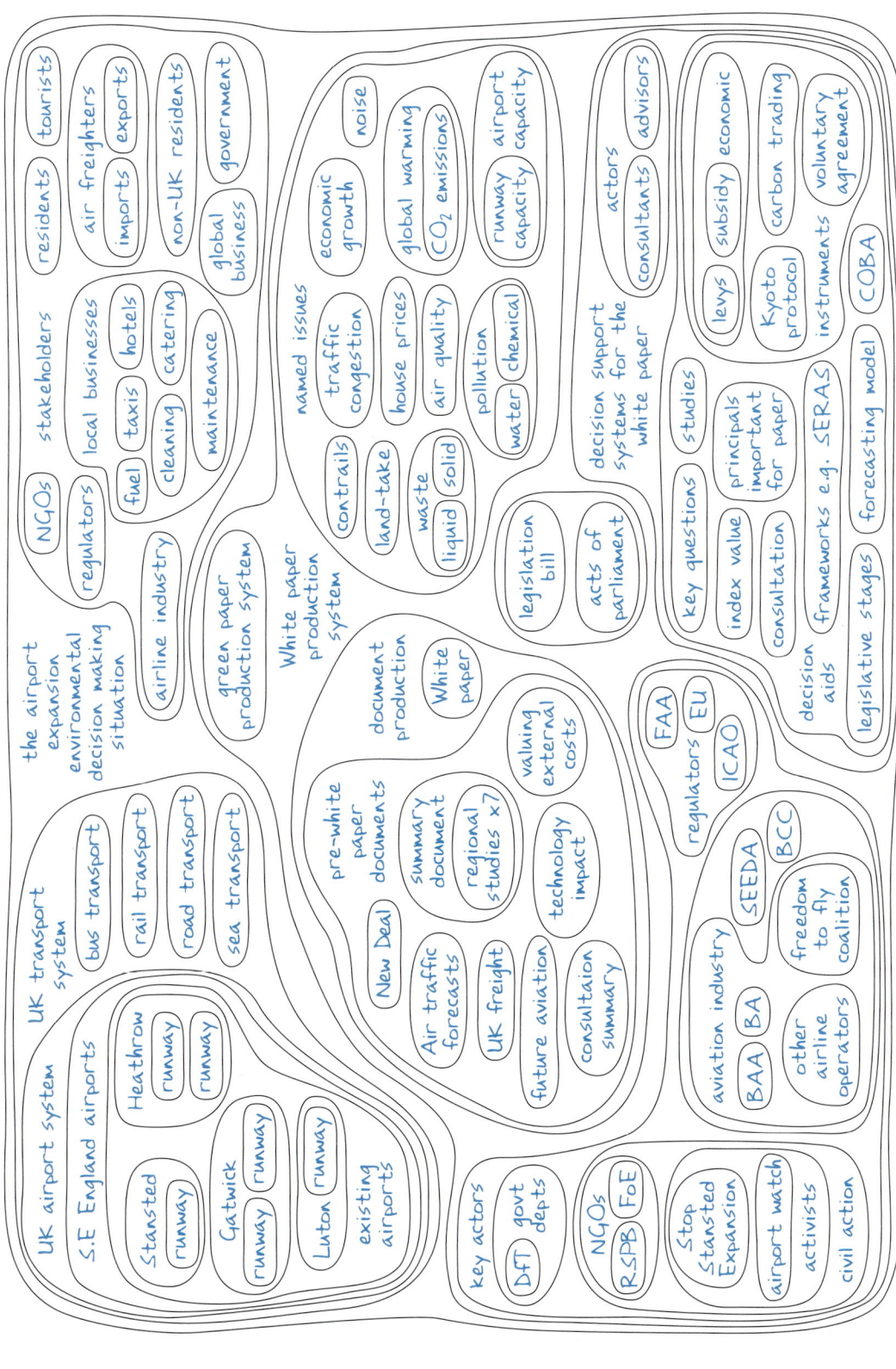

Figure 51 A set of elements in the case study situation and a first iteration systems map of the aviation expansion environmental decision-making situation

system from the other forms of transport: although, in my view, they should be considered together, they were not in the case of the aviation expansion case study. So really it would be better to move these other modes of transport to the environment of my system of interest (i.e. outside the boundary).

At the core of my map is a White Paper producing system. I first tried to capture all of the documents produced as part of the process leading up to the White Paper. These were different I felt to the actual legislation. My other main sub-systems were a 'key actors sub-system', a 'decision-support sub-system' and a 'named issues sub-system'. As you will see I have made a distinction between key actors (in the White Paper producing process) and stakeholders (which is another sub-system of my overall system of interest). I did this because I felt that as actors in the situation they were perhaps playing a different role to that of 'stakeholder', and that there were a large range of stakeholders not involved as actors. In my next iteration I am not sure I would want to keep this division and I now realise that it might be better to include a consultation sub-system somewhere. I felt particularly satisfied with my 'decision-support system' because I was able to capture the specialist roles as well as decision aids including policy instruments (or social technologies). Overall I found it a helpful sense-making procedure.

I did a second iteration of my systems map reducing some of the detail (Figure 52). I did this because I wanted to move from an analytical mode so as to use my map for communication purposes.

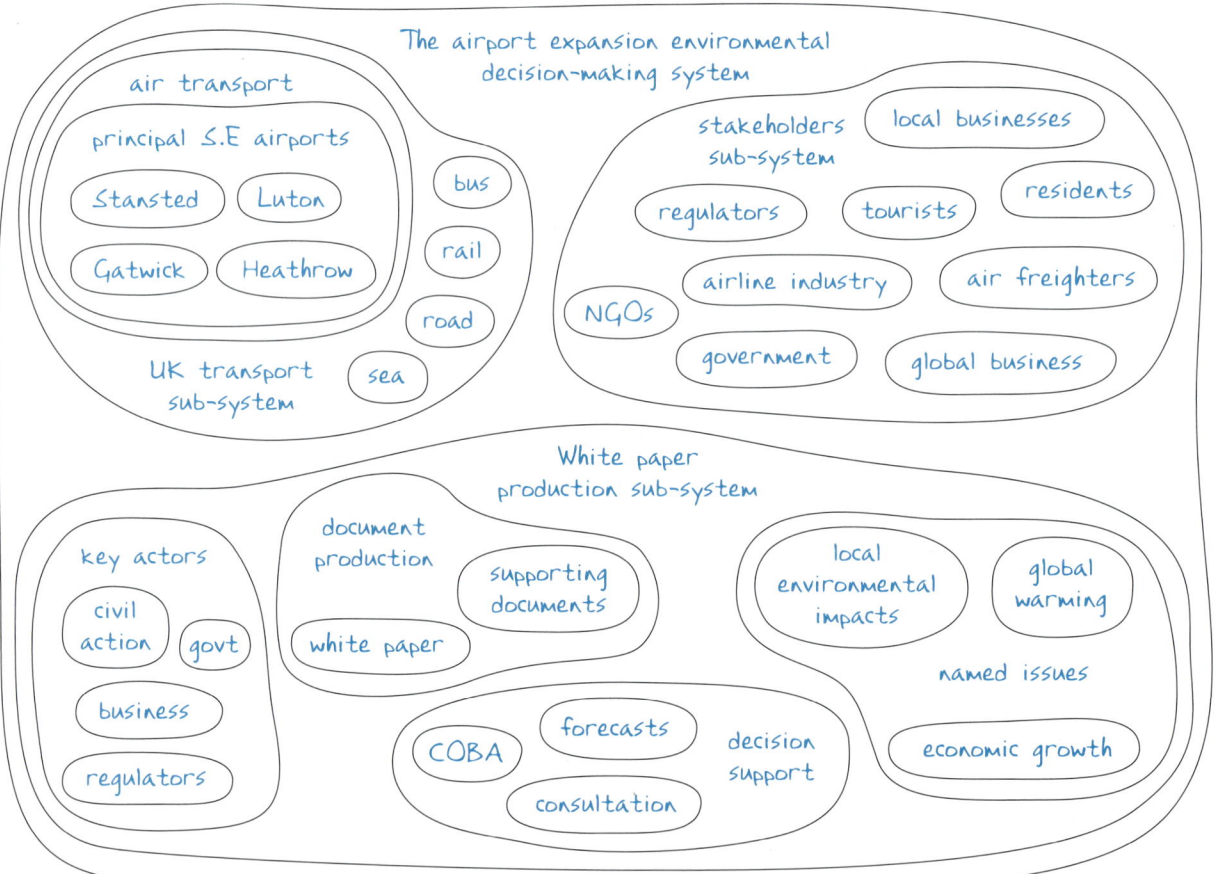

Figure 52   A revised systems map of the airport expansion situation simplified so as to aid communication

# Activity 5  Patterns of influence – influence diagramming

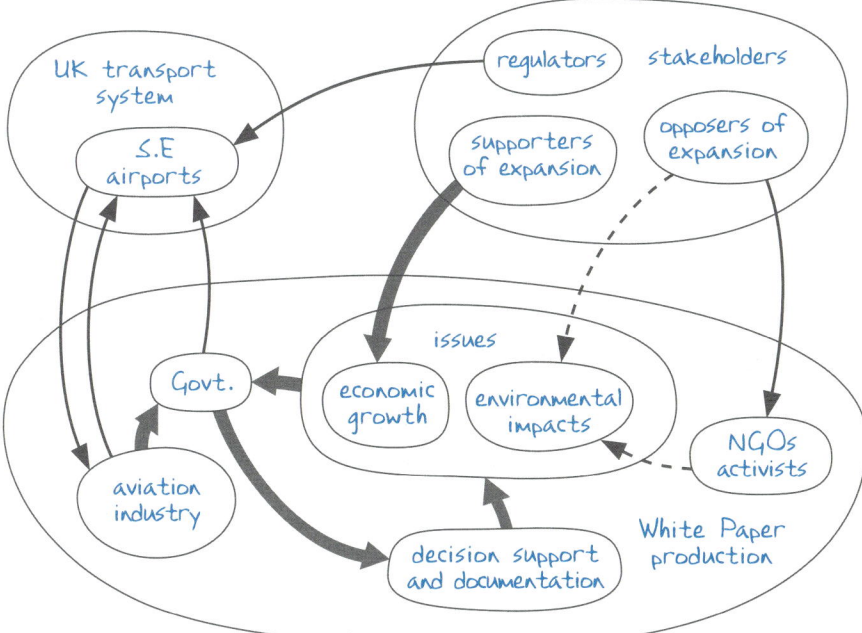

Figure 53  An influence diagram of the situation concerning airport expansion in south east England

I started my diagram by thinking about the systems and sub-systems that I peerceived as being key to this decision. As you will see, I have made the White Paper production process a key factor. The desire to maintain or increase economic growth and the strong influence of the aviation industry were other important factors. I was also conscious of what appeared to be a difference in the strengths of influence between the supporters and opposers of expansion.

# Activity 6  A simple multiple cause diagram

Figure 54  A multiple cause diagram that shows plausible relationships between the three factors volume of air traffic, demand for flights and cost of flights

## Activity 7 Multiple cause diagrams and feedback loops

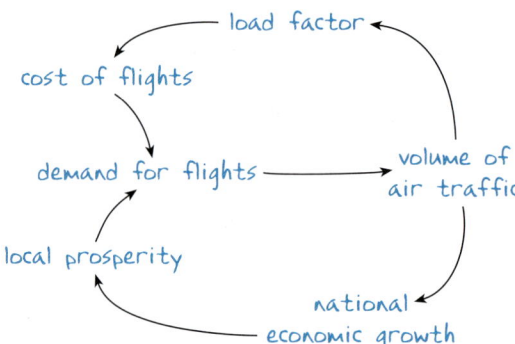

Figure 55 A multiple cause diagram showing two of the feedback loops associated with demand for air travel from Swansea

One loop that is suggested involves the effect of load factor on cost, and hence on demand. This has the form 'demand → air traffic → cost → demand'. The other loop concerns prosperity. The Government claimed in the debate over the White Paper that air traffic 'drives economic growth' and hence prosperity, which in turn affects demand for air traffic.

## Activity 8 Investigating feedback

The actions required to produce these graphs and the graphs themselves are on the DVD.

## Activity 9 Sign graphs

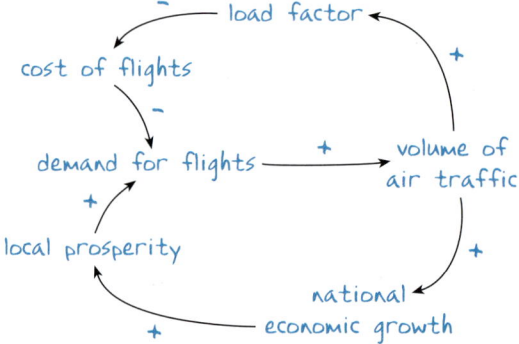

Figure 56 The interaction between some of the factors affecting demand for air travel, shown as a sign graph

## Activity 11   Developing diagrams

The range of diagramming techniques illustrated in this activity shows how these can be used together in a comprehensive exploration of a situation. The limitations imposed by each technique imply that it is recommended to use different approaches at different stages of an inquiry. Spray diagrams and rich pictures are extremely useful to brainstorm a situation at the beginning of an inquiry, but at some stage you may want to identify boundaries within a system of interest, and classify components within a nested set of boundaries. You may then want to take this initial structuring further by identifying the relationships between components through connecting arrows by developing your systems map into an influence diagram. We are now gradually moving away from a static representation of a situation to one which is increasingly dynamic.

A multiple cause diagram establishes cause and effect relationships between components, and a sign graph identifies positive and negative feedback mechanisms within the changing situation. The system dynamics diagram selects a specific sub-set of components whose relationship can be readily quantified and differentiates between levels (measurable quantities), rates (how these levels change over time) and auxiliary variables (factors which influence the rates of change).

As we move through the various diagramming techniques, there is a trend from divergent and exploratory modelling towards convergent and predictive modelling, but this should not imply that this is a one-way process. Convergent techniques may trigger off new insights and/or avenues of investigation which ought to bring you back to previous diagrams for modification or initiate a new set of exploratory diagrams altogether.

## Activity 14   Exploring a situation through metaphor

Using the metaphor of the hammerer, I have first chosen to look at the use of a long-term simulation of passenger numbers by Halcrow (Section 5.3 in Book 1). The tool (hammer) was simulation – we know very little about the hammerer (i.e. the simulation practitioners) other than their firm. I assume they were consultants. I have no knowledge of their professional training or of their personal perspectives – the fact that they coined the acronyms SPASM and SPAM suggests they may have had a sense of humour! We also know little about the mental models of the practitioners (i.e. the traditions of understanding out of which they thought and acted) that determined the criteria/assumptions around which the simulation was built. The assumptions and outputs can be used to gauge some of these – they engaged in forecasting not backcasting; they assumed unregulated growth; they did not build in any sensitivity analysis on varying oil prices; and they do not appear to have accounted for possible positive and negative feedback processes.

So what gets hammered? Well if the assumptions are wrong or questionable then it is the environment and citizens. If they are valid, then what gets hammered shut is the 'decision box' framed by the original starting questions or terms of reference for the White Paper.

I have already commented in the teaching text on the aviation expansion environmental decision in terms of the metaphor of 'a performance'. For me the best insights came from the material in Book 1 and the interview with staff of the DfT. From a historical point of view the 'music was composed' by a 1985 White Paper, the actions of a Transport Select Committee in 1996 and a set of civil servants who ran 'the performance' for a period of over seven years. In a sense, the civil servants were the 'conductors' although I could choose to see ministers as the ones who decided on 'the orchestration'. The following quote reveals aspects of the conducting role: 'the starting point has to be to understand the kinds of developments that might be required, then understand their impacts and then to try to find the right balance between those two things. ... developing ... the modelling tools, the analysis frameworks was quite a significant exercise before you could start looking at ranges of scenarios and options. And critical was that that analysis had to be objective ... it had to be thorough ... and it had to be capable of standing close scrutiny'.

In some sense, the conductors were prescribing the sort of performance it had to be in advance, and clearly objectivity was a major performance measure for them!

In the interview, it becomes clear at one stage that the conductors felt short of resources at several stages – in terms of the metaphor they were short of players of a particular type. One aspect of the interview was revealing – again in terms of the relationship between choice of music, score and orchestration: 'there were some ... broad policy questions ... the issue of just how much growth of aviation in the UK should there be taking account of, on the one hand ... the economic benefits ... both for UK businesses increasingly operating on an international and indeed global level ... and for ... attracting inward tourism to ... and, on the other hand ... the ... clear environmental impacts of aviation ... at both a local level and at a global level, not least in respect of global warming'.

Yet operationally these questions had been decided when the consultation exercise began: 'We didn't want to come with preconceived ideas as to what the best solution at a particular airport would be'.

The metaphor suggests three options for environmental decision making: (i) play someone else's music; (ii) negotiate over the music; or (iii) come together and make music and see what emerges.

### Activity 15 Factors that influence decision-making practices

If I use the image of hammering as a form of practice, then I could think of the 'hammerer' as the decision maker, the 'hammer' as decision support – tools and techniques – and the decision situation as 'that which is hammered', although I would rather express 'that which is hammered' in terms of the issue which has been agreed needs to be addressed (e.g. airport capacity or global $CO_2$ levels). Clearly it is the hammerer who can think in terms of problems or opportunities and, in relation to the situation, elucidate the decision criteria (this would be a classic situation to involve a range of stakeholders – by building in stakeholding processes people can be transformed from those affected to those who can take responsibility). Time can be a mental construct or a 'real' feature of the situation. The decision situation also has a history which is open to analysis as do the tools and techniques that can be employed. One factor that is clearly missing from this set is purpose – why are these practices to be carried out at this time in this situation? But purpose is not static and can be linked to levels in systemic terms.

For me acting with awareness of the history, the dynamics of the relationship between a 'hammerer', a 'hammer' and something that is 'hammered' and the questions of purpose would differentiate systemic environmental decision making from just environmental decision making. This image draws attention to a form of individual practice. The advantage of the image of a 'performance' is that it recognises in situations of complexity, uncertainty and interconnectedness that systemic environmental decision making has to be an emergent and concerted performance. For such a performance to emerge, stakeholders have to be able and willing to participate in the performance.

## Activity 16   Do you recognise 'traps' in thinking in the case study?

Engagement with other people is one of the best ways to become aware of one's own traps. From the perspective of the dominant paradigm, the trap in my own thinking could be that I undervalue decision making based on current views of economic growth, and that I also undervalue the role that technology can play in the future. From my perspective the civil servants involved in 'running' the White Paper process are in a trap when they claim that the process has to be 'objective'. As an example I often think of the great cathedrals of Europe and wonder whether decision makers at that time needed objective reasons to proceed. My own perspective is that objectivity, in a context such as the case study, can be a claim made to avoid us as citizens taking responsibility.

A potential trap I have fallen into when engaging with the case study is to assume that the outcome was the result of some purposeful and ill-conceived design. It is likely that those involved were also in traps in thinking and practice – i.e. they did not know how to do things differently. From my perspective, Jonathon Porritt identifies a trap that most government are in; he is possibly in a trap when he espouses the purpose of economic growth as delivering happiness. I think he could have drawn attention to how economic growth is dependent on the number and type of transactions that go on between human beings.

## Activity 17   Treating situations as messes

If setting up the simulation associated with the forecasting model had been considered as a mess rather than a difficulty, then it might have led to more attention being addressed to the main policy choices (economic growth or environmental impact) and a different process for the construction of the White Paper. Different assumptions would have emerged. This in turn might have attracted more resources to help with the decision-making process, recognising that it was a situation of complexity and uncertainty.

## Activity 19  Thinking in terms of transformations

Some examples of transformation processes that I would associate with a White Paper as a means to appreciate its purpose from a systemic perspective include:

- all the current facts about airport expansion not compiled → all the facts compiled
- all perspectives on airport expansion not known → all perspectives known
- all perspectives on airport expansion not heard and reported → all perspectives heard and reported
- case for airport expansion not made → case for expansion made
- decision-making rules not controlled → decision-making rules controlled

There are many, many more – how you answer this will depend on your perspective and your purpose.

## Activity 20  Stakeholder analysis using a systems map

I found I was able to draw on my answer to Activity 4 to do this. As you will see in Figure 57 there are some similarities between my systems maps. As I did this, I felt that in another iteration, if I wanted to be specific about further action, I would have to add names to some of these categories of stakeholders. Only then would I be really sure who were primary, intermediate and key (customers, actors, owners) stakeholders. Some names can be gleaned from the text in Book 1 and from the interviews on the DVD. I put Entebbe airport staff and travellers to the UK in the environment of my system of interest, as whilst they are potentially affected by the decision I do not see them as having a primary stake. As I reflect on my figure I realise I have left ministers out and that I am unsure as to how particular business groups might lobby decisions of this type. This raises the question of who the unseen stakeholders are: those who have meetings with civil servants and ministers? I am also unclear as to how much civil servants from different departments were involved.

## Activity 21  Possible contribution of stakeholder analysis

I have drawn on the limited material in Book 1 and also the interview with the civil servants responsible for the White Paper process which is on the DVD. In providing my answer, I have drawn on some of the transcript of the interview with the civil servants to give you a feel for what was involved in the process. The civil servants

# RESPONSES TO ACTIVITIES

Figure 57   A systems map used as a stakeholder analysis of the airport expansion decision-making process

claimed that in preparing for the consultation 'it was very important to not have preconceptions and to be able to ... consult upon ... the widest possible range and then use the consultation responses we got to help formulate and frame policy'.

Based on the evidence, I would claim that those responsible for the White Paper process had a limited appreciation of stakeholder analysis and processes of building stakeholding. The whole strategy was built on a thorough analysis (one might say paralysis by analysis), conceptions of objectivity and 'information' transfer, collection, collation and dissemination. (In Part 3, I refer to different understandings of human communication so you might like to re-think the consultation strategy when you get to it.) However, there were over half a million responses to the consultation, so clearly many were able to express, to some extent, their stakeholding. They generated a huge amount of data – it is hard to imagine how this was effectively dealt with and then passed to ministers who made the final decision. My own perspective is that some form of stakeholder analysis which led to the design of a process to articulate different perspectives and to frame different sorts of questions for the consultation may have been an improvement.

BOOK 2 STARTING OFF SYSTEMICALLY IN ENVIRONMENTAL DECISION MAKING

## Activity 22   Multiple perspectives in the case study situation

Figure 58   A spray diagram of the different perspectives held by some of the main 'actors' in the airport expansion decision-making process

## Activity 23  What was the problem/opportunity?

You may find that your answer to this activity is very similar to the one you gave for Activity 17 in Book 1. In Book 1 you were told that the UK Government decision-making process on airport expansion posed the following three fundamental questions:

1. How much extra airport capacity (defined as the number of passengers embarking on a flight per annum) will be needed over the next 30 years?
2. How will the environmental impacts be mitigated or paid for?
3. Based on the forecasted passenger number, where should the new airport capacity be located?

You may now recognise these statements as referring to difficulties rather than messes.

You may remember the following quote from the interview with the civil servants responsible for the White Paper process: 'But it was also around a series of questions within each of the documents ... we were trying to ask the key questions ... which, if you like, we were starting to ask ourselves and wanted to understand what the different views were ... which were going to be helpful in terms of ultimately formulating policy and seeking key decisions'.

My point here is that the question that had to be answered – i.e. the naming of the problem and opportunity – preceded the consultation process. Ministers and civil servants had framed the problem as a difficulty – how 'to maximise the significant social and economic benefits that growth in aviation would bring whilst paying for the environmental impacts' – and the situation was not engaged with as a 'mess'. There is also the question of whether or not the environment can be 'paid for' (i.e. consumed).

Given the opportunity, I would choose not to name the problem or opportunity but rather to bring together a range of people with different perspectives to contribute creatively to a systemic inquiry into the situation which I regard as a mess – and characterised by uncertainty, interconnectedness, complexity and conflict.

## Activity 24  Exploring your own perspective on problems and opportunities

I have addressed my own perspective in the teaching text. I rarely speak about problems these days, although I do refer to opportunities. Many years ago, I spoke about problem solving and assumed that problems existed independently of social processes. I now recognise that often one person's problem is another person's opportunity. So I try to be careful with my language and to avoid jumping to hasty assumptions about the nature of a problem/opportunity and hence what might constitute a solution. In fact, I rarely talk about solutions preferring 'situation improvement' instead, i.e. I tend to find that I treat most situations as messes.

## Activity 25  Ways of knowing

Epistemology is concerned with theories of knowledge (or more accurately 'knowing') but it is more than theoretical because we each have different epistemological positions whether we are aware of them or not – our epistemological position determines what we accept as valid knowledge. For me, epistemology is a very practical issue that I encounter every day – for example when two referees of a research bid make contrasting judgements it is often a matter of epistemology. The civil servants responsible for the White Paper take an epistemological stance when they claim that the process was objective. It is possible they were engaged – perhaps without awareness – in technocentric thinking (Quadrant 2 in Figure 29) which is characterised by a reductionist and positivist perspective. From this perspective in isolation, a claim to objectivity is a means of dismissing other perspectives.

It could also be said that a claim to objectivity is a means of avoiding responsibility. Ecocentric thinking (Quadrant 3) represents a positivist but also holistic perspective – in terms used in this course, a systematic perspective. In my experience, this perspective may be held by some ecologists and other environmental scientists and may be reflected in some of the NGO contributions to the decision-making process. My own perspective is close to that of the holocentric perspective (Quadrant 4), that is, a holistic and constructivist, systemic perspective. (The claim is that those with this perspective focus on 'the problem' as the outcome of human activity and on critical learning).

I find this figure useful/helpful in part – but I am loath to use it to label individual people. My own position is to value epistemological awareness – not any one position – so my interest is in using it to trigger reflection on practical questions associated with epistemology. It could, for example, be used to raise awareness amongst those responsible for managing an environmental decision-making process.

## Activity 26  Perspective on science and environmental decision making

My own perspective is similar to that articulated in Reading 5. It has developed from experience of being a scientist and reflecting on how science operates as a form of practice (i.e. I am interested in what scientists do when they do what they do!). A summary of my position is that scientific explanations when they are available are important for environmental decision making, but for me science is only one of many sources of explanations.

## Activity 27  Different forms of participation used in the case study

My answer is contained in the following adaptation of Table 7 from the teaching text.

# RESPONSES TO ACTIVITIES

| Form of participation | Evidence from the aviation expansion case study |
|---|---|
| 1 Passive participation | There were elements of this in the case study – the framing of the questions and posting of material to a website and even village hall meetings can be of this type if no feedback is obtained. |
| 2 Participation in information giving | There was a lot of information giving and gathering in the White Paper process. It is not clear that any of the 500,000 respondents to the consultation had a role in devising the methodology to interpret their comments. Nor is it clear what was actually passed to ministers by way of recommendations. It is clear that the consultation was not designed to be extractive, but it is not clear that the findings were shared or checked for accuracy. |
| 3 Participation by consultation | This was the primary mode employed in the case study. People participate by being consulted and external agents listen to views. These external agents define both problems and solutions, and may modify these in the light of people's responses. Such a consultative process does not concede any share in decision making, and professionals are under no obligation to take on board people's views. |
| 4 Participation for material incentives | This form did not seem to apply, although it is clear that some powerful interests contributed or lobbied with material interests at stake. |
| 5 Functional participation | The 'Freedom to fly?' coalition and some of the other stakeholder interest groups that formed during and after the White Paper process could be seen to fit this category. |
| 6 Interactive participation | I did not perceive any examples of this form of participation. |
| 7 Self-mobilisation | There were examples of people participating by taking initiatives independent of external institutions to change situations, e.g. Airport Watch. But as noted, such self-initiated mobilisation and collective action may or may not challenge existing inequitable distributions of wealth and power. |

## Activity 28   Perspectives on planning

I have answered this question from two perspectives.

1. I am a citizen of Milton Keynes (MK) which is one of the few cities in England that has been totally planned – although this happened well before I became a resident. In my daily life I experience the results of this plan. I experience MK as having many advantages and only a few disadvantages. I do not experience it as being easy to participate in the ongoing planning of the city or my neighbourhood, although I am aware that such opportunities exist and that there has been a history of attempting to involve residents in planning in MK. I am constrained by my family and work commitments, the priorities I set and, until recently, my relative agreement with most of what I see happening. I am increasingly concerned about the seeming imposition of plans for expansion of the 'city' by central Government at a time when traffic congestion is becoming worse and there are no obvious plans for enhanced public transport. However, what is important to me is having the feeling that I could participate more if I wanted to – although I also recognise that I could find this frustrating and I have no experience of the local authority and do not know whether they have a policy on participation.

2   I once worked as a soil conservationist with a public sector agency responsible for many aspects of conservation policy. This agency offered a service to landholders of developing conservation plans which, amongst other features, identified soil conservation practices and structures that were seen as necessary. These plans were developed on aerial photographs of the landholding; they looked particularly good mounted and hanging on the wall of the farm office, hall or living room. My experience with this agency and over subsequent years made me very sympathetic to Ackoff's approach to planning. When the plan was developed by a professional soil conservationist acting largely in isolation, or following minimal consultation, then often the plan remained in its cylinder, or at most was mounted on the wall. It rarely guided subsequent actions of the landholder. However, when the landholder and their family participated in its development and took ownership for its management implications then it became a guide for future activity. Plastic overlays could be used to make changes to the base plan, moving it from a static to a dynamic model. With this approach, the landholder could iterate through a process of learning involving planning and acting.

### Activity 30   Using CSH in 'ought' mode

My answer to this activity is in the form of answers to the 'ought mode' questions in Table 1 in the *Techniques* book. As advised I started with Question 2 – what ought to be the purpose of the consultation process thought of as a system (S).

**Sources of motivation**

1   Citizens in the South East and indirectly citizens in other parts of the UK who miss out because of the concentration of development in the South East.

2   As I considered this question I had to decide where conceptually to put the boundary of my notional system of interest, i.e. what was the purpose of consultation from my perspective? Consultation ought to have been about either (i) how can the long-term quality of life of citizens in the South East be enhanced and sustained? or (ii) what future role should air transport play as part of an integrated and sustainable transport system in the South East? Both these take as their starting point a different level of abstraction than used in the White Paper process. (I recognise that this set of questions could be used at different levels of abstraction and more or less instrumentally.)

3   As a result of consultation, actions are agreed that lead to improvements in the quality of life based on a more effective and less environmentally damaging, integrated transport system.

**Sources of control**

4   It may be better to take this away from central Government and give it to regional bodies (particularly if they have democratic power as in Scotland and Wales).

5   Resources, including expertise, to run an effective, participatory decision-making process based on citizens', not consumer, values.

6   Factors associated with globalisation and a transparent account of Treasury policy.

**Sources of expertise**

7   Systemic environmental decision makers.

8   Material incorporated into T863 as a basis for understanding and practices.

9   Publicly accountable narrative of how different perspectives were valued and employed in framing questions, interpreting results and arriving at decisions (deliberative democracy); widespread experience of invitations to participate (even if declined); mechanism to avoid control action being usurped by ministers which is contrary to emergent outcomes.

**Sources of legitimation**

10  Advocates for these interests can be trained and invited to participate – i.e. these perspectives can be institutionalised.

11  A genuine invitation is one that is (i) experienced as an invitation (ii) and is something that can be declined (otherwise it is coercion or a threat). We need more sophisticated practice and institutional arrangements to allow invitations to be issued, experienced and declined (the NHS consultation described in the teaching text is a move in the right directions but does not yet go far enough).

12  The underlying worldview on which my answers are based concern the relationship between responsibility and response-ability and my contention that the systemic understandings and practices to deal with this are in short supply.

## Activity 31   A critical assessment of systems practice for environmental decision making

I had a particular model of systems practice in my head as I read through the paper, making notes, which included (i) the practitioner – and their history (traditions of understanding) as well as espoused approach; (ii) the situation including stakeholders, institutional factors and the history of failure or success (as for example found in reports, literature, etc.); and (iii) the approach used to engage with the situation (methods, technique, tools) and how these were contextualised or adapted to the situation. In my first reading, I made notes of elements of practice and structure (Figure 59). I then developed a systems map of Martin Bunch's systems practice system (Figure 60).

I found it interesting that Martin stayed with the problem metaphor, but by using UNCHS' question in a workshop setting where many stakeholders were present he enabled the surfacing of a wide range of perspectives as to what the problem was – anyone who experienced that process would be left in little doubt that one of the 'problems' was to know and agree what the problem was! It also opens up a space for negotiation and prioritisation – clearly this was happening during the process.

I have not attempted detailed analysis of all the stakeholders mentioned in the paper – there are many named and it could be done. Martin is not explicit as to whether a stakeholder analysis as such was conducted, but they clearly had an appreciation of a wide range of organisational stakeholders as well as issuing public invitations. Martin acknowledges that slum-dwellers were not included in the workshops. No special workshop was conducted for them (that I am aware of). Understandings from Ulrich's boundary-setting questions might well have been employed to tease out some of the

Elements of practice/structure =
Notes on my first reading

Cooum River = situation = complex, interconnected, uncertain, conflicting multiple perspectives = mess

Martin Bunch = systems practitioner/systemic environmental decision maker

Named environmental issues = eg. pollution

Ecosystem approach based on tools and techniques from adaptive management and SSM
* expression of the problem situation → conceptual modelling
* comparison of conceptual models with real-world situation to stimulate debate about change

1. The situation is explored (who by?)
   - includes partial stakeholder analysis
   - past failures are related to ways of knowing (i.e. engineering approaches based on reductionist - positivist paradigm).

2. Adaptive ecosystem approach - includes systems concepts such as:
   Levels/hierarchy
   Emergent properties
   Feedback
   Control mechanisms
   Modelling
   Concept of 'socioecological systems'
   Combines systems approaches and collaborative (participative?) approaches
   Purposeful (intentional) operating of a learning cycle

3. Activities
   Stakeholder workshops
   Collaborative development of simulation models
   1998 workshop ⎱ → SSM style analysis ⎰
   1999 workshop ⎰        ⎱ → framework for a GIS-based
   exploratory management ⎰   DSS + environmental model
   scenarios

- Snowball technique
  - invitations → newspapers + direct approach
  - p187 → more stakeholders named
  - slum dwellers = affected but not involved (who were Guardians in CSH sense?)
- Indian cultural features an important aspect of the situation
  → local process observers/facilitators
- Rich pictures; CATWOE; mode 2 use of SSM = 'doing work using SSM'.
- Problem identification questions = 8 UNCHS questions
  → surfacing multiple perspectives on the nature of the problem/opportunity
- generation of Themes from questions and rich picture
  → moved 'problem' away from just biophysical to 'political, social and management aspects'.
  ("coordination and communication".
- Rich pictures developed collaboratively (kept open as a living picture for whole workshop).
  → Rescoping of perceptions of the situation
  → joint learning
- Comparison techniques used = formal questioning
  = informal debate/discussion
  = mapping of conceptual models to real model solutions (what/how comparisons) using GIS/simulation models (how?)
  focus on spatial elements
  through comparison phase eg Where do they occur? For how long?
  - Brainstorming → objectives of management
  - DSS → sewage dynamics
  - Iterating between systemic and systematic
  ⇒ Experiential learning a key!
    Was the ongoing-capacity to operate as an adaptive learning system institutionalised?

Figure 59

# RESPONSES TO ACTIVITIES

Figure 60   A first-iteration systems map of Martin Bunch's systems practice system

issues associated with ownership of S, power relations and who was affected but not involved, e.g. who might have played the guardian role. This would have made boundary judgements more apparent.

It is not clear to me that issues of power have been addressed explicitly – little is said about how the intervention came about in the first place, and it is not clear if invitations were widely experienced as invitations and boundary-setting questions were not explored. From my perspective, perhaps one of the main deficiencies – at least as reported – is the lack of explicit mention of how, if at all, monitoring and evaluation were built into practice. That said I thought it was a very good example of how systems practice can be used to effect environmental decision making.

## Activity 32   Conducting a systemic 'meta-inquiry'

As I re-read Reading 6, I generated the following transformations (T) for possible systems of interest (of the form 'a system to do P by Q to achieve R'). My aim was to generate a few that were of interest to me, and from my perspective best reflected what I perceived his purpose to be.

I started with three possible transformations (T).

1. An SSM and adaptive ecosystem approach not tested → SSM and adaptive ecosystem approach tested
2. Cooum River mess not improved → Cooum River mess improved
3. Systems practice not validated academically → Systems practice validated academically

I then expanded these into root definitions of the form do P by Q to achieve R:

1. A system to test SSM and an adaptive ecosystem approach by employing it in a real situation so as to evaluate the effectiveness of these approaches (I considered making R 'to justify the use of these approaches').
2. A system to improve the Cooum River situation by employing a systemic approach so as to bring environmental and social benefits.
3. A system to validate systems practice as research by submitting a paper for peer review and publication so as to justify its value and academic credentials.

I selected number 2 to start with as my system of interest and employed CATWOE to iterate between my original system description and a refined one:

C = Martin Bunch, Martin's department/university, Cooum River stakeholders

A = Martin Bunch, Martin's main collaborators, Cooum River stakeholders

T = Cooum River mess not improved → Cooum River mess improved

W = Improvement environmentally and socially can be achieved by taking a systems and collaborative learning approach

O = Martin Bunch (and/or Indian sponsor – not named?)

E = Past failure opens up opportunity to do something different.

I made some modifications to my system description after doing CATWOE:

A system conducted as a collaborative action research study by Martin Bunch to improve the Cooum River situation perceived as a mess by employing a systemic approach based on SSM and adaptive ecosystem management so as to bring environmental and social benefits as defined by the participants.

I then followed the example in Box 11 and the guidelines for conceptual models in the *Techniques* book (see Modelling: conceptual modelling) to develop a conceptual model. I started with the following list:

- know the (Cooum River) situation
- use action research
- know what constitutes an improvement
- identify stakeholders (potential collaborators)
- plan action research
- know how to use a systemic approach
- plan (develop a design for) the use of a systemic approach
- use SSM and adaptive ecosystem management
- monitor

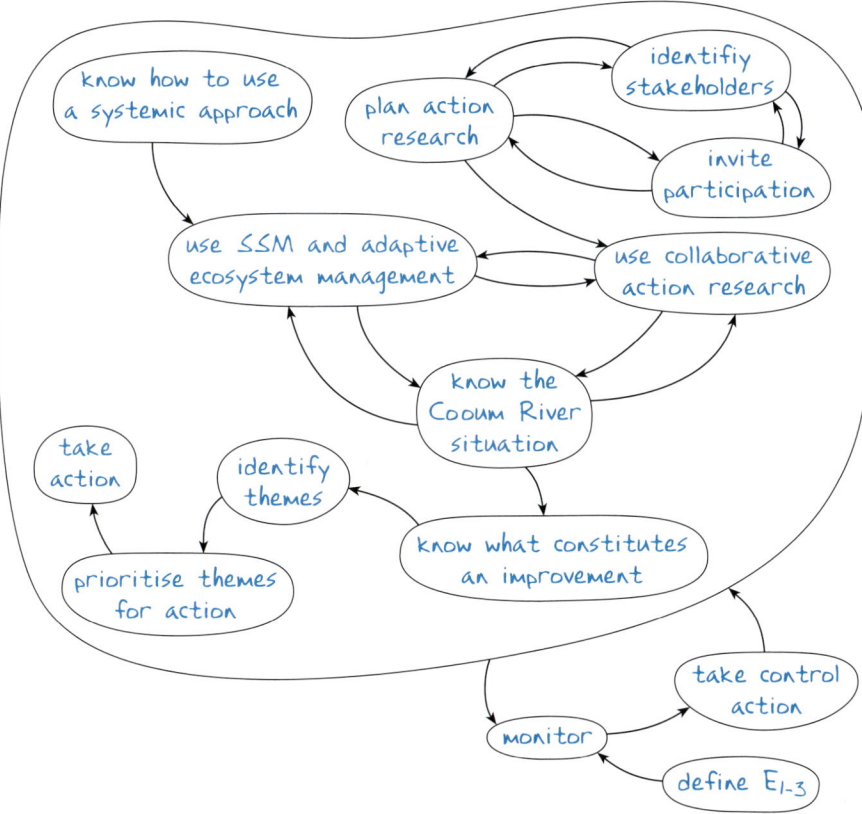

Figure 61  A first-iteration conceptual model based on my root definition of a Cooum River improvement system based on systems practice

- define measures of performance
- take control action.

As you will see from my conceptual model (Figure 61), I identified some additional activities whilst doing it. I call this a first-iteration model – I would normally go back and modify it in line with the logic of the root definition and I might also subsume several activities into a 'take action' sub-system so as to stay within the 7 +/− 2 rule (remember in further iterations each sub-system can be expanded further based on this same rule). When doing this, it is important not to fall into the trap of modelling activities in the situation but modelling activities that are conceptually valid for and consistent with the root definition.

The idea of levels influenced my thinking most as I began to build the conceptual model. For me, one of the main insights I gained out of doing this was to recognise that in a systemic, collaborative approach, knowing about the Cooum River situation was an output of the process (using SSM and collaborative action research) not an input to it. I also recognised that generating the list of activities for any conceptual model is not always easy so I have included Figure 62 as an additional aid for when you have to do it next time.

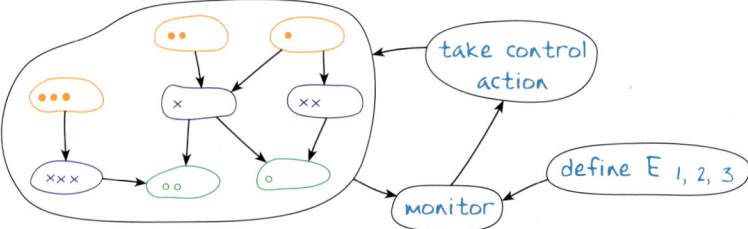

Figure 62    Some guidelines for developing conceptual models as part of SSM (Source: Checkland, 2000)

## Activity 33    Selecting relevant legislation

Taking an 'air travel expansion' system of interest, I see the following international environmental legislation as relevant:

(i)   the Climate Change Convention because aircraft emissions contribute to greenhouse gas concentrations

(ii)  the Aarhus Convention because it appears to cover who participates in deciding what is expanded as part of environmental decision making

(iii) the Kyoto Protocol – rate of expansion of air travel seems to be directly related to meeting targets to affect climate change as set under this protocol.

# Activity 35 Start an audit of your experience of environmental legislation and schemes

(i) I have chosen the categories of 'work' and 'home' as my frame of reference.

(ii) **Work**

Higher education environmental and sustainable development policy initiatives (OU and other)
UK Environmental Protection Act 1990
Agenda 21
Kyoto Protocol
Water Framework Directive
Common Agricultural Policy reform
ISO 14001

**Home**

Local authority environmental policy and Local Agenda 21
Bedfordshire Waste Management Strategy
The National Forest project

(iii) Becoming aware of or engaged in the initiatives I have identified under (ii) has affected my environmental decision making in some cases but not others. For instance Bedfordshire's Waste Management Strategy and work to meet targets for recycling has had a significant effect on how I manage waste at household level (re-use and recycling). Through a research project in which I was involved I became much more aware of issues concerning water at several levels (local, regional, national and European) and I now tend to make more informed choices regarding water. I also became involved in producing teaching and training materials in support of some of the legislation but this has not always directly affected my environmental decision making.

(iv) I would like to know how the Aarhus Convention will work in practice in the longer term, and whether or not it will open up new opportunities for participating in environmental decision making, particularly regarding planning developments in my area. My objective here initially is to check accounts of people's experiences with respect to the legislation at different levels.

I would also like to find out more about what my council intends as part of its waste management strategy and what that might mean for me as a householder in the longer term, e.g. I want to find a more satisfactory way of disposing of hedge clippings from my garden and what support is currently available and what might become available in future.

(v)

| Legislation or scheme | Objectives | 6 month check |
| --- | --- | --- |
| Aarhus Convention | Check accounts of experiences at different levels | |
| Bedfordshire Waste Management Strategy | Find out more detail current and planned | |

## Activity 36  Exploring the purpose of legislation and schemes

| Abstract | Declared purposes of legislation/scheme |
|---|---|
| Water Framework Directive | Holistic approach to managing Europe's water bodies including coordination for sustainable management of water resources. |
| Environmental management systems | Managing an organisation's significant environmental impacts. |
| Strategic environmental assessment | Considering the potential impact of proposed plans, policies and programmes on the environment. Contributing to sustainable development. |

## Activity 37  Identifying systems of interest

Some potential systems of interest I can identify in the extract from Karl Fuller include a policy and planning system in New Zealand and a policy and plan appraisal system in the UK. Without more detail I can only identify these potential systems of interest in general terms. One distinction I make between the two is that the purpose of the system of interest in New Zealand seems to be effects-based policy and plan making whereas the purpose of the system of interest in the UK seems to be appraisal of policy and planning from an environmental perspective.

(i) The New Zealand policy and planning system of interest seems to be of interest to those involved in the act of policy and plan making and potentially other stakeholders in those activities. (It also seems to be a system of interest to Karl Fuller for the purpose of cross-country comparison of SEA but this is different from the purpose of the New Zealand system of interest, so I assume Karl's overall system of interest is a different one.) The UK policy and plan appraisal seems to be of interest to those involved in environmental appraisal. (There isn't enough detail given for me to be more specific here.)

(ii) There is not enough detail given in this short extract for me to be able to deduce much about systems boundaries but in the process of drawing the following systems maps, I found myself asking questions about who stakeholders might be, the depth of consideration of SEA and what was involved in the process and what other activities besides SEA those involved in policy and plan making or appraisal were involved in. For accuracy I would need to check my assumptions regarding boundaries in the diagrams I have drawn with those involved in the activities but the diagrams may be a useful tool in that checking process.

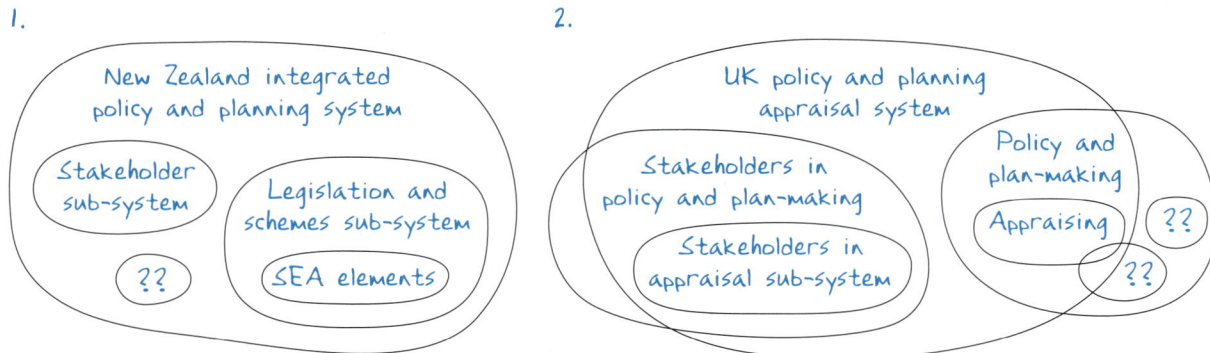

Figure 63  Systems maps of a New Zealand and a UK policy and planning system of interest

### Activity 38  Implications of the Aarhus Convention

(i) The emphasis on making information available to the public early in a decision-making process sounds as though it could enhance stakeholders' ability to explore environmental decision-making situations. I am however also mindful of Glasson et al.'s (2005) comments on disadvantages as well as advantages of public participation, and wonder who will use the information supplied and how and whether it will be to the benefit of a majority of stakeholders or just a few.

(ii) The provision of very broad-based environmental information could potentially enable stakeholders to approach environmental decision making more systemically, as it sounds less likely to focus immediately on narrow problems or from a limited range of perspectives. Including more information on context from which stakeholders can formulate and negotiate systems of interest sounds promising in terms of taking a systems approach. I do wonder, though, whether what will be provided is more likely to be data than information and how informative most stakeholders will find it. From the experience of past EU directives, I also think that even if we have EU directives and what is intended is written down, how it works in practice can be quite different from what is intended.

### Activity 39  Formulating questions to ask stakeholders

Five questions I would like to ask stakeholders in the three cases are:

(i) What were the roles and perspectives of those who drafted the scoping documents (mentioned in case studies 1 and 2)?

(ii) Which stakeholders in the new Dibden Bay Terminal were and were not included or represented in the 'interest groups' mentioned in the preliminary discussions?

(iii) What process of decision making preceded all three of the consultation processes presented in the case study?, i.e. were other options besides the new terminal, sea defences and extraction of sand and gravel at these particular sites considered? If so why were these rather than other sites selected?

(iv) Who decided what alterations to the Dibden Terminal proposal were 'realistic, practical and justified'?

(v) Did local stakeholders in the Dibden Bay and Bedfordshire EIA processes feel that they had been heard and did they think they had been included in the process early enough?

### Activity 40   Comparing EIA diagrams

(i) Figure 25(T): consideration of alternatives, action design, screening, scoping, preparation of the EIA report (description of action and environment, impact prediction, impact significance), mitigation, consultation and participation, reviewing the EIA report, decision making and monitoring action impacts.

Figure 42: project concept, site selection, environmental screening, initial assessment, scoping of significant issues, pre-feasibility, assessment of significant impacts, identification of mitigation needs, input to cost–benefit analysis, feasibility, design of mitigation measures, design and engineering, implementation of mitigation measures and environmental strategy, implementation, monitoring and post-auditing, monitoring and evaluation, changes in project management and lessons for future projects.

(ii) Similarities: all three process diagrams include stages of screening, scoping, monitoring, consideration of impacts and their significance, mitigation and review. Figures 41 and 25(T) have additional similarities by including consideration of alternatives, action description/design, consultation and participation, decision making, report or statement preparation/presentation/review and post-decision monitoring. In broad terms Figures 41 and 25(T) are similar. In terms of structure all three diagrams show an iterative process. Figures 41 and 25(T) also show iterative loops within the process and both indicate repetition of public consultation and participation at many stages. As all three diagrams show iterative rather than linear processes the 'initial stages' might involve re-exploring as well as exploring situations for the first time.

Differences: Figure 42 is most different from the other two, in terms of both elements and structure probably because it has a different purpose, linking the EIA process to a project cycle rather than just describing it. The process in Figure 42 is more cyclical than the other two and suggests multiple starting points shown by the incoming arrows, whereas the other two are structured as flow diagrams. There are more double-headed arrows in Figure 25(T) and no loop back from the post-decision stages in Figure 41. The clustering of the steps is different in the two diagrams.

(iii) As Figure 41 is a clear flow diagram, I identified the initial stages of the EIA process as the top box which includes screening, scoping, etc. though my eye is drawn to the box on the right (public consultation and participation) which could also be considered a starting point. I find it a little more difficult to work out the starting point of Figure 25(T) as the many double-headed arrows seem to suggest a highly dynamic process and I started to think how an individual could join the process at any of these stages. In the tradition of a flow diagram, I assume it is the stage of consideration of alternatives that is intended as the start, though consultation and participation and mitigation are linked to this so could also be starting points. In Figure 42, multiple starting points are clearly intended by the series of incoming arrows and, as the diagram is mapping one process with another, I found it difficult to work out where to break into the circle. As you will see from my list, I eventually decided on the 'project concept' stage. But I felt I could easily have started instead with taking account of the review stage implied in 'changes in project management and lessons for future practice'.

(iv) None of the diagrams indicate who is involved in any detail though Figure 42 does refer to public consultation and participation, so I assume that means broad involvement of stakeholders – but I can't really tell that just from the diagram. The processes shown are quite detailed and that raised a question for me about who, if anyone, is involved in all of it. And who goes round the cycle or cycles more than once carrying on what has been learnt? Or do different people mainly get involved at different stages? And if people are not involved in all stages of the processes or multiple cycles, then what means are used to link the stages? I found myself wondering how an individual would or could get involved. The idea of consultation suggests engagement of some people by others in the process. I recognise that I'd need to look at examples of EIA in practice to be able to answer these questions.

## Activity 41  A European Commission perspective on EIA

(i) Margot Wallström's role and quote are the only evidence of her perspective in the press release. She has a formal role as Environment Commissioner in the European Commission. She described EIAs as a very useful tool for promoting environmental protection with the potential to simplify decision making. She claimed the directive also enables citizens to take part in decision making. She disagreed with the view of some project developers that they were a bureaucratic obstacle.

(ii) Quite a lot of the shortcomings identified seem likely to affect how EIAs start off – those relating to screening and scoping, for instance, as these activities are in the early stages of an EIA and, if ineffective, may lead to an inappropriate focus for the EIA. Two further shortcomings that may affect how systemically EIA starts out are: (1) insufficient consideration of cumulative effects of projects – unrecognised cumulative effects from past and ongoing projects will affect the starting conditions for new projects and this shortcoming sounds as though the boundaries of EIA 'systems of interest' may be placed inappropriately to recognise systemic effects of the projects – and (2) processing of transboundary EIAs requires more consideration. This focus on transboundary issues makes me think that this shortcoming sounds relevant to the process of formulating problems, opportunities and systems of interest and hence also relevant to starting out systemically ... or not.

## Activity 42  Starting off in SEA and sustainability appraisal

The SEA and sustainability appraisals appear to start with a phase of 'setting the context and establishing the baseline' which corresponds to a planning stage of identifying the issues and options and preparing for consultation (although I am conscious that this table is just one rather linear representation of the process and there may be more to it, so I would need to check with policy makers and practitioners to be sure).

The purpose of this activity seems to be partially to explore the situation and to consider contextual factors, so it sounds as though there is some potential to start off systemically. Also a process of 'helping to identify SEA and sustainability problems, objectives and alternatives' is described and depending on how it is done that too could indicate potential to start off systemically. But the language of 'setting' the context rather than exploring it sounds more like a systematic and rather static placing of boundaries. So I would question what opportunity there is to explore the situation, before focusing in on very specific issues and related data. I would also need to understand who decides which are the key environmental and sustainability issues and on what basis to be able to judge whether the process starts off systemically.

## Activity 43  Effective RIA – a systemic and systematic approach?

All of the characteristics for RIAs that add value identified by the National Audit Office could be interpreted as part of both systemic and systematic approaches. Starting at an early enough stage sounds as though there is scope for a systemic approach with exploration of a situation before formulating problems, opportunities and systems of interest. Starting RIA early may also give more time for a rigorous and systematic approach if adequate resources are available for the appraisal. Consulting early and effectively sounds as though it has the potential for multiple perspectives of stakeholders to be taken into account in formulating problems, opportunities and systems of interest so may also support a systemic approach. It is probable that effective consultation is also systematic. While cost–benefit analysis often tends to be a systematic rather than systemic approach, it depends how it is used and perhaps has the potential to help the consideration of some of the wider effects and interconnections of regulations as well as direct effects. (You will find out more about the pros and cons of cost–benefit analysis in environmental decision making in Book 3.)

## Activity 44  Starting off in ISO 14001 and EMAS

(i) The spiralling process of continual improvement in the diagrammatic representation suggests an iterative process where a previous cycle of ISO 14001 activities provides the starting conditions for the next. It is not clear from the details provided how these cycles are interpreted, but if wanting to enhance systemic awareness among stakeholders this approach suggests to me that there would be potential to involve new and/or different stakeholders at different stages of the process and learn from understanding their perspectives, particularly regarding counterintuitive effects and unintended consequences which are central to developing systemic awareness (see Part 1 of this book). Environmental policy appears to be the first formal stage of ISO 14001 according to Box 22 so developing the policy through a multistakeholder process may also enhance systemic awareness. Understanding connectivity for developing systemic awareness may not emerge from a multistakeholder process. Rigorous and systematic inquiry and becoming conscious of gaps in understanding and taking steps to generate knowledge to fill those gaps may also be part of developing systemic awareness.

(ii) EMAS adds 'meeting the needs of the market and stakeholders' and 'environmental reporting and green claims' to the environmental management system ISO 14001. Both these additional areas of activity appear to be relevant to starting off systemically if reporting feeds back into an iterative process that affects starting conditions and supports re-exploration of a situation, and if meeting the needs of stakeholders includes taking account of their perspectives in formulating problems, opportunities and systems of interest.

## Activity 45  Different interpretations of phrases in ISO 14001 and EMAS

The following terms and phrases could be interpreted differently by different people:

- environment and environmental aspects
- environmental reporting and green claims
- continual improvement
- management system.

The arrows on the ISO 14001 diagram do not make it clear whether there is iteration between stages, which would be expected for continual improvement to be achieved.

## Activity 46  Identifying more scope for exploring and formulating

Designing a process for stakeholder involvement in the development of the standards would allow scope for situations to be explored at many different stages. It is difficult to tell from the diagrams alone as they do not give enough detail. The environmental statement presumably indicates a wish to communicate what is being done but it is not clear who is communicating what to whom nor whether and where stakeholders are drawn into the process. Some of the stages that seem to me to imply a need for stakeholder involvement are the review, policy, audit and definition of objectives.

EMAS suggest iteration in the audit cycle every three years, so that would presumably provide an opportunity to re-explore the context of environmental issues. The checking and corrective action stage of ISO 14001 also suggests iteration, as does the notion of continual improvement.

## Activity 47 EMAS and Kirklees Metropolitan Council

(i) Kirklees Metropolitan Council (KMC) used a SWOT (strengths, weaknesses, opportunities, threats) analysis to reflect on their experience and learning after achieving EMAS accreditation. SWOT analysis and its variants are included in the *Techniques* book and have already been mentioned in Part 1 of Book 1.

(ii) KMC recognised that before the introduction of EMAS, the council had no corporate provision to ensure compliance with environmental legislation, so they conducted a review of each department to identify applicable legislation and compiled it into a register which is reviewed annually. No details are given as to who did this and how, but the legislative situation was clearly explored in that process.

The report refers to increasing enthusiasm and commitment to environmental protection from employees following the EMAS process, so by implication these were at lower levels on starting out.

'At the beginning EMAS was seen as a stand-alone system.' A corporate group of senior and middle managers then worked on integrating EMAS with other schemes. This sounds to me like some re-exploration and re-negotiation of systems of interest.

In the first phase of verification, poor operational control at depots was identified as contributing to non-conformance (presumably with EMAS). Interactions with frontline staff and training followed. Both could be seen as opportunities to re-explore a situation and re-formulate problems, opportunities and systems of interest.

Responsibility for EMAS lay initially with the Environment Unit. It sounds as though stakeholder involvement increased in time with a resulting increased sense of ownership by departments rather than by the unit. I would be surprised if re-exploration of the situation and re-formulation of problems, opportunities and systems of interest did not occur in this process.

The comments on 'impacts scoring' suggest a developing appreciation (a re-formulation or re-conceptualisation?) of the nature of environmental impacts.

(iii) To identify signs of systems thinking, I looked for signs of developing systemic awareness among stakeholders, particularly in increasing understanding of cycles, counterintuitive effects and unintended consequences (as discussed in Part 1). Recognition that KMC had unexpected areas of non-compliance in legislation regarding waste and water management and their subsequent consultation with the Environment Agency and Yorkshire Water to address the arising issues sounds to me like an increase in systemic awareness. Similarly, I would interpret recognition of the links between EMAS and other schemes and the need for integration as deepening systemic awareness, though this may have been evidence of a more systematic rather than systemic approach. It would depend on the nature of the interactions that resulted. The whole SWOT analysis is an example of KMC's evaluating. Negotiations and re-negotiations sound to have taken place at several stages of the process. The example of departments gradually taking ownership of EMAS mentioned above is clearly one where some re-negotiations occurred. Modelling is evident in several parts of the report, e.g. cost–benefit analysis and environmental statements can be thought of as models.

I found in this report examples of systems thinking, evaluating, negotiating and modelling that took part at different stages of the process, not just at starting out. The iterative nature of the process and the evaluation through a SWOT analysis do, I think, provide some evidence of a systemic approach overall, though I find it hard to tell just from this report how systemic the process was at its start.

(iv) I would like to know a little more about who initiated the EMAS process and how, from the perspectives of several levels in the organisation (senior and middle management and other staff working in individual departments). What were the drivers for EMAS? I would be interested to hear how KMC management and department are now responding to both the opportunities and threats they identified and how they are dealing with the continual improvement.

## Activity 48    Framing a situation and practices through an environmental statement

(i) I think the statement from Councillor Hall frames the situation in the London Borough of Sutton as one where there are local environmental problems that contribute to regional and global issues, such as those relating to climate change, wastes and loss of biodiversity. It isn't clear to me just from this statement how the London Borough of Sutton has formulated its environmental problems. A wide range of examples is given on actions being taken to address impacts, so I think the statement also frames the situation in terms of action. Environmental 'targets' alongside those for economic and social well-being also suggest a systematic approach.

(ii) Stakeholders mentioned in the statement include Sutton Council (including presumably Councillor Hall himself), the local community (including residents who are mentioned specifically), businesses, other authorities and partners. The statement is clearly intended as information for residents and other stakeholders so it is not clear how this relates to individuals' own practices. I would expect to find actions and targets linked to specific practices in the detail of the statement.

## Activity 49    Issues and uses of CSR reporting

(i) Some of the issues of CSR reporting are around:
- whose interests these reports serve – companies or society or both?
- the roles of wider stakeholders in CSR and its reporting process – are they largely public relations exercises and/or genuine attempts at transparency in decision making?
- what the criteria are against which company performance and 'best practice' are judged, and how were those criteria arrived at?
- whether environmental factors are included or not, along with others, in CSR?

(ii) A CSR process in which stakeholders as well as shareholders are involved in a process of dialogue sounds as though it does have potential for exploring situations and systems of interest, but it would depend on the nature of the process and how and when perspectives of stakeholders are included. If the reporting process is a dynamic process which facilitates this dialogue among stakeholders then perhaps it could also have a role in exploring situations and formulating systems of interest. But the nature of CSR reports is such that they seem to present already formulated systems of interest, so I question how useful they may be in starting off systemically in environmental decision making.

(iii) I think some of the issues regarding the process of reporting may be similar in environmental and CSR reporting but they do seem to me to have some different purposes and benchmarks. The contexts of achieving EMAS or ISO 14001 or demonstrating more general corporate responsibility are different, e.g. regarding processes of external verification and continual improvement. I think environmental reporting could easily form a part of corporate responsibility reporting.

## Activity 52   Control models

I have not reproduced the labelled control model here – you can check your labelling by going to 'Diagramming: control model diagrams' in the *Techniques* book. As I have not done the course, I provide here some of the sorts of questions that the control model could be used to answer.

Control models are a useful way of investigating purpose and the means in place to achieve it. So are you able to articulate a purpose for studying T863 and the nature of the transformation that you are hoping for? You might like to consider the inputs into and outputs from this transformation process. Also, how will you know when the transformation has been achieved? In your own circumstances, what might you choose to regard as the comparator and the actuator?

There are no right answers to these questions – this is just a device in this context to trigger questions about your own understandings and practices. Control model diagrams provide a structure for exploring these questions. The drawing of the model allows you to decide whether the elements are in place to support the achievement of the purpose and whether they are the right elements.

## Activity 53   Communication ideas influence understandings of control

Your answer is likely to differ from anything I write, so I will merely make the observation that some of the best examples of language use that implies particular understanding of human communication and thus control comes from the interview with the civil servants responsible for the White Paper process. For me the container, conduit and control metaphors were very apparent in their language.

## Activity 54   Re-exploring the T863 environmental decision-making framework

I have not attempted a response to this activity as it will depend on your own understanding and circumstances.

## Activity 55   A systematic review of concepts associated with a 'systems' approach

I have not provided an answer to this question as it is designed for your own personal revision. There will be more opportunities to engage with these concepts in Books 3 and 4, so do not worry if you found it difficult at this stage of the course.

## Activity 56   Monitoring your own situation

I have not provided an answer to this question. The distinction between what is systemically desirable and culturally feasible will be taken up in Book 3.

# Answers to Self-Assessment Questions

## SAQ 1  Biophysical environments

River diversion and associated habitat maintenance (for fish, mussels, eels, etc.) as well as waste/materials management were the main area of focus. A joined-up transport hub and the planned focus on public transport could also be seen as encompassing environmental concerns. If a broader meaning to environment is taken, then health and safety and risk management might be included.

## SAQ 2  Environmental impacts

The main additional points made were global warming and human induced climate change leading to temperature changes, sea-level rise, flooding, need for new flood defences, aviation induced pollution of air and water (including groundwater), increase in noise, loss of amenity, loss of biodiversity (e.g. through loss of trees and some habitat).

## SAQ 3  Earth and the greenhouse effect

Any object, including the earth, exchanges heat with its environment. In the case of the whole earth, its environment is outer space. Heat flows to the earth from the sun, but it also flows from the earth's surface out into space. The rate of loss into space depends on the surface temperature of the earth, but also on the composition of the atmosphere. If the earth had no atmosphere, its average surface temperature would be some 30 °C lower than it is currently. This is because gases such as carbon dioxide in the atmosphere in effect trap heat emitted from the solid surface of the earth and act like a blanket, so that the surface temperature is at the familiar higher level. This is the 'greenhouse effect'.

## SAQ 4  Evidence for climate change

It is claimed that the average global surface temperature of the earth has risen by 0.7 °C over the last century. In several recent years, summer temperatures including those in the UK have been at or above the highest previously recorded levels. Mountain glaciers and the Arctic sea-ice appear to be melting and retreating, as illustrated by the experience of the journalist in *Reach for the Sky*. A specific pattern of weather off the Pacific coast of South America (El Niño) has recently become more frequent and intense.

## SAQ 5  Key uncertainties about climate

Changes in the amount of tiny particles, clouds and water vapour in the atmosphere also affect heat balance, in a complex way that it has not so far been possible to predict. Other changes, such as in the amount of ice and snow and in the way the oceans circulate, are also difficult to predict. But possibly the key uncertainties are those associated with the amount of carbon dioxide in the atmosphere, which is influenced by human decisions, but also by the way carbon (which combines with oxygen to form carbon dioxide) is cycled around the globe by living organisms and other processes.

## SAQ 6  Key processes affecting $CO_2$

The key processes are:

- the anthropogenic addition of $CO_2$ to the atmosphere by burning of fossil fuel and other materials
- the interchange of $CO_2$ between green plants (plus some other organisms, such as algae) that are able to synthesise more complex materials involving carbon
- respiration of carbon-containing compounds by humans, animals and microorganisms, releasing $CO_2$ into the atmosphere
- solution and degassing of $CO_2$ between the oceans and the atmosphere.

These processes all occur on relatively short timescales. Over very long timescales, some of the carbon-containing compounds in the ocean sink to the bottom and become unavailable for interchange with the surface ocean, so reducing the degassing effect.

Several of these processes, notably those involving living organisms, are affected by a wide range of factors, and so it is very difficult to predict how they will affect the level of $CO_2$ in the atmosphere, which is key to predictions of future climate. Even what are relatively simple physical processes such as absorption and degassing in the surface ocean are difficult to measure or predict across the whole of the world, and since the atmosphere is in constant movement, local changes can have global effects.

## SAQ 7  Models used in the case study

Examples that I noted included:

- the 'web-based project-flow software' used to provide a model of the construction process for scheduling the different activities and implicit models of what the diverted rivers should look like, which determined that there should be 'natural river banks', 'in-channel flow enhancement' and the 'use of pre-grown native plants'
- CAD models of components shown in the risk management section, used to communicate between different parties and to optimise designs
- the 'trial run' erection of part of the abutments could be regarded as an iconic model, again used for an optimisation process
- use of models of the geophysics, maps of the site and virtual reality re-creations by the archaeologists. The geophysics models were used to predict likely sites for detailed examination, while the maps and re-creations were used mainly for communication
- cost modelling, underlying all of the cost–benefit analysis, depended on a whole range of implicit models of the changes in the volume and nature of air traffic and associated ground traffic, of the likely emissions from all this traffic and, as we will see in Book 3, more general estimates of other environmental impacts. These were models used for prediction, but the cost modelling itself is claimed to be about optimisation
- implicit in some aspects of the CBA, and certainly underlying much of the argument about the effects of aviation expansion on climate, is a whole range of predictive models of the earth's atmosphere, carbon cycling and interactions between land, sea and air.

### SAQ 8 Factors affecting air traffic in south east England

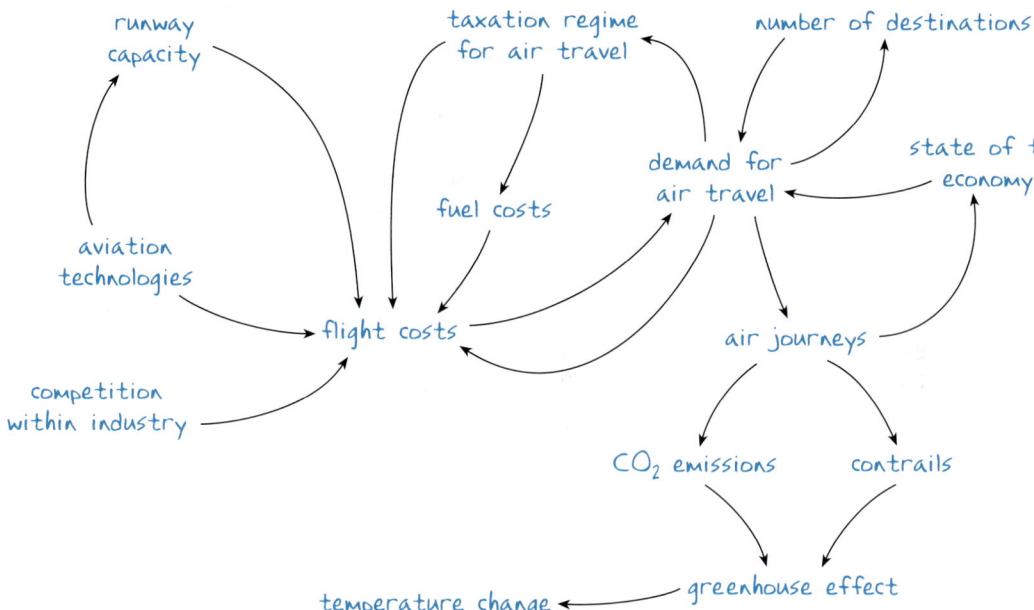

Figure 64 A multiple cause diagram of factors affecting air traffic in the south east of England

### SAQ 9 Feedback loops

There are two loops, involving the flow of carbon from the terrestrial biosphere to the atmosphere, through plant respiration, and the flow from the terrestrial biosphere to the soil. In both cases, these flows directly affect the amount of carbon in the terrestrial biosphere, as they represent direct losses from this to the other compartments, and the rate of loss in each case also depends on the amount of carbon that is present in the biosphere.

### SAQ 10 More feedback loops

Three further loops are those concerned with degassing, downwelling and biopump aspects of surface ocean carbon.

### SAQ 11 Diagram differences

An influence diagram can be regarded as a more general version of a multiple cause diagram, in that it identifies general 'influences' between components and sub-systems of the chosen system. It also shows a defined system boundary, which is usually only implied in a multiple cause diagram. Multiple cause diagrams tend to be more detailed and specific, and deal with particular aspects of the situation, looking at the factors that influence that one aspect, although they may draw in various other interrelationships involving different processes.

## SAQ 12  Diagrams – compare and contrast

A systems map concentrates on the structure of the identified system of interest, showing clearly the proposed boundary and the sub-systems that those drawing the map regard as important. In contrast, a multiple cause diagram, as noted in the preceding answer, looks more specifically at a particular set of interrelationships within the chosen system.

Using a systems map to explore a situation is likely to highlight the perspectives of those involved, and to provide a relatively complete (at least from the perspective of whoever draws the maps) summary of the chosen system. It deliberately does not name specific issues, but names a system that is related to the whole situation. A multiple cause diagram is likely to concentrate on specific issues, and so may be more restrictive in terms of exploring the situation. However, it does provide a more rigorous interpretation of some of the processes surrounding the chosen issue, and if done well, can also lead back to considering the wider set of issues.

## SAQ 13  Boundaries in a system dynamics diagram

The system dynamics diagram of the carbon cycle has a series of boundaries that can be characterised according to the following criteria:

1. Space – the focus is clearly global. This is in stark contrast to the previous diagrams which focused on the local and national.
2. Time – the components represented in the diagram have a relatively slow rate of change compared to components identified in previous diagrams; tens to hundreds of years need to elapse before significant change occurs.
3. Quantifiable and measurable – the components selected can readily be assigned a numerical value. This therefore excludes the ambiguous and emotive aspects highlighted in the previous diagrams.

## SAQ 14  Time and space in aviation expansion

The virtual reality model of Terminal 5 shows a relatively small spatial area of a few hundred square metres at most. It does not show how the area represented relates to other areas – the implication of the commentary is that the facilities needed for departure are all close together, but the model does not confirm this. It shows in a few seconds a passenger movement that would probably take several minutes. Both space and time aspects are chosen to present a positive picture of what is likely to be encountered in the actual terminal.

The cost–benefit model considers much greater time and area. The benefits are calculated on a regional scale, or even national scale. Costs are mostly calculated on a rather smaller spatial scale of the area around the proposed expanded airports, although notionally the costs of effects attributed to climate change are global in extent. The timescale used is notionally 30 years, about one human generation. However, as you will see in Book 3, the mechanics of the cost–benefit model are such that effects occurring at the end even of this short period are greatly reduced compared to more short term effects, so the effective timescale covered is less than this. You may like to consider whether this use of specific scales of time and space may distort subsequent decisions.

## SAQ 15 Differences between a dualism and a duality

A dualism is an either/or pair in which self-negation operates whereas a duality is a complementary pair that create a greater whole. The pair subjective–objective is a common dualism. In some circles it is common for explanations to be rejected because they are not considered objective. When this happens, a negation is operating (in fact any claim for objectivity is a claim by whoever makes it for their version of 'truth' and is also a device to undermine an argument). The pair 'predator–prey' can be regarded as a whole (i.e. a duality) or a dualism. Dualisms (actually dualistic thinking) can entrench fixed perspectives and fail to deal with higher levels of complexity that are common in environmental decision-making situations.

## SAQ 16 Using metaphors in your practice

Schön (1979) described the creative, or generative, function of metaphors with the example of the development of a new paintbrush with synthetic bristles that failed to apply an even coat of paint. Somebody observed that 'a paintbrush is a kind of pump'. This was taken as an invitation to start to consider a paintbrush as a pump. Certain aspects of the paintbrush and its performance 'came to the foreground'. Attention then focused on the spaces between the bristles, and these were then thought of as channels through which paint could flow. Other ideas followed from thinking of a paintbrush in terms of a pump. A conclusion was that instead of wiping paint onto a surface, a paintbrush could pump the paint. It was not so much the image of a pump that was important, but the invitation to consider a process of pumping. In the UK a common way of describing the countryside is 'as a tapestry' because of the network of fields, hedges and different colours but the metaphor conceals the smells, frequency of farm accidents, noise, etc. that are also a feature of the UK countryside.

## SAQ 17 Distinguishing metaphors

The authors claim that metaphors are central to our ways of understanding and also that different stakeholders have different understandings. They argue that these differences need to be accommodated within practice and this can be done by distinguishing metaphors because this can help to explain, appreciate and create different understandings. By introducing an awareness of metaphors into practices, new understandings can emerge and different or alternative metaphors can be considered. They point out that no metaphor is 'right' – each metaphor will reveal and conceal different aspects of our understandings.

## SAQ 18 Environmental decision making as a practice

An environmental decision-making situation, a decision maker or makers, other stakeholders, an environmental issue, decision support tools, performance criteria (for decision and for evaluation).

## SAQ 19 Constructing a timeline

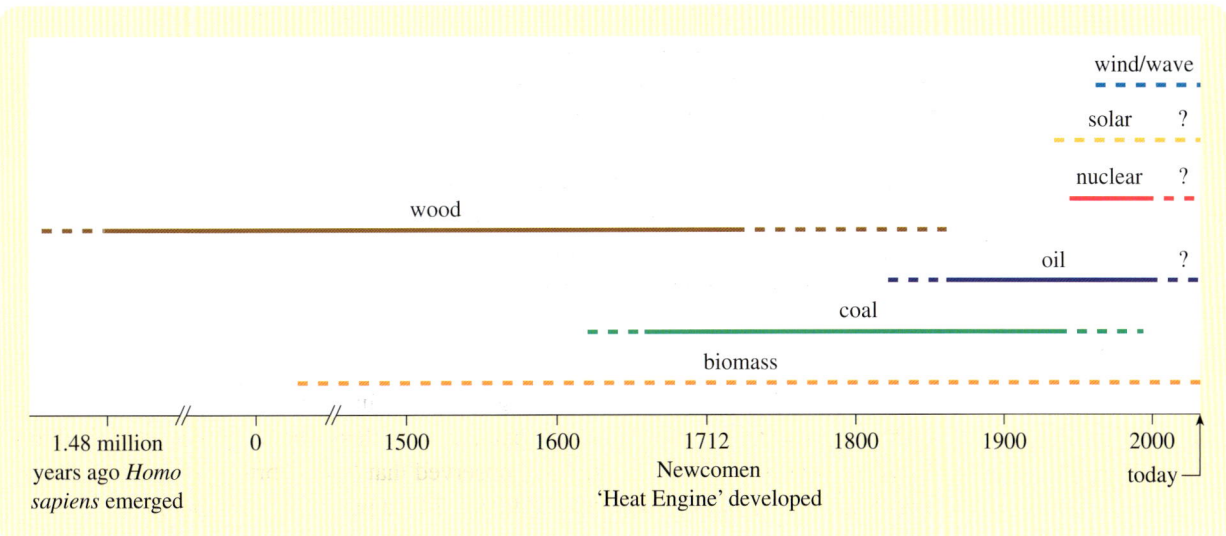

Figure 65   Timeline for human use of energy

## SAQ 20 What is a social technology?

Social technologies involve people, artefacts and practices – they are often invisible because they are embedded in daily practices, including our language and use of numbers. They are made up of procedures and rules designed to standardise behaviour – or in other words, sets of techniques used routinely without awareness of the origins of, and implications of the use of, such techniques, the role of the practitioner and the need for contextual understanding about the situation.

Social technologies are often embedded in our society in ways that we are not aware of – they can structure how we think and act and thus determine how decisions, including environmental decisions are made. One of the most powerful is cost–benefit analysis – see the *Techniques* book (Economic evaluation: cost–benefit analysis) and also Book 3.

## SAQ 21 The importance of history

Each human being has a history which is both biological (we grow and develop) and social (we live in particular families, societies and have different experiences which lead us to think and act differently). It is biologically impossible to have exactly the same experience as another person, but we can talk about our experiences, just as some of the different stakeholders in the airport expansion case study have done in their interviews on the DVD (but neither I nor they can guarantee that the meaning they intended is the meaning that you made out of what was said – this will depend on your history). Situations also have a history, but history must be interpreted by someone at a particular moment in time. The aviation expansion case study was written at a particular moment in time – the history and context of the author influenced what he did and paid attention to, just as your own experience and context have influenced how you have interpreted the case study situation. Elements in the situation also have a history. Take, for example, the history of using oil and the possibility that the world may be facing a post-oil future. Understanding these different facets of history is, in my view, critical to understanding the case study (and thus environmental decision making) from a systems perspective.

## SAQ 22   What is a trap?

We are in a trap in situations beyond the limits of what we can 'see and value and do'. Many of them have deep roots in our experience and upbringing and in the society in which we live. The example given was that for almost the whole of the twentieth century, the problem of increasing demand for energy was met by increasing the supply. However, in the 1980s, a few people saw the problem differently and argued that it would be better solved by energy conservation. Whatever the particular advantages or disadvantages of this, it is clear that it is an alternative. More interestingly, it is one that was genuinely not apparent to all those concerned with energy supply over a very long period. This is because people who defined the problem as one of increasing supply, and devoted their efforts to doing this, simply did not see or value ways of reducing demand.

## SAQ 23   Mess and difficulty

The three main features a practitioner might use to distinguish a difficulty from a mess are:

1. Messes are made up from a network of problems and opportunities that will be described differently by different people engaged in the situation. By contrast, a difficulty will be described much the same by different people, even from a diversity of perspectives.

2. The improvement in a mess is not just the sum of the improvements in its component parts. The improvements in a difficulty are easier to identify and describe, and it is easier to identify how they came about.

3. Because a mess is a set of external conditions that causes dissatisfaction, a judgement about whether or not it has been improved, and by how much, will depend upon the perspective of the people involved. The improvement in a difficulty will be generally agreed upon by people with a range of perspectives.

To deal with messes requires a holistic or systems approach; therefore it makes little sense to distinguish one feature as more important than another. A core concept at the heart of the idea of mess is, however, that of emergence, meaning the whole is different from the sum of its parts.

## SAQ 24   Relationship between boundary and levels

I can use a systems map as an example for my answer. All systems maps will have a system and one or more sub-systems each of which will involve making a boundary judgement (that is what makes them a 'map' of a system of interest). So most systems maps will have a structure comprising at least two levels but sometimes three (i.e. sub-sub-systems).

## SAQ 25 How does backcasting differ from forecasting?

Forecasting means starting where you are now and predicting possible futures based on past trends. For backcasting, you imagine possible future situations and then work out how to get there.

The first step in backcasting is putting yourself at some point in the future; maybe six months, a year or several years ahead depending on the circumstances. Then you think imaginatively about what your alternative situations are there, and what the possibilities are for getting to that situation. Having explored the possibilities, you then ask yourself what alternatives are really open to you. This means acting within reasonable constraints that you need to be aware of.

## SAQ 26 Activity modelling

For activity sequence diagrams, the activity at the tail of an arrow must logically precede that at the head of the arrow; the boxes or nodes represent activities or events, i.e. the commencement or completion of an activity; the time between activities can either be written on the connecting line, or dates for start and completion for each activity are noted on the relevant node; loops are permitted on activity sequence diagrams but not network drawings or critical path analyses.

Conceptual models comprise:
- a large circle representing the purposeful activity
- numbered blobs
- words (verbs) describing an individual action
- arrows linking the actions
- title.

The conventions are: (1) start by drawing a large circle or boundary; (2) individual activities (i.e. phrases with a verb) are placed within blobs; (3) link the blobs by arrows; (4) number the blobs according to the sequence implied by the root definition – a description of a system of interest. More than one action may lead into a subsequent action and (5). It is essential to write down the root definition as the title of the purposeful activity system which the activities cause to happen.

These forms of diagram are similar but differ in that conceptual models: (i) are strictly concerned with activities and not events; (ii) use only blobs and not boxes; (iii) the conventions about labelling the arrows are different as conceptual models follow the logic of input–output diagrams and transformation as described in the teaching text.

## SAQ 27 Transformation types

Number (i) is an example of a physical transformation achieved by the transformation of 'painting' whereas (ii) is an abstract transformation achieved by the transformation 'meeting a need'.

### SAQ 28 Stakeholder and stakeholding

Stakeholders are those who have a 'stake' – a real, material interest, from their perspective – in the situation or in the resource under consideration. A person's stake can be formed in any number of ways: for example, as a resident, domestic water user, angler, farmer, professional water manager or government official. Stakes may also overlap. Stakeholding expresses the idea that individuals actively construct, promote and defend their stake. A stakeholder also can assert influence by not participating in key multistakeholder events. In the case of groups, stakeholding implies a shared interest among group members, although individual members might still perceive their own stakes in different ways.

### SAQ 29 Stakeholder analysis

The basic steps in SA (stakeholder analysis) are usually:

1. drawing up a table or 'map' of those stakeholders considered to be primary, intermediate and key (customers, actors, owners), on the basis of information presently available
2. assessing stakeholders' importance with regard to the situation, problem or activity addressed by the analysis, and their relative importance or influence
3. identifying assumptions about how stakeholders might affect relationships, outcomes or the viability of the proposed activity.

### SAQ 30 Purposeful and purposive – examples

Both (a) and (d) exemplify purposefulness because each demonstrates examples of willed action and/or changing behaviour in response to learning. Scenario (b) exemplifies purposiveness – the attribution of purpose by someone outside the context. For me, scenario (c) has elements of both purposefulness and purposiveness. The former is indicated by the phrase 'my company has adopted'; whereas purposiveness is indicated by the way standards are often imposed from the outside in ways that are unhelpful because they are not sensitive to the local situation.

### SAQ 32 Participation and levels of power

Category 1 represents 'power over'. Categories 2–4 represent a gradation of consultation, and also represent, in my view, 'power over', although clearly the results of extractive surveys, etc. could ultimately be used in other ways. Categories 5 and 6 represent 'power with' whilst category 7 can represent 'delegating power to'. These are not hard-and-fast distinctions and you will need to consider the many variations on these that are possible in practice.

### SAQ 33 Handing over the stick

The metaphor of handing over the stick is concerned with aspects of power and responsibility. It can be seen as a manifestation of Heron's 'deciding with' or, perhaps more so, delegating 'deciding to' in which responsibility is facilitated amongst local people (as a counter to expert or bureaucratic holding of the stick). The metaphor conceals notions of what can happen when anyone wields the stick – i.e. what is the stick that is being handed over – and also assumes there is something to hand over!

# SAQ 34  Stages and principles of SSM

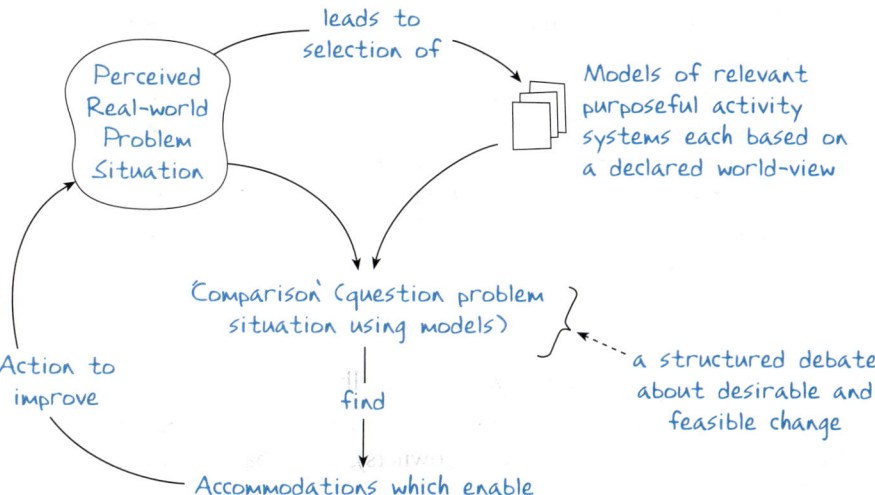

Principles

- real world: a complexity of relationships
- relationships explored via models of purposeful activity based on explicit world-views
- inquiry structured by questioning perceived situation using the models as a source of questions
- 'action to improve' based on finding accommodations (versions of the situation which conflicting interests can live with)
- inquiry in principle never-ending; best conducted with wide range of interested parties; give the process away to people in the situation

Figure 66

# SAQ 35  PQR and a root definition

P = communicate (what), Q = writing and posting letters (how), and R = maintaining good relations with Mum (why) and each are expressed in the root definition in the form do P by Q in order to achieve R.

# SAQ 36  Blobs in a conceptual model

Each blob has a single-headed arrow either leaving it or arriving at it (always drawn from or to the boundary) and each blob has an activity associated with a verb – e.g. decide, organise, obtain, monitor, etc.

# SAQ 37  Worldviews

As explained in earlier parts of Book 2, different people will see the same situation differently (Figure 26). They will thus formulate different systems of interest and attribute different purposes – think of one person's freedom fighter being another person's terrorist! So a system of interest is only relevant in the context of a specific worldview – if the worldview is changed then so will the system and the activities that constitute it. SSM forces those using it to be explicit about their own worldview but also enables them to experiment by choosing other worldviews as part of the process of formulating systems of interest.

### SAQ 38    Activities in conducting a systemic inquiry

The activities start with: (i) set up structured exploration of situation considered problematical (i.e. explore and re-explore the situation); then (ii) make sense of situation by exploring context, culture (politics) using systems models as devices (e.g. Snappy Systems); (iii) tease out possible accommodations between different interests; (iv) define possible actions to change that are systemically desirable and culturally feasible; (v) take action to change – creating a new situation; (vi) monitor; (vii) define criteria: efficacy, efficiency, effectiveness; and (viii) take control action (the last three activities are discussed in Part 3).

### SAQ 39    Where next for EU environmental policy?

(i) A reduced appetite for further environmental lawmaking is attributed to changes in Europe, as it has expanded eastwards and 'old' Europe has taken an economic downturn.

(ii) Responsibility for addressing environmental issues is shared between the EU and its member states. The EU relies on the unanimous support of its member states to take forward action concerning environmental issues.

(iii) The thematic areas being addressed by the strategies included in the EU's sixth environmental action are air pollution, sustainable use of natural resources, waste prevention and recycling, the marine environment, soil protection, pesticide use and the urban environment.

(iv) Stavros Dimas insisted that better regulation doesn't mean weaker regulation and standards but instead genuine consultation of all stakeholders and rigorous assessment of costs and benefits, removing complexities wherever possible and acting in a strategic rather than ad hoc manner.

(v) Command and control, co-regulation, market instruments, financial measures, voluntary agreements and other measures are mentioned as different forms environmental policy initiatives can take.

(vi) Advantages of voluntary agreements perceived by regulators are that they require less resources and time to negotiate and the burden of policing them falls on industry. From the perspective of businesses, they provide flexibility to come up with cost-effective solutions and allow costs to be spread across sectors. Disadvantages in the context of the car industry are that people have to stick at them to make them work, and experience has shown this doesn't always happen, so they may need to be abandoned in favour of legislation. An OECD study suggested this experience extended outside the EU also.

(vii) Some of the issues of integration mentioned in this article include institutional deficiencies such as a lack of clarity in roles and responsibilities and patchy leadership. Flaws in the system of reviewing and reporting have been a particular obstacle, and the strategies themselves were of variable quality and, because most councils saw them as one-off exercises, soon became outdated. The European Environment Agency claims that effective integration will require greater coherence between and within departments, clear mission statements and reporting based on indicators. Extra resources and capacity building with more information and transparency was also seen as required. Cross-compliance, tying funding to policy goals and legislation, was seen by WWF's director of its European policy office as a powerful tool in support of integration.

## SAQ 40  SEA and its application

(i) Karl Fuller suggests that SEA can be interpreted differently in terms of scope, role and purpose.

(ii) Karl Fuller gives a range of examples from different countries to illustrate how they have focused their use of SEA differently. The EIA-based approach from the Netherlands sounds quite different from the integrated policy and planning system of New Zealand. However it is not clear in this extract whether 'within country variation' may mean that the range of approaches used in the two countries may have similarities as well as differences.

(iii) An example of 'within country variation' in use of SEA comes from the Netherlands where an EIA-based approach seems to differ from a dual-track system.

## SAQ 41  New EU directives to implement the Aarhus Convention

(i) The three principal 'pillars' of the Aarhus Convention are identified by Andrew Ryan as:

(a) access to information

(b) public participation in environmental decision making

(c) access to justice in environmental matters.

The three EU directives derived from the convention cover the same areas.

(ii) *Access to environmental information*: Public authorities have a duty to supply information relevant to the environment, when requested, within a strict time limit. Their definition of environmental information is broad.

*Public participation in environmental decision making*: Requires that information is provided free of charge early on in the process and when all possible options are open for consideration.

*Access to justice in environmental matters*: The public have a right to challenge a decision by a public authority not to supply environmental information.

## SAQ 42  Consultation and participation in EIA case studies

(i) Preliminary discussions, scoping documents and reports, a planning application, an updating newsletter, forum meetings, presentations, exhibitions, working groups, a round table and meetings were all used for consultation and participation in the case studies. Some of these sound interactive and others more one-way, but the level of interactivity depends on how they were used. For instance, a newsletter can be used to put forward just a few perspectives or many.

(ii) Most of the documents, plans and representations at exhibitions or events could be thought of as models.

(iii) The early stages of the consultation process are not shown as iterative, but there are several two-headed arrows indicating iteration once the detailed studies and reports have been drawn up. There also appears to be iteration early on in the project design process (presumably after the decision has been taken that the project will go ahead). There is also iteration in expert consultation and in some of the later stages of project design and the environmental statement.

(iv) In Dibden Bay, Associated British Ports was consulting with local authorities, industry and the community. In Strangford Lough, it is not entirely clear from the brief extract, but presumably the proposers of the sea defences were consulting with the 29 organisations mentioned and later with the wide range of interest groups.

(v) At Dibden Bay, mitigation measures were incorporated into the scheme and in some cases adjusted as a result of the consultation. Alterations were also made to the scheme, design and layout of the proposals. At Strangford Lough, a working group with representatives from interest groups was established, which appeared to be taking a key role in an iterative process of scoping and considering options. In Bedfordshire, the planning application was modified with a reduced extraction period, improved screening and changes in the phasing of extraction.

### SAQ 43  Screening

(i) Screening is a process whereby those projects that are considered to have little or no environmental impact are 'screened out' so that they can proceed in the planning consent process without additional assessment on environmental grounds. Projects and programmes that are not screened out will require an EIA.

(ii) Annex I is the list of projects for which EIA is mandatory. Annex II shows projects where EIA is required when the project is likely to cause significant environmental effects, a judgement made by EU member states using guidelines and criteria set down in the EIA Directive.

### SAQ 44  Scoping

(i) Scoping in the context of an EIA is where key significant issues are identified by considering all of the possible impacts of a proposed development and alternatives to that development.

(ii) It is in the spirit of EIA that all stakeholders' perspectives are sought and considered, and the perspectives of those who may not be stakeholders but may have previous experience that will help stakeholders recognise potential impacts. These people may include developers, consultants, government agencies, members of the public, representatives of organisations, specialists in, for example, health and safety, or environmental conservation, monitoring, pollution prevention or control.

(iii) Practices vary on how scoping is done in different countries. A variety of means is usually used including formal and informal meetings, expert panels, questionnaires and surveys. It is often the developer or a consultant employed by the developer who is responsible for bringing forward different perspectives on scoping which are recorded in an environmental impact statement. In some countries there are 'statutory consultees' and a requirement for public participation.

## SAQ 45  Everything you already know about EIA

(i) Beattie is an academic in the Massachusetts Institute of Technology in the USA, with an understanding of the perspective of environmental professionals.

(ii) (a) that EIAs are not science

(b) that EIAs will always be political

(c) that EIAs always contain unexamined and unexplained value assumptions.

(iii) Because they represent a public attempt to document and evaluate the environmental effects of projects and policies. When done properly, their systematic organisation of pertinent information makes them valuable additions to any decision-making process.

(iv) 
- To write EIAs in ways that explicitly describe the assumptions and premises that have gone into the selection of data, the use of models or the projection of impacts. Public criticism of assumptions could then lead to improvements that allow models used to reflect values outside professional cliques.

- Do more to involve a wide range of people in the scoping process so that the issues of most analytical concern are incorporated into the EIA. If an issue arises that is outside the scope of the EIA, professionals should be able to explain in plain language why it is outside the EIA and where people should turn to get that issue addressed.

- Unless there is public discussion of how EIAs are used in the real world – their weaknesses as well as their strengths – environmental professionals will compromise their usefulness as a policy-making tool.

## SAQ 46  Exploring effects of environmental legislation

1 Some environmental legislation, such as the EC directive for EIA, actually requires an exploration of issues before a decision is made, but whether this exploration takes place before problems and opportunities are formulated is questionable.

2 The interpretation of legislation may affect which perspectives are heard in the early stages of an environmental decision-making process. Alder suggested that English law combined with the vagueness of the European directive for EIA was inadequate to ensure compliance with principles of scoping, screening and participation. While some aspects have improved with the amended directive, Glasson et al. still include scoping and participation as current issues.

3 There are different degrees of flexibility in legal frameworks of different countries, and hence presumably different attitudes to compliance, which may affect the way in which environmental decision making starts off.

## SAQ 47  Evolution of environmental assessment

According to Sadler (1994), environmental assessment evolved from a limited project review phase before 1970 and pre-EIA, through methodological development and introduction into developing countries in the early 1970s, through a phase where social dimensions began to be included in the late 1970s. In the early 1980s, there was process and procedural redirection, which included efforts to integrate project environmental assessment with policy planning, focusing on effects of monitoring, audit and process evaluation and on mediation and resolution of disputes and adoption of EA by international aid lending agencies. In the late 1980s, evolution incorporated the 'sustainability paradigm'. Since 1990, I would suggest that many of these trends have continued with increased integration of environmental assessment, in particular EIA, with other forms of assessment, and a continuing proliferation of assessment techniques.

## SAQ 48  Considering McCulloch's objection

McCulloch considers that the way in which environmental assessment is characterised encourages us to think of it in narrow terms, as part of project management or as self-contained. He implies that feedback from the environmental assessment should be directed into the wider environment within which the process takes place, and that this feedback should be used as a resource for society to learn from.

## SAQ 49  Decision making and strategic environmental assessment

(i) The authors consider that environmental assessment, in general, provides a prescriptive approach for decision makers who want to think systematically about environmental factors in decision making.

(ii) Critiques of rationalism include that it portrays decision making as normative and as an ideal. Empirical findings contradict assumptions that individuals can rationally maximise behaviour to achieve an expected utility. Rationalism is critiqued because in practice its use is found to be limited. Rationalism is also critiqued by some (e.g. Zey, 1998) because it is difficult to explain issues such as power, conflict and trust. It is also argued that decision making takes place in complex systems characterised by aspects such as uncertainty, the involvement of mutually dependent organisations and lack of knowledge. Methodologies related to rational choice and their use to lend authority to particular viewpoints and attempts to portray policy making as value-free have also been critiqued. A point was made by Miller (1984) that the rational model of decision making is useful at different levels of (organisational) analysis to explore an actor's position in a complex decision-making process.

(iii) Incremental models focus on the process of political negotiations and coalitions, and see decision making as a process of gradual change. They were developed to overcome some of the problems connected with the rationalist approach.

(iv) Impact-driven approaches come from the EIA tradition with predetermined stages. Decision-driven approaches are more tailored to the decision context.

(v) According to the authors, SEA often seems to fail because it is not sufficiently tailored to the decision context, and is too heavily structured.

(vi) The authors have identified steps that need consideration but do not suggest that they take place in sequence or that they are used in a heavily structured manner (sounds to me a bit like how we intend the T863 framework to be used).
The steps are

environmental and social context

specifying the issue

goal setting

information collection and processing

alternatives

evaluation

decision

implementation.

(vii) While the authors don't intend the steps to be used necessarily in sequence, they do suggest that consideration of the decision context may come early in the process.

(viii) Nilsson and Dalkmann's main conclusions are that SEA practices are highly variable and are still difficult in many countries because actors involved have difficulty in seeing the added value of the approach. They think SEA needs to adopt quite a different role from EIA, to incorporate environmental factors into strategic decision making. They also think the practice of SEA has much to learn from other fields, such as decision-making sciences, policy analysis and risk assessment. They conclude that an approach to SEA that recognises bounded rationality and behavioural constraints is needed.

## SAQ 50     The purpose of RIA

Kirkpatrick and Parker quote the National Audit Office to suggest that the purpose of RIA is to 'explain the objectives of the [regulatory] proposal, the risks to be addressed and the options for delivering the objectives'. (They also refer to the need for transparency and regarding costs and benefits in this process but this relates to process rather than purpose.)

## SAQ 51     Comparing EMSs and quality systems

The primary objective of a quality management system such as ISO 9001 is to maintain the quality of a product to deliver a customer specification, whereas the primary objective of an environmental management system is continuous improvement in environmental performance.

## SAQ 52     London Borough of Sutton – environmental reporting

I understand the purpose of the London Borough of Sutton's statement to be to inform residents and other stakeholders of the environmental performance of their council.

## SAQ 53     Why does CSR matter?

(i) Taylor Woodrow give three reasons why CSR matters to them. Firstly, stakeholders are interested in the broader performance of their company. Secondly, there are legislative, fiscal, customer, investment community and societal drivers for adopting a positive CSR agenda. Thirdly, good performance on CSR will benefit the company, wider society and the environment. An example later given is that good CSR performance will enhance their credentials with ethical investors. BAA has existing policies on sustainable development and ethics that are guiding their approach to corporate responsibility. From the extract selected, they seem to link CSR with best practice and performance and their relationship with their stakeholders, including investors and community groups.

(ii) In both cases, the reports seem to be aimed at stakeholders. Taylor Woodrow identify two groups of stakeholders, those with whom they already have a significant dialogue about CSR and other stakeholders interested in their wider activities. The BAA report mentions different groups of stakeholders in many parts of the text – investors, community groups, Government, employees, travellers/passengers, staff, business partners, etc. This extract does not explicitly state who this report is for, but in answering this question I am wondering if those details are given elsewhere – perhaps on their website? The title of the piece suggests that they are trying to let others know that they are 'doing the right thing'. How these reports affect early stages of environmental decision making is not clear from these extracts. In both cases, the statements could be read as indications of already formulated environmental or social problems, opportunities and systems of interest. The statements clearly follow some process of dialogue and previous exploration of situations with stakeholders. There are also many indications of values underpinning the statements. But what scope there may be to re-explore the situations, question assumptions and re-formulate problems and opportunities is not clear.

### SAQ 54  Corporate social responsibility – a debate

(i) Tom Burke is an environmental policy adviser, currently with a company, previously with the UK Government. He also has an academic role and previously led two environmental NGOs. Joel Bakan has a background in law. He has an academic role in Canada and is an author focusing on 'the corporation'.

(ii) Bakan describes CSR as an oxymoron because he finds a contradiction in the implication that a company's responsibility to society can take priority over its responsibility to make money for shareholders.

(iii) Burke accepts that public trading companies have conflicting responsibilities but says that there is no imperative for companies to put their shareholders' financial interests above all other considerations. He claims that many businesses go beyond compliance with the law in discharging their social responsibilities.

(vi) Burke focuses on legal and social responsibilities, arguing that nothing in corporate law permits a company to ignore its other legal responsibilities in discharging those to shareholders. He sees a clear link between company law and other laws. Breaking an environmental law can also mean a breach in company law if there is no adequate assurance process. Breaking the law is not in company interests, but not all legal regulation is effective, and compliance with the law doesn't necessarily lead to corporate responsibility. Constructive debate is needed to look at alternatives that would improve this situation. He sees the movement for CSR as an effort at re-negotiation of the relationship between business and society.

Bakan claims CSR meets corporate rather than society's needs, as the strategic scope of CSR means it has very little capacity to protect social and environmental interests from corporate harms. He concedes that there are some tangible environmental and social benefits of CSR, and that many of those adopting CSR are sincere. Company law gives primacy to the interests of the company and the interests of shareholders. Responsibilities to stakeholders rather than to shareholders comes through regulatory law, which comes from outside the company not from company law. So if regulatory law is ineffective, then corporate self-interest created by company law can go unchecked. Breaking a regulatory law may be in the interests of the company and penalties are often small. Bakan appears to be more sceptical about CSR than Burke, but both agree about the need for a public, democratic and effective regulatory system.

## SAQ 55   Evaluating what?

The three Es that were introduced as measures of performance in Box 11 were efficacy, efficiency and effectiveness. Patton (1990) says that 'When one examines and judges accomplishments and effectiveness, one is engaged in evaluation. When this examination of effectiveness is conducted systematically and empirically through careful data collection and thoughtful analysis, one is engaged in evaluation research'. Patton's focus for evaluation is effectiveness which is, of course, related to purpose. Efficiency is a measure – one could, of course, evaluate how effective someone was at being efficient!

## SAQ 56   Measures of performance

Checkland initially describes three Es but adds another two possibilities (although there may be others as well). His additional ones are ethicality – is this transformation morally correct? – and elegance – is this an aesthetically pleasing transformation? (Note here that the Es refer to the transformation process not the outcomes of the transformation.)

## SAQ 57   Systemic and systematic

This was a hard choice for me, as many distinctions are understandably interconnected. I chose the following distinctions: 'The espoused role and the action of the decision-maker are very much part of the situation. How the researcher perceives the situation is critical to the "system" being studied. The role is that of participant-conceptualiser' (systemic) and 'The espoused role of the decision-maker is that of participant-observer. In practice, however, the decision maker claims to be objective and thus remains "outside" the "system" being studied' (systematic). I chose this set because issues of ethics and responsibility flow from it.

## Acknowledgements

Grateful acknowledgement is made to the following sources:

### Text

Box 5: Extract from McClintock, D., Ison, R., and Armson, R. (2003), 'Metaphors for reflecting on research practice: researching with people', *Journal of Environmental Planning and Management*, Vol. 46, issue 5, September 2003. Reproduced by permission Taylor & Francis Group.

Box 7: Porritt, J. 'Odd Couple', *The Guardian*, 9 July 2003, Guardian Newspapers. © 2003 Jonathon Porritt.

Box 10: Russell, D. B. and Ison, R. (2000) 'The research-development relationship in rural communities: an opportunity for contextual science', in Ison, R.L. and Russell, D. B. (eds) *Agricultural Extension and Rural Development: Breaking Out of Traditions,* Cambridge University Press.

Box 14: Brady J. (2005), 'Policy and Legislation', *Environmental Management in Organisations: The IEMA Handbook*, IEMA.

Box 16: Case Study 1: Smith, A. 'Scoping, Public Participation and the Consultation Process', *Environmental Assessment,* Vol. 5, No. 4, 1997.

Box 17: Glasson J. et al. (2005) 'EIA Systems Worldwide', *Introduction to Environmental Impact Assessment*, Routledge, Taylor & Francis Group.

Box 21: Kirkpatrick, C. and Parker, D. 'Editorial: Regulatory Impact Assessment – An Overview', *Public Money & Management*, October 2004, Vol. 4, No.5, Blackwell Synergy.

Boxes 22 and 23: Permission to reproduce extracts from BS EN ISO 14001: 2004 is granted by British Standards Institute.

Box 24: Hall, C. 'London Borough of Sutton Annual Environmental Statement 2003/ 04', IEMA Reading Room website.

Box 25: Taylor Woodrow plc. (2003) *Taylor Woodrow Corporate Responsibility Report 2003.*

### Tables

Table 9: Roe, D. et al. (1995) *A Directory of Impact Assessment Guidelines,* IIED, after Sadler, B. (1994) *Proposed Framework for the International Study of the Effectiveness of Environmental Assessment,* Federal Environmental Assessment Review Office (FEARO), Canada and the International Association of Impact Assessment.

Table 12: After Krippendorff, K. 'Major metaphors of communication and some constructivist reflections on their use', *Cybernetics and Human Knowing,* Vol. 2, No. 1, 1993, Imprint Academic.

## Figures

Figure 3: O'Brien, B. (1990) *Consequences*, Wakefield Press.

Figure 5: Keeling, C. D. and Whorf, T. P. (2005) 'Atmospheric $CO_2$ records from sites in the SIO air sampling network', in *Trends: A Compendium of Data on Global Change*, Carbon Dioxide Information Analysis Center, Oak Ridge National Laboratory, U. S. Department of Energy.

Figure 8: Reproduced from the Ordnance Survey 1:500000 OS map of the area of around Stansted Airport with the permission of Ordnance Survey on behalf of The Controller of Her Majesty's Stationery Office. © Crown copyright. The Open University, Milton Keynes, Licence No. 100018362.

Figure 9: Stansted Expansion Campaign – the Map Room, 'Stansted noise map for 2 runways in 2030 with two 'Modal Split' halves recombined to show the total area which gets noise nuisance at some time', www.stopstanstedeexpansion.com.

Figures 10 and 11: Adapted from figure at http://www.shodor.org/mvhs/carbon.gif, Shodor Education Foundation, Inc.

Figure 14: Svensson, M. (2005) 'Archetypes in System Analysis' (online) Lund University Centre for Sustainability Studies.

Figure 15b: © Paul McConnell/Getty Images.

Figures 16 and 47: Wadsworth, Y. (1997) *Do it Yourself Social Research,* Allen & Unwin Book Publishers.

Figures 19, 20, 29: Courtesy of the SLIM Project.

Figure 25 top: © Getty Images; bottom: © Martin Bond/Photofusion.

Figure 27: Courtesy of Ray Ison.

Figure 30: Leunig, M. (1985) *Ramming the Shears: A Collection of Drawings by Michael Leunig,* Penguin Books Australia Ltd. Copyright © Michael Leunig.

Figure 32: Collins, K. B. et al. and Environment Agency (2005) 'River Basin Planning Project: social learning', *Science Summary.*

Figure 38: Airports Council International, (2004) 'Airport and Land/Ground-Centric Environmental Impact', Airports and Environmental Legislation.

Figures 39 and 41: Glasson J. et al (2005) 'EIA Systems Worldwide', *Introduction to Environmental Impact Assessment*, Routledge, Taylor & Francis Group.

Figure 40: Institute of Environmental Management and Assessment, (2002) 'Guidelines on Participation in Environmental Decision Making', IEMA.

Figure 44: Permission to reproduce extracts from BS EN ISO 14001: 2004 is granted by British Standards Institute.

Figure 48: Adapted from Checkland, P. andScholes (1990) in Stuth, J.W. and Lyons, B. (eds). (1993) *Decision support systems for the management of grazing lands: EmergingIssues. UNESCO's Man and the Biosphere Book No. 11*, UNESCOPublishing/Parthenon Publishing.

Figures 21 and 62: Checkland, P. (2000) 'SoftSystems Methodology: A Thirty Year Retrospective', *Systems Research andBehavioural Science, 17*(1), Wiley Interscience. Copyright © 2000 John Wiley & Sons Ltd.